Remembering the Liberation Struggles in Cape Verde

Remembering the Liberation Struggles in Cape Verde: A Mnemohistory takes as its reference from the anti-colonial struggles against the Portuguese colonial empire in Africa in the 1960s and 1970s and the ways this period has been publicly remembered. Drawing on original and detailed empirical research, it presents novel insights into the complex entanglements between colonial pasts and political memories of anti-colonialism in shaping new nations arising out of liberation struggles. Broadening postcolonial memory studies by emphasising underdeveloped research cases, it provides the first comprehensive research into how the liberation struggle is memorialised in Cape Verde and why it changes over time. Proposing an innovative approach to thinking about this historical event as a political subject, the book argues that the "struggle" constitutes a mnemonic device mobilised while negotiating contemporaneous representations related to the Cape Verdean nation, state and society. As such, it will appeal to scholars of history, sociology, anthropology and politics with interests in memory studies and public memory, postcolonialisms and African studies.

Miguel Cardina is a permanent researcher at the Centre for Social Studies of the University of Coimbra, Portugal. He is a European Research Council (ERC) grantee with the project CROME – *Crossed Memories, Politics of Silence. The Colonial-Liberation Wars in Postcolonial Times*. His publications include books, book chapters and journal articles on colonialism, anticolonialism, the colonial wars and liberation struggles in Portugal and Africa; political ideologies in the 60s and 70s; and the dynamics between history and memory.

Inês Nascimento Rodrigues is a researcher at the Centre for Social Studies of the University of Coimbra, Portugal. She is co-coordinator of the Observatory of Trauma in the same institution and a member of CROME's team. Her publications and research interests are focused on postcolonial and memory studies, cultural history and the debates on the representation and evocation of the Colonial-Liberation wars, particularly in S. Tomé and Príncipe, Cape Verde and Guinea-Bissau.

Memory Studies: Global Constellations
Series editor: Henri Lustiger-Thaler
Ramapo College of New Jersey, USA and Ecole des Hautes Etudes en Sciences Sociales, France

The "past in the present" has returned in the early 21st century with a vengeance, and with it the expansion of categories of experience. These experiences have largely been lost in the advance of rationalist and constructivist understandings of subjectivity and their collective representations. The cultural stakes around forgetting, "useful forgetting" and remembering, locally, regionally, nationally and globally have risen exponentially. It is therefore not unusual that "migrant memories"; microhistories; personal and individual memories in their interwoven relation to cultural, political and social narratives; the mnemonic past and present of emotions, embodiment and ritual; and finally, the mnemonic spatiality of geography and territories are receiving more pronounced hearings.

This transpires as the social sciences themselves are consciously globalizing their knowledge bases. In addition to the above, the reconstructive logic of memory in the juggernaut of galloping informationalization is rendering it more and more publicly accessible, and therefore part of a new global public constellation around the coding of meaning and experience. Memory studies as an academic field of social and cultural inquiry emerge at a time when global public debate – buttressed by the fragmentation of national narratives – has accelerated. Societies today, in late globalized conditions, are pregnant with newly unmediated and unfrozen memories once sequestered in wide collective representations. We welcome manuscripts that examine and analyse these profound cultural traces.

Titles in this series

22. **Memory and Identity**
    Ghosts of the Past in the English-speaking World
    Edited by Linda Pillière and Karine Bigand

23. **Remembering the Liberation Struggles in Cape Verde: A Mnemohistory**
    Miguel Cardina and Inês Nascimento Rodrigues

For more information about this series, please visit: https://www.routledge.com/sociology/series/ASHSER1411

Remembering the Liberation Struggles in Cape Verde
A Mnemohistory

**Miguel Cardina and
Inês Nascimento Rodrigues**

LONDON AND NEW YORK

First published 2022
by Routledge
2 Park Square, Milton Park, Abingdon, Oxon OX14 4RN

and by Routledge
605 Third Avenue, New York, NY 10158

Routledge is an imprint of the Taylor & Francis Group, an informa business

© 2023 Miguel Cardina and Inês Nascimento Rodrigues

The right of Miguel Cardina and Inês Nascimento Rodrigues to be identified as authors of this work has been asserted by them in accordance with sections 77 and 78 of the Copyright, Designs and Patents Act 1988.

The Open Access version of this book, available at www.taylorfrancis.com, has been made available under a Creative Commons Attribution-Non Commercial-No Derivatives 4.0 license.

Trademark notice: Product or corporate names may be trademarks or registered trademarks, and are used only for identification and explanation without intent to infringe.

British Library Cataloguing-in-Publication Data
A catalogue record for this book is available from the British Library

Library of Congress Cataloging-in-Publication Data
Names: Cardina, Miguel, 1978- author. | Rodrigues, Inês Nascimento, author.
Title: Remembering the liberation struggles in Cape Verde: a mnemohistory / Miguel Cardina, Inês Nascimento Rodrigues.
Description: 1 Edition. | New York, NY: Routledge, 2022. | Series: Memory studies: global constellations | Includes bibliographical references and index.
Identifiers: LCCN 2022023992 | ISBN 9781032201924 (hardback) | ISBN 9781032208459 (paperback) | ISBN 9781003265535 (ebook)
Subjects: LCSH: Cabo Verde--Historiography. | National liberation movements--Cabo Verde--History--20th century. | Cabral, Amílcar, 1924-1973--Influence. | Decolonization--Cabo Verde. | Collective memory--Cabo Verde.
Classification: LCC DT671.C25 C37 2022 | DDC 966.58/02--dc23/eng/20220728
LC record available at https://lccn.loc.gov/2022023992

ISBN: 978-1-032-20192-4 (hbk)
ISBN: 978-1-032-20845-9 (pbk)
ISBN: 978-1-003-26553-5 (ebk)

DOI: 10.4324/9781003265535

Typeset in Times New Roman
by KnowledgeWorks Global Ltd.

CONTENTS

List of Figures	vii
Introduction: The Liberation Struggle as a Mnemonic Device	1
Notes 10	
Bibliography 12	
1 The Struggle as the Cradle of the Independent Nation	15

*Building the Nation State and the centrality of the
    struggle 17*
The "return to Africa" through music 28
*The end of the union with Guinea-Bissau and its
    impacts 35*
Recalibrating memory 37
Between two ruptures 42
Notes 43
Bibliography 53

2 The Struggle in the Mnemonic Transition	59

The political transition: causes and processes 61
The return of removed images 64
A new paradigm of remembrance 69
The change in national symbols 72
The mnemonic transition: reasons and circumstances 77
Notes 78
Bibliography 86

3 The Struggle and the Image of the Combatant	90

Constructing the liberation struggle combatant 91
Public recognition and political disputes 99

vi *Contents*

The diversification of the image of the "combatant" 105
A composite memorial framework 111
Notes 112
Bibliography 118

4 The Struggle and Cabral's Afterlives   121

Crossroads of memory 123
Questioning Cabral 131
Alternative representations 135
The new heirs: Protest and appropriations 141
Notes 147
Bibliography 154

Epilogue   158
Acknowledgements   160
Index   162

FIGURES

0.1	Map of Cape Verde	2
1.1	"Ceremony to Proclaim the Independence of Cape Verde, in Praia", Fundação Mário Soares e Maria Barroso / Arquivo Amílcar Cabral	16
1.2	"Amílcar Cabral Portrait", Fundação Mário Soares e Maria Barroso / Arquivo Amílcar Cabral	26
1.3	"Amílcar Cabral Portrait", Fundação Mário Soares e Maria Barroso / Arquivo Mário Pinto de Andrade	27
2.1	Statues of Diogo Afonso (Mindelo) and Diogo Gomes (Praia)	67
2.2	Bust of Camões (Mindelo)	68
2.3	Coat of Arms before 1992 and after 1992	73
2.4	Cape Verde Flags: The Post-Independence Flag *and* the Current Flag Since 1992	73
2.5	500 Escudos Banknote, Issued in 1989, with Amílcar Cabral's Image and 500 Escudos Banknote, Issued in 1992, with Baltasar Lopes da Silva's Image	77
3.1	Tarrafal Penal Camp, Nowadays Transformed into a Museum of Resistance	98
3.2	Mural in Honour of Pedro Pires at ACOLP	99
3.3	In Memoriam: Mural to the Late Liberation Struggle Combatants at ACOLP	104
4.1	Mausoleum of Amílcar Cabral. Forte de Amura, Bissau (Guinea-Bissau)	122
4.2	Cultural Centre in Cape Verde	124
4.3	Amílcar Cabral Memorial, Praia	125
4.4	Trial textbooks for the History and Geography of Cape Verde, 5th and 6th grades, Ministry of Education	128
4.5	Mural by Rabelados, at Achada Grande Frente (Praia)	130
4.6	Mural of Amílcar Cabral, painted in 2019 by Portuguese artist Vhils, at Achada Grande Frente (Praia)	130

viii *Figures*

4.7 The Presence of the PAIGC Flag in Artwork Done by
Youth From the Rabelados Community in Espinho
Branco, May 2019   140
4.8 *Marxa Kabral* and Official Ceremony of Homage to
Cabral, 20 January 2019   145
4.9 8th *Marxa Kabral*, 20 January 2020   146

INTRODUCTION
THE LIBERATION STRUGGLE AS A MNEMONIC DEVICE

This book examines the memory of the liberation struggle in Cape Verde.[1] It seeks to demonstrate the ways in which the *struggle* has been expressed through different public practices, symbolic meanings and political appropriations. More than 40 years of the archipelago's post-colonial life are observed to show how the historical birth certificate of this independent nation – the liberation struggle against Portuguese colonialism – has become a "mnemonic device", that is, an intermittent heritage recognised as foundational to the State and that in its successive manifestations, silencing processes, and modulations extensively defines its own representations and the power structures of any given socio-political present.

Lying off the west coast of Africa, the Cape Verde archipelago consists of ten islands, nine of which are inhabited (Figure 0.1). Santiago, together with Fogo, Maio and Brava constitute the Sotavento islands. On Santiago, the largest island and the first to be occupied, is the city of Praia, today the country's capital. Barlavento consists of the islands of São Nicolau, Boa Vista, Sal, Santo Antão, Santa Luzia (currently uninhabited) and São Vicente. The latter island gained in importance in the second half of the 19th century as a coaling station and stopover for ships crossing the Atlantic, becoming a cultural and economic centre of some prominence. The geography, history of occupation and social formation of each island all imbue them with specific characteristics. The country shares two languages: Portuguese, mostly used in formal situations, instruction and in the mainstream media, and the Cape Verdean, a result of Portuguese and African languages, nuanced with regional differences, and widely spoken in day-to-day life.

In 2021, the population of the islands was close to 500,000. In 1975, the year the country became independent, there were fewer than 300,000 inhabitants. The two largest cities – Praia (on the island of Santiago) and Mindelo (on the island of São Vicente) – have been growing significantly over the last few decades, despite the significance of long, structural migratory dynamics. Today, it is estimated that a greater number of Cape

DOI: 10.4324/9781003265535-1

2 *Introduction*

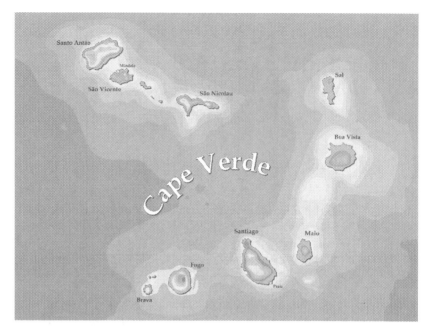

Figure 0.1 Map of Cape Verde.
Source: Artwork by André Queda.

Verdeans or their descendants are living in other parts of the world. The insular dimension, centuries-old economic deprivation and the relatively small size of the islands, makes networks of complicity, family ties and solidarity a key feature of the archipelago and its distinct diaspora communities. Added to this is a strong social stratification that has tended to solidify elites over time not always as the holders of capital but rather the possessors of reputation and property.

The Portuguese were the first to settle on the islands, between 1460 and 1462 – initially in Santiago and later in Fogo – although it is very likely that Africans from the coast had known and visited the islands prior to this. Santiago, in particular, became an important staging post for the trafficking of enslaved people, mainly from the Gulf of Guinea, to be "ladinised" there, that is, to learn the rudiments of Portuguese, to be baptised and catechised, and to have a Christian name imposed on them. From there, they were taken to other places: first Portugal and Spain, and later Brazil and the Antilles. While only a minority remained in Cape Verde, serving as an internal labour force, the number of enslaved people always far exceeded the numbers of the white or mixed-race population, especially on the island of Santiago.[2] As António Correia e Silva states, "Cape Verde was not only a slavocrat society, similar to those that existed in the Americas, but also the first of its kind in the Atlantic world".[3]

Introduction 3

This slavocrat society was established consisting of a minority elite of European white men – gradually replaced by a local creole elite – and a significantly more sizeable group of black individuals, which decisively affected the racial composition of the archipelago.[4] The creole landowning minority, also known as the "whites of the land," in many cases benefited from slavery, which was especially strong between the 15th and 17th centuries. However, this endogenous elite was denied access to the higher echelons of the State, particularly from the 18th century onwards until very close to independence, and this became a traditional demand of the local elites. These circumstances would determine the ways in which the identity *of* and *in* Cape Verde was imagined. The image of Cape Verdean exceptionality, which generations of intellectuals have shaped particularly since the 19th century, was expressed in different ways, and tended to be based on the combination of two archetypes: Europe (or Portugal), symbolising reason, fatherhood, and science; and Africa, seen as a place of emotion, motherhood, and tradition.[5]

The independence of Cape Verde was part of the broad movement that, with the end of World War II, ushered in a wave of anti-colonial struggles around the world and a range of political processes leading to the independence of colonised territories. In 1960 alone, known as the "year of Africa," the continent saw the emergence of seventeen new nations, made independent from British, French and Belgian rule. By then, the Portuguese obstinacy in maintaining its colonial presence in Africa led to protracted wars that would only end with the overthrow of the *Estado Novo* dictatorship on 25 April 1974. In the so-called "Carnation Revolution", the old Portuguese regime, established in the 1930s, fell into the hands of the Armed Forces Movement (MFA), a movement made up of middle-ranking officers from an army tired of a long cycle of fighting that had been going on since 1961. In 1974/75, Portugal saw a revolutionary dynamic that would genetically mark its democracy. At the same time, five new African nations emerged from the collapse of this late colonial Empire: Angola, Mozambique, Guinea-Bissau, Cape Verde and São Tomé and Príncipe.

Although Cape Verde's independence was not the result of a process of armed struggle in the archipelago, it was a direct consequence of this historical context and of the struggle of the PAIGC (African Party for the Independence of Guinea and Cape Verde). Since at least the mid-1950s, anti-colonial feeling had been rising among fringes of the population, and it occasionally made its presence felt in the territory and among its significant diaspora. The emergence of the PAIGC attested to the growing presence of the independentist ideals. In this case, marked by the peculiar aim of fighting for the joint liberation of two territories: Guinea and Cape Verde.[6] Led by the charismatic figure of Amílcar Cabral, between 1960 and 1962 the movement prepared the ground for the transition to armed struggle, while trying to gain international support and recognition.

4 Introduction

Amílcar Lopes Cabral was born in 1924, in Bafatá (Guinea), son of Cape Verdean parents. When he was eight years old, he went to Cape Verde, settling with his family in Santa Catarina, in the interior of Santiago Island. He finished primary school there, and then moved to Mindelo, with his mother and siblings, where he finished secondary school. In 1945 he obtained a scholarship to study Agronomy in Lisbon, where he graduated in 1950. Involved there in anti-colonial political activities, he took part in the House of the Students of the Empire, a common house created by the regime to integrate African students. There, he socialised with several African political leaders – among whom the Angolans Agostinho Neto and Mário Pinto de Andrade and the Mozambican Marcelino dos Santos – and later actively participated in agglutinating structures of the liberation movements, such as the MAC (Anti-Colonial Movement), the FRAIN (African Revolutionary Front for National Independence) and the CONCP (Conference of Nationalist Organizations of the Portuguese Colonies). He returned to Guinea in 1952 to work as an agronomist, which gave him a detailed knowledge of the socioeconomic structure and cultural mosaic of the territory. He then became the leader of the PAI (African Party for Independence) and its successor, the PAIGC.

In Cape Verde, the PAIGC's position clearly managed to overcome competing initiatives emerging in those years which advocated independence without a linkage to Guinea. On the Guinean side, linking up with Cape Verde was also a source of friction, especially due to the presence of Cape Verdeans in the Portuguese colonial administrative apparatus. From 1963 onwards, the PAIGC began to conduct an armed struggle from the Guinean territory. The first attacks were followed by a series of political decisions, military actions and diplomatic successes. The geography of Guinea – with its dense forests and an ecology hostile to Portuguese troops – facilitated guerrilla action, supported also by the new nations bordering it: Léopold Senghor's Senegal and, above all, Sékou Touré's Guinea Conakry. In Guinea, during the late 60s and early 70s, the PAIGC gained control of a significant portion of the territory.

On 20 January 1973, an event occurred that would deeply mark the liberation struggle but also the post-colonial history of the two future countries: Amílcar Cabral was assassinated in Conakry by PAIGC member Inocêncio Kany, revealing the high tensions existing between the Cape Verdeans and Guineans and leaving unresolved the involvement of other actors, specifically the Portuguese secret police, which had already tried to assassinate him some years earlier.[7] What is certain is that, following Cabral's death, the armed struggle entered a very intense phase. From March 1973, the availability of Strella anti-aircraft missiles, supplied by the USSR, reinforced the heavy artillery that the PAIGC already had and took air supremacy away from the Portuguese forces. On 24 September 1973, the PAIGC unilaterally declared Guinea's independence at a meeting inside the country in the presence of international observers.

Introduction 5

Plans to extend the armed struggle to Cape Verde were considered on several occasions. In 1967, after two years of military training in Cuba, the Cape Verdean Armed Forces were formed there, with the aim of carrying out a land assault on the islands.[8] The plans, however, never came to fruition. In Guinea, several Cape Verdeans joined the armed struggle. Others participated in the mobilisation and clandestine struggle in Portugal or in Cape Verde, and some of them were arrested and convicted as a result. Others carried out diplomatic and political work from exile either in Europe, in France, Holland or Sweden, or elsewhere in Africa, in Senegal, Algeria, Conakry.[9] The political landscape that opened up with the Carnation Revolution on 25 April 1974 led to a new situation. In Cape Verde, political mobilisation came out into the open, competing blueprints for a new society were aired, militants from the struggle returned to the archipelago and the PAIGC consolidated its hegemony, in some cases with generational and ideological differences that were still barely perceptible at the time but became evident in the years that followed. On 5 July 1975, the new Republic of Cape Verde was officially declared.

*

The analysis presented in this book is grounded in the literature that is dedicated to studying the ways in which colonial pasts and their post-colonial ramifications shape both the new countries emerging from liberation struggles and the former colonising powers. In fact, if we focus on the reminiscences of empire in Portugal and in its former African colonies, we will uncover two substantially different ways in which the rupture with colonialism is inscribed in the public memory. In Portugal, a "politics of silence" historically prevailed with regard to the war and colonial violence perpetuating, in significant sectors of the population, the image of a country of *brandos costumes* [mild manners] and its benevolent presence overseas. The reverse side of this representation is that slavery, exploitation, domination or racism tended to be transformed into socially denied realities. In Portugal, the imaginary of empire still retains strong traces of explicit or implicit nostalgia combined with resentment about the abruptness by which the break with colonialism was effected. In contrast, in the African countries that were once Portuguese colonies, a certain memory of the liberation struggle has predominated, one that recognizes the centrality and justice of the anti-colonial struggle and objectively serves to reinforce the political and symbolic legitimacy of the movements that conducted the liberation wars. These movements became one-party regimes in the various post-independence periods.[10]

With their very distinct post-colonial histories, Angola, Mozambique and Guinea-Bissau are examples of this. Considering FRELIMO and the Mozambican case, João Paulo Borges Coelho has identified what

6   *Introduction*

he terms the *Liberation Script,* a fixed narrative by which the historical past of the struggle can be read and interpreted.[11] This script would consist of a sequential and fixed discursive framework, to a large extent orally transmitted and based mainly on dichotomous thinking structured around binary opposites such as fair / unfair, nationalist / colonialist, revolutionary / reactionary, modern / traditional, military / civilian or rural / urban.[12] The script was an *apparatus* or *dispositif* – Borges Coelho makes direct reference to Michel Foucault and Giorgio Agamben – that interwove power relations and knowledge relations.[13] He therefore sees it as a grand strategic narrative, teleological in nature, and as a political instrument used to legitimise and consolidate the authority of the former liberation movements.

The case of Cape Verde presents singularities, for various reasons – because of its own colonial history, due to the fact that it had no armed struggle on its territory, and because of the processes of multiparty change in the post-1990 period. In Cape Verde, the memory of the struggle both assumed political centrality and became subject to particular contestations. The central argument of this book is that the liberation struggle, through its uses, symbols and meanings, is configured as a "mnemonic device" that interacts with the (re)production of national imaginaries and with the definition of the challenges that Cape Verdean society had to and will face. The notion of "mnemonic device" that we outline here is in partial dialogue with the reflection offered by João Paulo Borges Coelho, although it differs from the clearly hegemonic and stable constraint presupposed by his concept of "Liberation Script" and its application to the Mozambican case.

By "mnemonic device" we mean the constellation of representations that radiate from a particular historical past and the way in which the device lends itself to appropriations and disputes that transform it into a decisive – and fluctuating – political agent.[14] Indeed, mnemonic devices are summoned from multiple elements: from narratives, memorial landscapes, myths and commemorative practices, symbologies, power relations or moral hierarchies. The historical process of a given society, the logic of the State and its agents, the political, ideological, cultural, religious, economic or regional positions of certain groups, as well as the relationship between the national context and international constraints all influence their concrete re-presentation.

The inescapability of the struggle as a mnemonic device does not lie in the fact that it is an uncontested memorial subject, but rather that it marks the terms by which debates are produced and has a decisive presence in them. Even when the memory of the struggle is so diluted that it appears to be absent, this simulacrum of absence is often no more than a paradoxical attestation of its presence. It is to this extent that the struggle as a mnemonic device can be activated or deactivated, celebrated or erased, remembered or forgotten, as we will show in the following pages.

Introduction 7

By putting forward the notion of the "mnemonic signifier," Gregor Feindt et al. have highlighted the ways in which the past is subject to narrative input that, according to specific contexts, can be intersected by different and even conflicting meanings. According to the authors, the analysis of "mnemonic signifiers" must be accompanied and expanded through a mnemography: the act of tracing the set of discourses that cover them over time.[15] The notion of "mnemonic device" includes a diachronic dimension that finds expression in discursive ways of representing the past, but also in various modes – discursive, material and performative – of political appropriation. The struggle as a "mnemonic device" offers markers that translate the development, transformation and power disputes over the memory of the struggle, from the (re)definition of memorial landscapes related with it, into performances of social protest that operationalise this historical event according to current objectives and needs.

Analysing the evocations of the struggle thus implies decisively attending to the diachronic expression of memory, what Jan Assmann, from a predominantly culturalist viewpoint, calls "mnemohistory".[16] According to Assman, mnemohistory would examine "the entanglements of tradition, the webs of intertextuality, the diachronic continuities and discontinuities of reading the past".[17] In support of Assman's formulation, Marek Tamm also argues that "mnemohistory studies not so much the routine reception of events, but also their haunting effect".[18] It is this "haunting effect," as present as it is spectral, that we will seek to identify in the case of the liberation struggle in Cape Verde.

As Berber Bevernage and Nico Wouters define it, the production of a nation's past is a mnemonic capacity activated in different spheres, contexts and scales by what they call the "memorialising State," which refers to the multiple, intertwined and complex ways in which States successfully mobilize their power and resources to create particular histories and regimes of memory.[19] According to the authors, States can do this not only as legislators, but through three other central domains: as the funders of memorials, foundations, scholarships, museums, schools, archives, etc.; as entities with the power to appoint and consecrate certain individuals and specific ideas or causes; and finally, as holders of jurisdictional powers, which allows them to act as arbiters of what are the legitimate and illegitimate interpretations of the past or to define what the positive and negative aspects of a country's history are.[20] Naturally, an analysis of the role of the State and the political and institutional space cannot be detached from the more diverse and multifaceted dynamics of appropriating and remembering that past, to which this book will also pay due attention.

In other words, memory becomes a "battlefield" in which actors and representations assert themselves and clash. This dispute is marked by a combat for the hegemony of certain groups around the mobilisation,

8   *Introduction*

diversification or selection of history. Berthold Molden proposes that we think about this aspect by using the concept of "mnemonic hegemony," based on a "encompassing analysis of the dialectics between memory and politics" which attends to the "intersection between material structures, social experience, and discursive practices".[21] In his view, "any sign, word, or memory can be multivocal and be put to use differently by different speakers, according to their experience, context, and needs". As a consequence, Molden alerts us to the need for analyses that observe the multifaceted ways in which power dynamics shape narratives, discourses and hegemonic and counter-hegemonic spaces, sometimes conflictive, sometimes polyphonic.[22] This book seeks to contribute to this dialogue, starting from the political memories of colonialism and anti-colonialism in Cape Verde.

*

Our study is structured around four intertwined axes: the memorialization of the struggle in the immediate post-independence political order; the transition to a multiparty system and the contested legacies of anti-colonialism; the construction of the "combatant" between recognition and invisibility; and finally, the public mobilization of Amílcar Cabral and the mnemonic battles for history. These central analytical points are translated into four chapters as outlined below.

Chapter 1 focuses on the country's first 15 years as an independent nation. The liberation struggle became the great mnemonic device capable of defining a new beginning for Cape Verde and Cape Verdeans. Focusing on the new state-building phase, it will be shown that activating the struggle as the cradle of the independent nation worked in two ways. Firstly, as a multidirectional response to the experiences of suffering and violence that preceded and drove it: the spectre of hunger that cyclically resurfaced in Cape Verde. Secondly, as a moral reserve of resistance that was evoked during the difficulties and constraints that the new independent nation faced. It is within this context that a national narrative came to be formed in those years which included an attempt towards "re-Africanization," particularly in the area of culture. The end of the unity with Guinea-Bissau and the outbreak of some social contestation *in opposition to* and *within* the ruling party were accompanied, particularly in the latter half of the 1980s, by a series of mnemonic and political transformations, which aimed to combine the struggle with the cultural and intellectual legacies that preceded anti-colonial nationalism.

Chapter 2, entitled "The Struggle in the Mnemonic Transition," discusses the profound changes that occurred with the adoption of a multi-party system and the defeat at the polls of PAICV. The political transition that took shape in 1991 was followed by a specific "mnemonic transition".[23] It involved replacing the hitherto dominant memoryscape

Introduction 9

of the struggle with a new public memoryscape. We explore the ways in which this new memorial landscape produced in Cape Verde in the 1990s erased the centrality of the anti-colonial heritage and the connection to Africa and began to recover pre-independence events and figures, in a process that Márcia Rego has called the "de-Africanization" of national symbols.[24] The struggle as the cradle of the independent nation was directly challenged here by anti-anticolonial representations that were part of a redefinition of Cape Verde and its history.

Chapter 3 focuses on the figure of the "combatant" and how this figure has been invested with different public meanings and appropriations. The figure of the combatant has shaped ideas of citizenship, as well as the moral categorisations of heroism, resistance and suffering that established a symbolic grammar anchored in the struggle. We will therefore attempt to reflect on the trajectory of this concept by highlighting how it is developed according to archetypes that define different ways of legitimising the State, the nation and its protagonists. The combatant's legal status occupies, in this case, a very significant place: the changes in legislation and in the discursive representations of the figure of the "combatant" in Cape Verde accompany the country's political, social, and economic transformations and reveal the ambivalence with which the past is socially and imaginatively disputed in the country on a scale that swings between celebration and erasure.

Chapter 4 examines the memory of the struggle through the current representations of Amílcar Cabral. The fact that he was the main architect of the PAIGC, the great strategist and the face of the armed struggle against Portuguese colonialism made him the "father and founder of the nation," expressions used to characterise Cabral both in Cape Verde and Guinea-Bissau. Particular attention will be given to the unrealised plan for a large cultural centre dedicated to Amílcar Cabral and designed by the Brazilian architect Óscar Niemeyer, and then to the building of the Amílcar Cabral Memorial, inaugurated in 2000, in the city of Praia and offered by China. Firstly, we will seek to understand how the memorial could be put in interaction with monuments from the colonial period still standing in the nation's capital. Then we will attempt to identify the ways in which Cabral is subject to different appropriations by different communities, political elites, and protest movements, signalling the symbolic, ideological and affective asymmetries at play in the co-production of the public memory of the struggle and mobilising and re-signifying Cabral's image.

*

Like all texts, this book is anchored in a series of contingencies. As Portuguese researchers, our perspective was necessarily marked by the fact that we did not grow up in the archipelago nor have been exposed over

10 *Introduction*

the years to its political, social and cultural vicissitudes and contexts. Our study was carried out in a delimited period of time, between 2017 and 2022. During these years, we made regular trips to Cape Verde, where we carried out fieldwork, particularly in the islands of Santiago and São Vicente. There we were able to develop our hypotheses, conduct interviews, do participant observation and consult various visual and written sources. We owe a warm and heartfelt thanks to all the institutions and people in the country that helped us. We have made many friends and this unpayable debt alone is enough to make this task meaningful. The list is long and we have decided to include proper acknowledgments in a final note. As it is common to say on these occasions, without them this book would not be possible at all, although possible omissions or less successful interpretations are our responsibility. We hope that the book succeeds in conveying the essential point that, from the beginning, motivated us to write it: showing how the liberation struggle is a conflictual heritage that continues to play a role in reconfiguring Cape Verde's past, present and future.

Notes

1 This work was produced as part of the CROME project – *Crossed Memories, Politics of Silence. The Colonial-Liberation War in Postcolonial Times*, funded by the *European Research Council*, under the European Union's Horizon 2020 Framework Programme for Research and Innovation (StG-ERC-715593) based at the Centre for Social Studies of the University of Coimbra.

2 In 1582, of the total number of inhabitants on Santiago, which was estimated to be around 13,500, about 13% were free citizens (whites, *mestiços* and freed blacks), while 87% were enslaved people. On Fogo, of the 2,300 inhabitants, 2,000 were enslaved (which would correspond to roughly the same percentage). Cf. Iva Cabral, "O processo de formação da sociedade cabo-verdiana (finais do séc. XV a finais do séc. XVIII)", in *Radiografia Crioula. Um diagnóstico político e social de Cabo Verde*, org. Bruno Carriço Reis (Lisboa and Faro: Universidade Autónoma de Lisboa / Sílabas & Desafios, 2016), 29–47.

3 António Leão Correia e Silva, *Noite Escravocrata. Madrugada Camponesa. Cabo Verde, sec. XV–XVIII* (Praia: Rosa de Porcelana, 2021), 17.

4 António Carreira, *Cabo Verde. Formação e extinção de uma sociedade escravocrata (1460–1878)* (Praia: Instituto Cabo-verdeano do Livro, 1983); Luís de Albuquerque and Maria Emília Madeira Santos, ed., *História Geral de Cabo Verde, vol. X* (Lisboa and Praia: Instituto de Investigação Científica Tropical / Direcção-Geral do Património Cultural de Cabo Verde, 1991); Iva Cabral, *A Primeira Elite Colonial Atlântica. Dos "homens honrados brancos" de Santiago à "nobreza da terra". Finais do séc. XV – início do séc. XVII* (Praia: Livraria Pedro Cardoso, 2015).

5 José Carlos Gomes dos Anjos, "A condição de mediador político-cultural em Cabo Verde: intelectuais e diferentes versões da identidade nacional", *Etnográfica* 7, no. 2 (2004): 273–295; João Vasconcelos, "Espíritos Lusófonos numa ilha crioula: Língua, poder e identidade em São Vicente de Cabo Verde", in *A persistência da história: Passado e Contemporaneidade em África*, ed. Clara Carvalho and João Pina Cabral (Lisboa: Imprensa de

Introduction 11

Ciências Sociais, 2004), 149–190; Rego, *The Dialogic Nation of Cape Verde*; Rui Cidra, "Cabral, popular music and the debate on Cape Verdean creoleness", *Postcolonial Studies* 21, no. 4 (2018): 433–451; Eurídice Monteiro, "Crioulidade, colonialidade e género: as representações de Cabo Verde", *Revista Estudos Feministas* 24, no. 3 (2016): 983–996.

6 According to the official narrative, the party, then called PAI (African Independence Party) was founded in Bissau on 19 September, 1956. Julião Soares Sousa raises a series of doubts about whether the PAI was effectively constituted on that date. He suggested that its creation was in 1959, at a time that MLG (Guinean Liberation Movement) already existed. This group had been created months before, and some of the main supporters of PAI were collaborating with it. The designation PAIGC, as well as its programme, appeared publicly in 1960. See Julião Soares Sousa, *Amílcar Cabral (1924–1973). Vida e morte de um revolucionário africano* (Praia: Spleen, 2013), 184–235. Tomás also considers it unlikely that the party was founded on 1956, noting that Cabral makes no reference to its existence until 1960 in his correspondence with the MAC (Anti-Colonial Movement). António Tomás, *O Fazedor de Utopias. Uma biografia de Amílcar Cabral* (Lisboa: Tinta-da-China, 2007), 107–108. Aristides Pereira's explanation is that the date 19 September, 1956 was chosen later in Conakry by Aristides Pereira, Amílcar Cabral, and Luís Cabral to appease Léopold Senghor, who thought they were a branch of the Senegalese PAI, founded in 1957. It was therefore thought appropriate to add a "GC" and set a date when Cabral would have been in Bissau and actually met with prominent comrades. Cf. José Vicente Lopes, *Aristides Pereira. Minha Vida, Nossa História* (Praia: Spleen, 2012), 175.

7 On the life and death of Amílcar Cabral, see for example: Mário de Andrade, *Amílcar Cabral: essai de biographie politique* (Paris: François Maspero, 1980); Patrick Chabal, *Amílcar Cabral. Revolutionary leadership and people's war* (London: Cambridge University Press, 1983); Mustafah Dhada, *Warriors at work: how Guinea was really set free* (Colorado: University Press of Colorado, 1993); José Pedro Castanheira, *Quem Mandou Matar Amílcar Cabral* (Lisboa: Relógio D'Água, 1995); Tomás, *O fazedor de utopias.*; Sousa, *Amílcar Cabral (1924–1973)*; Daniel dos Santos, *Amílcar Cabral: um Outro Olhar* (Lisboa: Chiado Editora, 2014); Peter Karibe Mendy, *Amílcar Cabral. A Nationalist and Pan-Africanist Revolutionary* (Ohio: Ohio University Press, 2019).

8 See, for example, Ângela Benoliel Coutinho, "Criação, em Cuba, das Forças Armadas de Cabo Verde", in *As Voltas do Passado. A guerra colonial e as lutas de libertação*, ed. Miguel Cardina and Bruno Sena Martins (Lisboa: Tinta-da-China, 2018), 172–177.

9 See, for example, José Vicente Lopes, *Cabo Verde. Os Bastidores da Independência* (Praia: Spleen Edições, 1996); Ângela Benoliel Coutinho, *Os Dirigentes do PAIGC. Da fundação à rutura. 1956–1980* (Coimbra: Imprensa da Universidade de Coimbra, 2017).

10 Cf. for example, Miguel Cardina, "O Passado Colonial: do trajeto histórico às configurações da memória", in *O Século XX Português. Política, Economia, Sociedade, Cultura, Império*, Fernando Rosas et al. (Lisboa: Tinta-da-China, 2020), 357–411; Miguel Cardina and Bruno Sena Martins, "Memorias cruzadas de la guerra colonial portuguesa y las luchas de liberación africanas: del Imperio a los Estados poscoloniales", *Endoxa* 44 (2019): 113–134.

11 João Paulo Borges Coelho, "Politics and Contemporary History in Mozambique. A Set of Epistemological Notes", *Kronos* 39, no. 1 (2013): 20–31.

12   Introduction

12 Coelho, "Política e História Contemporânea em Moçambique", 8–9.
13 Coelho, "Política e História Contemporânea em Moçambique", 4–5.
14 Besides its use in the field of psychology, the concept has been also mobilized by other scholars, although in a sense that does not coincide with the one we have outlined here. For example, starting from an analysis of name plaques commemorating the dead, Ana Lúcia Araújo takes them as "mnemonic devices" for aiding – or enabling – the recognition and remembrance of the victims of slavery in the US. Ana Lúcia Araújo, "Raising the Dead: Walls of Names as Mnemonic Devices to Commemorate Enslaved People", *Current Anthropology* 61, no. 22 (2020): 328–339.
15 Gregor Feindt et al., "Entangled Memory: Toward a Third Wave in Memory Studies", *History and Theory* 53 (2014): 31–32.
16 Jan Assman, *Moses the Egyptian: The Memory of Egypt in Western Monotheism* (Cambridge and London: Harvard University Press, 1997), 24–44.
17 "Unlike history proper, mnemohistory is concerned not with the past as such, but only with the past as it is remembered. It surveys the story-lines of tradition, the webs of intertextuality, the diachronic continuities and discontinuities of reading the past", Assman, *Moses the Egyptian*, 9.
18 Marek Tamm, ed., *Afterlife of Events. Perspectives on Mnemohistory* (London: Palgrave Macmillan, 2015), 3.
19 Berber Bevernage and Nico Wouters, eds., *The Palgrave Handbook of State-Sponsored History after 1945* (London: Palgrave Macmillan, 2018), 5.
20 Bevernage and Wouters, *The Palgrave Handbook*, 6.
21 Berthold Molden, "Resistant pasts versus mnemonic hegemony: On the power relations of collective memory", *Memory Studies* 9, no. 2 (2016): 127–130.
22 Molden, "Resistant pasts", 130.
23 A previous analysis of this phenomenon was made in Miguel Cardina and Inês Nascimento Rodrigues, "The mnemonic transition: The rise of an anti-anticolonial memoryscape in Cape Verde", *Memory Studies* 14, no. 2 (2021): 380–394.
24 Rego, *The Dialogic Nation of Cape Verde*, 77.

Bibliography

Albuquerque, Luís de and Maria Emília Madeira Santos, eds. *História Geral de Cabo Verde, vol. X*. Lisboa and Praia: Instituto de Investigação Científica Tropical / Direcção-Geral do Património Cultural de Cabo Verde, 1991.

Anjos, José Carlos Gomes dos. "A condição de mediador político-cultural em Cabo Verde: intelectuais e diferentes versões da identidade nacional". *Etnográfica* 7, no. 2 (2004): 273–295.

Araújo, Ana Lúcia. "Raising the Dead: Walls of Names as Mnemonic Devices to Commemorate Enslaved People". *Current Anthropology* 61, no. 22 (2020): 328–339.

Assman, Jan. *Moses the Egyptian: The Memory of Egypt in Western Monotheism*. Cambridge and London: Harvard University Press, 1997.

Bevernage, Berber and Nico Wouters, eds. *The Palgrave Handbook of State-Sponsored History after 1945*. London: Palgrave Macmillan, 2018.

Cabral, Iva. "O processo de formação da sociedade cabo-verdiana (finais do séc. XV a finais do séc. XVIII)". In *Radiografia Crioula. Um diagnóstico político e social de Cabo Verde*, edited by Bruno Carriço Reis, 29–47. Lisboa and Faro: Universidade Autónoma de Lisboa / Sílabas & Desafios, 2016.

Introduction 13

Cabral, Iva. *A Primeira Elite Colonial Atlântica. Dos "homens honrados brancos" de Santiago à "nobreza da terra"*. *Finais do séc. XV – início do séc. XVII*. Praia: Livraria Pedro Cardoso, 2015.

Cardina, Miguel and Bruno Sena Martins. "Memorias cruzadas de la guerra colonial portuguesa y las luchas de liberación africanas: del Imperio a los Estados poscoloniales". *Endoxa* 44 (2019): 113–134.

Cardina, Miguel and Inês Nascimento Rodrigues. "The mnemonic transition: The rise of an anti-anticolonial memoryscape in Cape Verde". *Memory Studies* 14, no. 2 (2021): 380–394.

Cardina, Miguel. "O Passado Colonial: do trajeto histórico às configurações da memória". In *O Século XX Português*. *Política, Economia, Sociedade, Cultura, Império*, edited by Fernando Rosas, Francisco Louçã, João Teixeira Lopes, Andrea Peniche, Luís Trindade and Miguel Cardina, 357–411. Lisboa: Tinta-da-China, 2020.

Carreira, António. *Cabo Verde. Formação e extinção de uma sociedade escravocrata (1460–1878)*. Praia: Instituto Cabo-verdeano do Livro, 1983.

Castanheira, José Pedro. *Quem Mandou Matar Amílcar Cabral*. Lisboa: Relógio D'Água, 1995.

Chabal, Patrick. *Amílcar Cabral. Revolutionary leadership and people's war*. London: Cambridge University Press, 1983.

Cidra, Rui. "Cabral, popular music and the debate on Cape Verdean creoleness". *Postcolonial Studies* 21, no. 4 (2018): 433–451.

Coelho, João Paulo Borges. "Politics and contemporary history in Mozambique. A set of epistemological notes". *Kronos* 39, no. 1 (2013): 20–31.

Coutinho, Ângela Benoliel. "Criação, em Cuba, das Forças Armadas de Cabo Verde". In *As Voltas do Passado. A guerra colonial e as lutas de libertação*, edited by Miguel Cardina and Bruno Sena Martins, 172–177. Lisboa: Tinta-da-China, 2018.

Coutinho, Ângela Benoliel. *Os Dirigentes do PAIGC. Da fundação à rutura. 1956–1980*. Coimbra: Imprensa da Universidade de Coimbra, 2017.

de Andrade, Mário. *Amílcar Cabral: essai de biographie politique*. Paris: François Maspero, 1980.

Dhada, Mustafah. *Warriors at work: how Guinea was really set free*. Colorado: University Press of Colorado, 1993.

Feindt, Gregor, Félix Krawatzek, Daniela Mehler, Friedemann Pestel, and Rieke Trimçev. "Entangled memory: Toward a third wave in memory studies". *History and Theory* 53 (2014): 24–44.

Lopes, José Vicente. *Cabo Verde. Os Bastidores da Independência*. Praia: Spleen Edições, 1996.

Mendy, Peter Karibe. *Amílcar Cabral. A Nationalist and Pan-Africanist Revolutionary*. Ohio: Ohio University Press, 2019.

Molden, Berthold. "Resistant pasts versus mnemonic hegemony: On the power relations of collective memory". *Memory Studies* 9, no. 2 (2016): 127–130.

Monteiro, Eurídice. "Crioulidade, colonialidade e género: as representações de Cabo Verde". *Revista Estudos Feministas* 24, no. 3 (2016): 983–996.

Rego, Márcia. *The Dialogic Nation of Cape Verde. Slavery, Language and Ideology*. New York and London: Lexington Books, 2015.

Santos, Daniel. *Amílcar Cabral: um Outro Olhar*. Lisboa: Chiado Editora, 2014.

14   Introduction

Sousa, Julião Soares. *Amílcar Cabral (1924–1973)*. *Vida e morte de um revolucionário africano*. Praia: Spleen, 2013.

Tamm, Marek, ed. *Afterlife of Events. Perspectives on Mnemohistory*. London: Palgrave Macmillan, 2015.

Tomás, António. *O fazedor de utopias: uma biografia de Amílcar Cabral*. Lisboa: Tinta-da-China, 2007.

Vasconcelos, João. "Espíritos Lusófonos numa ilha crioula: Língua, poder e identidade em São Vicente de Cabo Verde". In *A persistência da história: Passado e Contemporaneidade em África*, edited by Clara Carvalho and João Pina Cabral, 149–190. Lisboa: Imprensa de Ciências Sociais, 2004.

1 THE STRUGGLE AS THE CRADLE OF THE INDEPENDENT NATION

On 5 July 1975, Cape Verde proclaimed its independence in a ceremony in the capital city, Praia, attended by thousands of Cape Verdeans, along with international organisations, liberation struggle combatants, journalists, State representatives from foreign countries and representatives of African independence movements (see Figure 1.1). In the Várzea stadium, where the six-hour ceremony was held, processions of young people wore clothes with Amílcar Cabral's face printed on them and waved placards with slogans such as "Amílcar Cabral, People's Hero", "Down with imperialism" or "Our land is for our people".[1] There was a parade of the People's Revolutionary Armed Forces (FARP) and cultural expressions such as *tabanka*.[2] In front of the tribune of honour was a large poster with a portrait of Amílcar Cabral and the phrase *"Cabral ca mori"* – "Cabral did not die". Later, after the agreement on the independence was signed, the Portuguese flag was lowered and handed over to Vasco Gonçalves – then Portuguese Prime Minister – and replaced by the flag of the new country, raised to the sound of the new national anthem of Cape Verde.[3]

In the proclamation of independence, Abílio Duarte, first president of the People's National Assembly, announced the end of colonialism and declared the PAIGC to be the leading "force, light and guide" of Cape Verdean society.[4] Praising Amílcar Cabral as the "founder and foremost militant of the PAIGC" and "immortal guide", Abílio Duarte asserted the principle of the unity of Guinea and Cape Verde forged in the struggle. The unity echoed a common past – by the "communion of blood, of martyrdoms and of history" – shared since the days of slavery.[5] Now that colonial domination and subjugation were broken, Duarte went on, Cape Verde freely choose its "African destiny". The *freedom* to choose the path of independence, as part of the wave of anti-colonial struggles that were then being waged in Africa, was guided by the idea of a *destiny* that was being fulfilled: Cape Verde was now aligned with the "winds of history".

In this chapter, we will try to identify the ways in which the notion of *struggle* – especially its armed dimension – acquired centrality in the first years of independence, while it also invoked very disparate meanings,

DOI: 10.4324/9781003265535-2

16 *The Struggle as the Cradle of the Independent Nation*

Figure 1.1 "Ceremony to Proclaim the Independence of Cape Verde, in Praia", Fundação Mário Soares e Maria Barroso / Arquivo Amílcar Cabral.
Source: Author unknown.

political uses and chronologies. The struggle as a mnemonic device thus acquired a redemptive and multi-directional function. Establishing itself as a concrete possible response – cultural, social and political – to a past of violence, the struggle carries with it the promise of new futures and beginnings. We aim at analysing the ways in which, in the first 15 years of independence, the struggle provided other keys for interpreting Cape Verdean history. This process will be observed from two memorial flows. The first, in which the exalting mobilisation of the memory of the struggle organised the past and defined the identity of the independent State. In this phase, the activation of the struggle gave visibility not only to colonial violence, as exemplified by the cyclical famines that hit the archipelago, but also to the successive acts of resistance to which it gave rise. It also refocused the new country's relationship with the African continent and with the meaning of the anti-colonial experience, process for which the affirmation of music as an expression of cultural independence works here as an example. A second memorial flow is associated with a movement to relegitimise the State and calibrate memory, particularly evident from the second half of the 1980s. Here, the narrative drawn by the struggle showed signs of losing explanatory power as a result of the

The Struggle as the Cradle of the Independent Nation 17

rupture with Guinea-Bissau in 1980, challenges to the single-party State and the evocation of other pasts that, for example, valued miscegenation in defining Cape Verdean history and culture.

Building the Nation State and the centrality of the struggle

On the eve of 5 July, the National Assembly met for the first time to approve the text of the proclamation of independence and to nominate Aristides Pereira and Pedro Pires, senior PAIGC leaders, as President of the Republic and Prime Minister of Cape Verde, respectively. At the same meeting, it was decided to approve the LOPE (Law on the Political Organisation of the State)[6] and the law awarding "Comrade Amílcar Cabral the title of Founder of the Nationality", establishing 12 September, the date of his birth, as a National Day and giving his name to the highest honour of the State. A few days earlier, on 30 June 1975, the election of 56 deputies to the parliamentary assembly of the new country had taken place, with a turnout of nearly 90% of the population. Of these, 92% approved the single list presented by the PAIGC, thereby legitimising the party in power.[7] The tensions that had occurred in the previous months, especially in the interval between 25 April 1974, the date of the revolution in Portugal, and 5 July 1975, the date of the proclamation of independence in Cape Verde, seemed to have been left behind. During this period, there were several conflicts with political organisations – particularly the UPICV (Union of the People of the Cape Verde Islands) and the UDC (Cape Verdean Democratic Union) – who had different plans and solutions for the archipelago.

The UPICV, which enjoyed some support on the island of Santiago, advocated immediate independence, but without the link to Guinea-Bissau. It had been founded in 1959, and its main leader was José Leitão da Graça who had been politically active first in Cape Verde and then in Senegal, where he had prepared the first draft of the movement's statutes. Material was sent from Dakar, where a group linked to him was formed, to Rhode Island, where his brother (Aires Leitão da Graça) founded the Providence branch. The organisation gradually adopted Maoism, and was always opposed to unification with Guinea. The leader of the UPICV only returned to Cape Verde in August 1974, while his wife, Maria Leitão da Graça, also a ruling member of the party, had arrived only shortly before. This made it even more difficult to establish a structure amongst the political turmoil and when the PAIGC already had undeniable hegemony.[8]

The UDC, in turn, had been created in May 1974, in São Vicente, following the 25th April revolution in Portugal, and brought together intellectuals, landowners, merchants, civil servants and members of the clergy.[9] It also opposed unification with Guinea and supported a phased

18   *The Struggle as the Cradle of the Independent Nation*

self-determination for the archipelago, but only after a referendum and a more gradual path.[10] As the group noted, "the right to independence is the highest aspiration of a people, who have lived for centuries under colonial domination", although it was necessary to reject what was seen as a "premature independence", which would be a "reckless adventure".[11]

In the year or so that preceded the independence of Cape Verde, the political and social tensions between these groups and the PAIGC intensified. There were exchanges of insults and accusations on both sides, culminating in the banning of a demonstration organised by the UPICV in November 1974 and the taking of *Rádio Barlavento* – an arena for criticising the PAIGC, backed by the UDC in Mindelo, on the island of São Vicente – by popular groups led by the PAIGC in December of the same year.[12]

Following these episodes, dozens of militants from both organisations were imprisoned in the former Tarrafal camp by the Portuguese authorities, who had already recognised the PAIGC as the legitimate representative of the Cape Verde people in the "Algiers Agreement" signed on 26 August 1974.[13] Like other anti-colonial movements that started liberation struggles, the PAIGC claimed to be the legitimate founder of the state. And, in fact, this is how it was perceived by the international community, including the UN (United Nations) and the OAU (Organization of African Unity).

At the same time, the Cape Verde combatants who had taken part in the armed struggle in Guinea had been gradually returning to the archipelago. The popular unrest in the islands and the strengthening of the PAIGC's position in the negotiations with the Portuguese government through the signing of the "Lisbon Agreement" on 19 December 1974 – which provided for the appointment of a transitional government and set the date of independence – consolidated their hegemony. It distanced the opposing groups once and for all and created the preconditions for the PAIGC to establish itself as the leadership of the new State.[14] According to Ângela Coutinho, more than half of the PAIGC's senior military officers went on to assume positions of high responsibility within the party and the State after independence, and so, some of the experiences of the armed struggle found expression in the early years of Cape Verde's post-colonial life.[15]

Some aspects of this continuity were announced from the beginning. At midnight on 5 July, hours before the ceremony that would proclaim Cape Verde's independence, Aristides Pereira, secretary-general of the PAIGC, read a message to the population of the islands over the microphones of *Rádio Voz do Povo* and *Rádio São Vicente*. In it, he evoked the glorious example of Amilcar Cabral, as well as the names of other liberation struggle combatants who had died during the war.[16] Pereira also took the opportunity to pay homage to all those who had been victims of colonialism over the centuries. He asked that the sacrifice of those who

The Struggle as the Cradle of the Independent Nation   19

had resisted and fought for so long should not be belittled, so that the archipelago could be transformed from then on into a place where there would never again be hunger, from where Cape Verdeans would never again have to emigrate, and where injustices would no longer take place.[17]

Aristides Pereira's communication at the dawn of independence leaves explicit and implicit three elements: first, that the anti-colonial struggle and the independence to which it gave rise constitute a rupture with the colonial past with a dimension of redemption, allowing a "before" and an "after" to be enunciated; second, that the struggle created hierarchies of citizenship, based on the figure of the combatant; and third, that the experience of the struggle allowed for the articulation and definition of solutions to the great threat, and also the great challenge, that had long hanged over the archipelago: its viability.

In fact, few considered it possible for Cape Verde to survive the periodic droughts and famines that had marked the archipelago's history. Most of the islands had poor arable soil, buffeted by a tropical climate, with strong winds and very little and uncertain rainfall. The increase in population and livestock with the consumption of the existing vegetation for firewood and furniture has aggravated the country's ecological vulnerability. Hunger had therefore become a constant. At particularly critical moments, up to a third of the islands' population might die, as may have happened between 1863 and 1866, when there were 30,000 deaths out of a population that numbered barely 100,000 inhabitants.[18] In the 20th century, during the 1940s, there were two severe famines – 1941/1943 and 1947/1948 – which caused more than 45,000 deaths and led to another 15,000 people being forced to migrate, mostly to the coffee and cocoa plantations of São Tomé and Príncipe.[19] This African archipelago in the Gulf of Guinea, also colonised by the Portuguese, had been transformed into a lucrative plantation economy sustained first by enslaved subjects and then by forced labour, a practice that would become a historical feature of Cape Verdeans' migratory experiences.

Although the population faced regular periods of both control and uncertainty, famines and death had already been a recurring focus for protest and criticism in Cape Verdean pamphlets and press articles from the final decades of the 1800s. When the Portuguese Republic was replaced by a military dictatorship in 1926 newspapers in Cape Verde were subject to tighter censorship, particularly evident from the 1930s onwards, under the Estado Novo regime (1933–1974).[20] Denouncing poverty, starvation, colonial abandonment and forced migration became a role assumed and consolidated predominantly by literature, literary magazines and music.[21] It was through cultural representations that the suffering and history of Cape-Verdean people was then publicly witnessed and recorded. While the issue of hunger and droughts was mobilised by Cape Verde's intellectual elites as a way of monitoring the actions of the colonial administration from the beginning of the 20th century, the uses

20   *The Struggle as the Cradle of the Independent Nation*

of this memory in terms of the anti-colonial struggle acquired distinct and strategic meanings. In a recent book about the spectre of famine and the political responses to it in Cape Verde since the 1940s, journalist José Vicente Lopes states the profound impact of hunger to Cape Verdean nationalism, as a social element representing the extreme abandonment and violence perpetrated by colonialism in the islands.[22] From early on, the PAIGC configured the struggle as an element of continuity in the ancestral resistance to slavery and then to famines and consequent migrations southwards.

These experiences were, therefore, evoked with renewed vigour during the years immediately preceding the transition to armed struggle and during the struggle itself, particularly in Amílcar Cabral's texts and speeches and in official PAIGC documents. In 1961, in a report on the national liberation struggle presented at the Conference of Nationalist Organizations of Guinea and the Cape Verde Islands, held in Dakar, Amílcar Cabral explicitly highlighted this symbolic association, which would later resurface in several of his future speeches:

> In the Cape Verde Islands, numerous revolts have signalled the people's hatred of Portuguese rule since the slave era. The people rose up on several occasions against the landlords and against foreign rule, especially in Santiago, Santo Antão and São Vicente, through demonstrations, strikes and revolts. Our struggle is the continuation of the one that was started by our people against the Portuguese colonialists. In Guinea and the Cape Verde Islands, the situation is getting progressively worse due to the escalation of Portuguese oppression and as a result of the development of our liberation struggle.
> [...].
> In the Cape Verde Islands, in addition to the repressive measures taken by the colonial administration and the PIDE, the Portuguese government once again left around 10,000 people starve to death in 1958–1959. The Cape Verdean population, which in a period of only six years (1942 to 1947) fell by thirty to forty thousand people, decimated by famine, continues at the mercy of 'agricultural crises' and is subjected to the export of thousands of its children as hired labourers to the Portuguese plantations in the other colonies.[23]

From this perspective, the struggle was outlined as a response to successive waves of violence that, more or less distant in time, the colonial presence caused in the archipelago. The experiences of famines and forced labour in the plantations then became part of the narrative of the anti-colonial struggle led and mobilised by the PAIGC, reinforced by the fact that several of its main militants retained memory of them and enounced them as the main cause that sparked their decision to act against colonialism.[24] Years later, Pedro Pires, a commander in Guinea and first Prime

The Struggle as the Cradle of the Independent Nation   21

Minister of Cape Verde, explicitly mentioned them as the traumatic circumstances that catalysed his political mobilisation and awareness.

> There are three facts that disturbed me as a young man: the first was the famine of 42–43, which made me witness horrible scenes and to see directly how badly people lived. The second was in Praia, when I watched the return of labourers from São Tomé. And the third bad memory was in São Vicente when I saw labourers embarking, also to São Tomé. That was in 1955–56. That day I had the impression that the whole city was traumatised, the people sad and disoriented. People were leaving, they didn't know where, but they had to go. All this led me to think and later to choose a path... [the struggle for independence].[25]

By configuring itself as a mnemonic device that reorganised the past, the activation of the memory of the struggle in the first years of independence led to encounters with other memories, convergent but related to other times, spaces and actors. Stimulating the memory of the struggle is, in this context, also a way of reclaiming the more distant memories of famines and their legacies, and more broadly of colonialism itself. By intertwining these elements of suffering and resistance in a dialogic exercise, they can be read as part of the same history, in a movement close to that which Michael Rothberg calls "multidirectional memory".

Rothberg's popularised concept has substantially reconfigured the understanding of collective memory, highlighting the possibilities of activating a "multidirectional memory" that articulates different pasts (for example, the memory of the Holocaust and the memory of slavery and colonialism) and which goes beyond a "competitive" perspective, that is, "as a zero-sum struggle over scarce resources".[26] The notion of "multidirectional memory" would thus allow to productively contrast different memories with common aspects. Stressing the mobility of memory and the dislocations that mark any act of remembering, Rothberg thus draws attention to its multi-directional character, that is, the way in which particular stories engage with each other, "subject to negotiation, cross-referencing and borrowing".[27] In this gesture, the role of imagination and the framing of memorial acts within the context of the power relations that are socially established at any given moment is decisive.

In this particular case, multi-directionality also establishes a teleological path that enables tracing a narrow thread of continuity between the famines and the liberation struggle. The two memories feed back on each other because they become part of a common memorial frame: the odyssey that establishes the independent nation. It is not without foundation, therefore, as Victor Barros emphasises, that the commemorative acts of the nation in the post-independence period tend to associate the emergence of the anti-colonial consciousness in Cabral with the scenario

22 *The Struggle as the Cradle of the Independent Nation*

of hunger as a true precursor to the revolt and the desire to abolish the colonial regime.[28] The idea of combating hunger as a political priority in the immediate post-independence period is mentioned by José Vicente Lopes in *Cabo Verde. Um corpo que se recusa a morrer. 70 anos contra fome, 1949–2019* (Cape Verde. A body that refuses to die. 70 years against hunger, 1949–2019). In this book, published in 2021, the author shows the strong investment of the new State in the dynamization of socioeconomic structures such as EMPA – *Empresa de Abastecimento Público* (Public Supply Company) and FAIMO – *Frentes de Alta Intensidade de Mão-de-Obra* (Labour-Intensive Work Fronts), aimed at employing population in need and dealing with the spectre of systemic food shortages.[29]

In the first years following independence, cooperatives and public companies were formed for oil, water and electricity, schools were built and education was democratised. The health care network was expanded and a process of ecological viability was introduced to modernise and reconfigure agriculture and introduce agrarian reform. The Bank of Cape Verde was created, people's courts were formed, a telecommunications system was developed and a maritime transport company set up to connect the islands and facilitate travel between them.[30] So-called Labour-Intensive Work Fronts (FAIMO) were organised, with the dual objective of reducing unemployment and implementing the government's strategies in the areas of infrastructure and public works. FAIMO was a foreign aid-supported programme focused mainly on supply and assistance – through job creation – to rural populations threatened by droughts.

At the same time that the struggle as a mnemonic device enabled other ways of reading the past, it also established itself as a particular mechanism for constructing the present and the future. It is in the context of a weak economy, continuous droughts, food shortages, arid soils, famine, but also illiteracy and difficulty of accessibility between islands that, soon after independence, the young State embarked on a development-focused agenda and made efforts to combat the spectre of Cape Verde's unviability as an independent country. Combating food shortages through soil protection, reforestation and effective water infiltration – along with heavy investment in health and education – was one of the State's priorities in the immediate post-independence period. Opting for a single-party regime, termed "revolutionary national democracy", and for a centralised economy, the new leading cadres also assumed pragmatic management of the newly sovereign State. This was based, among others, on a foreign policy of non-alignment, against the backdrop of the Cold War following the end of World War II and the decolonisation processes that followed. Being part of the Non-Aligned Movement allowed the country some autonomy to cooperate with any of the blocs and benefit from different international funding, and economic and food support programmes. It also meant not antagonising the various countries with significant Cape Verde emigrants around the world.

The Struggle as the Cradle of the Independent Nation   23

Facing various challenges, the question was no longer a struggle for liberation, but a broader struggle, for which the first would serve as a metaphor: a struggle for a more robust economy, for ecological sustainability, for political and cultural affirmation and for contact with its multiple diasporas (in Europe, Africa and America). In 1984, for example, following severe floods that devastated the islands, Aristides Pereira established this parallel, stating that "just as our glorious struggle for national liberation, this persevering and arduous struggle to construct a viable state, to develop and build a dignified life in our country has its heroes and martyrs", so too do those "who lost their lives at their posts, as true combatants whose memory remains engraved in our spirit as martyrs".[31]

The semantic lexicon of struggle and some of its innovative experiences, particularly those tested in the liberated areas of Guinea, now emerged, in part, as defining models of state-building and its institutions, not only in ideological and discursive terms, but also in areas such as justice (with particular focus on the issue of popular participation), education and health.[32] A similar process also happened, to a large extent, with the hierarchies inherited from the struggle. In effect, there was a political legitimacy and symbolic recognition produced by the participation in the liberation struggle which extended to the movement that had led it. This process was not, however, consensual. Besides the disputes between those who did or did not want immediate independence or about the path that should be followed, as mentioned above, there were also divergences among militants of various sensibilities and origins within the PAIGC itself, both amongst those who had waged the armed struggle in Guinea, and between these and militants who had remained underground. In this last group, there were, roughly speaking, also disputes among militants who had participated in clandestine actions internally, in Cape Verde, or outside the archipelago, in Portugal.[33]

The leadership's option for a policy of rapprochement with both the West and the socialist bloc was one focus of tension within the PAIGC, particularly with a group of younger party members associated with Trotskyism, consisting of former students who, in essence, had become politicised and undertaken clandestine activities in Portugal.[34] Between 1976 and 1979, some of these elements dissented from the party, taking a stand against what they considered to be an autocratic State, although their departure and / or distancing were also taken by some to be the result of years of personal rivalries, generational and ideological differences, or disputes over political turf.[35] In Cape Verde, "Trotskyism" became a label used to characterise a group of militants and leaders in the post-independence period who were committed to deepening the socialist and anti-imperialist stance and to accentuating the dynamics of participation, and who generally distanced themselves from office, from the party and, in some cases, from the country.[36]

24   *The Struggle as the Cradle of the Independent Nation*

These internal tensions revealed the different ways in which the various groups in the PAIGC had experienced the struggle. This had a decisive influence on their conceptions of the nation, governance styles and the idea of the State to be built: the military experience of the combatants in the armed struggle (in Guinea) was substantially different from the political experience of the clandestine militants in Portugal, which was different again from that of the clandestine militants within Cape Verde, all three existing in turbulent cohabitation. Cláudio Furtado notes that the combatants' hegemony became visible in the dispute for positions within the PAIGC's leading structures even before independence, as early as March 1975. Of the 32 members who were now part of the National Commission of Cape Verde (CNCV), the most important party-political decision-making body, 19 were combatants from the armed struggle, and of those, 15 occupied the top positions in the hierarchy. There were nine representatives from the "Lisbon group", mostly associated with the Trotskyists.[37] In the CNCV Permanent Secretariat, the five names in this top structure were all prominent fighters from the "old guard", i.e. historical leaders of the PAIGC (Pedro Pires, Abílio Duarte, Silvino da Luz, Osvaldo Lopes da Silva and Olívio Pires).[38] It was therefore mainly combatants with experience of the struggle in Guinea and top political positions in the liberation movement who came to constitute the new Cape Verdean leadership structure, at the top of the PAIGC and occupying most ministerial posts. They functioned as the repository of political legitimacy in the newly independent country.

The State apparatus also included a bureaucratic elite, with a command of the Portuguese language and stable employment anchored to the State.[39] As Crisanto Barros stressed, the political-administrative elite, as well as a good proportion of the ruling party's leadership structure, was paradoxically a result of the investment in education brought about by the implantation of the Republic in Portugal in 1910 and encouraged, especially from the 1950s on, by Christian congregations, Catholic and Protestant, and more decisively by the expansion of the late-colonial State.[40] By allocating resources and expanding public administration to curb the anti-colonial sympathy that raged internally and externally, the late-colonial State eventually prepared the ground for a new *eliticised* social class that mobilised around the struggle and the PAIGC.[41]

The ruling elite in the first decade of independence – those who held positions at the highest level of responsibility in State institutions (ministers, head of State, president of the National Assembly, etc.) – would have the armed struggle as their experiential reference point. Ângela Coutinho notes that a significant proportion of this new political elite was descended from an upper-middle or upper social class, possessing cultural (although not necessarily economic) capital that their descendants reconfigured into symbolic capital.[42] It is from among these families, with connections predominantly associated with the State and the Catholic

The Struggle as the Cradle of the Independent Nation 25

Church, that the future leaders of the revolutionary movement emerged, almost all of them educated at the Gil Eanes High School in Mindelo, the only secondary school in the archipelago between 1917 and 1960.[43] From 1975 on, they became important agents in nation state-building, bringing the anti-colonial process into everyday life and making it meaningful.

From there, in the immediate post-independence period, a memory of the struggle was formed comprising discursive, visual and political spaces in which the value of this past predominated. The independence brought its own symbols and its pantheon of "heroes", a series of characters and individuals who were deemed worthy of being valued and honoured. Cláudio Furtado designates them as the "uncommons", that is, those who had experiential references that constituted "an important capital for them and for their party".[44] In these years, qualities were attributed to combatants that distinguished them from other Cape Verdean citizens. They were called "the best sons of Cape Verde" or "the worthiest sons of the land" for having given their lives or sacrificed the years of their youth to the anti-colonial cause. They were referred to in the press, in music, and in political speeches as "liberators" for their participation in the victorious struggle against Portuguese rule. In this case, the evocation of the struggle functioned as a mnemonic device that was activated for the purposes of political legitimation. The memory of the struggle was thus established as a generator of symbolic capital, prestige and recognition, attributed both to the PAIGC and to the members who waged the struggle within it.

In the case of Cape Verde (and, in different ways, also Guinea), the hierarchies of power and citizenship were confronted with the existence of a superlative hero, Amilcar Cabral, who was always present during these years.[45] For a number of reasons, he occupies the role of the greatest figure in the independent nation: he was the historical leader of the PAIGC and of the struggle against Portuguese colonialism, and was internationally recognised for his political and diplomatic skills, with a reputation that endures to this day; he was assassinated before Guinea and Cape Verde gained their independence, which gives him the aura of a martyr; he is praised as a shrewd strategist and an astute intellectual and theoretician, who added a series of broader cultural, social and political teachings to the concept of struggle that still reverberate today.

Amílcar Cabral became a permanent presence in the first decade of independence: his name and his life are constantly evoked in the Cape Verdean popular songs and mentioned by structures created by the PAIGC. Some examples of this include the Abel Djassi Pioneers Organization, inspired by Cabral's war name, for children between 9 and 14 years old; the PAICV staff training school, named after him, the Amílcar Cabral Institute (IAC);[46] or the designation of the youth branch of the party, JAAC (Amílcar Cabral African Youth). His portrait appears on the currency (the Cape Verdean *escudo*) and the newspaper

26 The Struggle as the Cradle of the Independent Nation

Voz di Povo regularly publishes excerpts from his writings, speeches and interviews. In the press and in political speeches, Cabral is referred as an example to be followed and honoured in official State celebrations, especially on the holidays of 20 January, the date of his assassination and consecrated National Heroes' Day; 5 July, the anniversary of national independence; and on 12 September, the Nationality Day, signalling the moment of its birth.

In an analysis of commemorative stamps of Cape Verde issued up until 1980, Ângela Coutinho notes that Amílcar Cabral is the only figure portrayed on them in a double-meaning representation. On some stamps, the image of the guerrilla fighter and revolutionary is reproduced, with the national flag in the background waving in the wind and Cabral's smiling face, with sunglasses and a *sumbia* on his head – the traditional cap worn by men in Guinea-Bissau and other neighbouring countries. On others, the image of Cabral as a politician and diplomat is reproduced, dressed formally in a suit and tie, with a serious countenance (both mimicking famous photos of Cabral as depicted in Figures 1.2 and 1.3).[47]

The armed struggle and its leader were thus forged with particular intensity in the immediate post-independence period as the "birth

Figure 1.2 "Amílcar Cabral Portrait", Fundação Mário Soares e Maria Barroso / Arquivo Amílcar Cabral.

Source: Bruna Polimeni.

Figure 1.3 "Amílcar Cabral Portrait", Fundação Mário Soares e Maria Barroso / Arquivo Mário Pinto de Andrade.

Source: Author unknown.

certificate" of the post-colonial nation. The flag, the coat of arms, and the Cape Verdean anthem are, along with the public appreciation of its key participants, also particularly expressive of the choice to affirm the centrality of the struggle. The national flag adopted by the archipelago, very similar to that of the PAIGC, was comprised of three rectangular stripes in yellow, green and red, and included in its emblem two ears of corn, a shell, and a black star symbolising the liberation of the African Man. The national anthem – *Esta é a nossa pátria amada* [This is our beloved homeland] – shared with Guinea-Bissau and with lyrics attributed to Amílcar Cabral is a text that praises the ancestors and the nation, but also exalts the liberation struggle and exhorts the people to defeat colonial domination:

>Sun, sweat, verdure, and sea,
>Centuries of pain and hope;
>This is the land of our ancestors!
>Fruit of our hands,
>Of the flower of our blood:
>This is our beloved homeland.

28   *The Struggle as the Cradle of the Independent Nation*

Long live our glorious country!
The banner of our struggle has fluttered in the skies.
Forward, against the foreign yoke!
We are going to build
Peace and progress
In our immortal country! (x2)

Branches of the same trunk,
Eyes in the same light:
This is the force of our unity!
Sing the sea and the land
The dawn and the sun
That our struggle has borne fruit.

Long live our glorious country!
The banner of our struggle has fluttered in the skies.
Forward, against the foreign yoke!
We are going to build
Peace and progress
In our immortal country![48]

The "return to Africa" through music

The historical process of the struggle allowed a critical reassessment of the imaginaries constructed about Cape Verde during colonialism, whether they were the Portuguese discourse – the archipelago as a paradigmatic model of an exemplary and specific type of colonisation – or those of the Cape Verdean elites.[49] In the latter case, the positions came to oscillate between proposals for political autonomy – in some instances proposed almost at the dawn of independence – to desires at claiming a status of adjacency to Portugal, assuming the Lusitanian status of Cape Verde. This claim resulted from the perception of a Cape Verdean exceptionality in relation to other African colonies, but was also stimulated by the perceived economic unfeasibility of the islands. We will return to this later.

From the mid-1950s on, a generation clearly committed to political Independence and the connection to Africa would emerge. With the struggle and until the 1980s, there was effectively, as João Vasconcelos says, a construction of Cape Verde identity against the grain, that is, an attempt to "re-Africanise the spirits". This aspect has to be understood not only within the general framework of African independence and the ideals of Pan-Africanism and negritude that had spread across the African continent but also in the context of the bi-national unity between Cape Verde and Guinea-Bissau.[50]

In a quote that is still widely reproduced today, Amílcar Cabral affirmed that "the national liberation struggle is, above all, an act of

The Struggle as the Cradle of the Independent Nation 29

culture".[51] The primacy of culture was rooted in an intention to rediscover an Africanity that was perceived as having been mutilated and erased by colonial domination. To this end, and in addition to other practices, PAIGC equipped itself with instruments capable of spreading its emancipatory message. The party set up *Rádio Libertação*, published and disseminated protest literature and oral poetry collections, and recorded albums with revolutionary songs that circulated among Cape Verdeans within the diaspora. *Rádio Libertação* started its regular official broadcasts in 1967, after Sweden provided the PAIGC with a new transmitter and mobile studio, enabling the radio to expand and achieve its goals as a "mouth cannon", as it became known.[52]

This radio station, which started by broadcasting music and messages from the liberation movement, became an important instrument in the "war arsenal". Programmes in different languages such as *Comunicado de Guerra* [War Bulletin], *Soldado Português* [Portuguese Soldier], *M Pidi Palavra* ["I request the floor"] or *Blufo* (aimed at a child audience) "enabled direct contact with PAIGC fighters, with Portuguese soldiers and with the great masses of the people, breaking the monopoly of the information broadcast by the colonialists' radio".[53] They passed on statements encouraging Portuguese troops to refuse the war, broadcasting testimonies from deserters and tried to encourage listeners to join the fight for the independence of Guinea and Cape Verde. Some of its broadcasts had a markedly cultural and pedagogical aspect, such as the programme *Vamos conhecer a nossa terra* [Let's get to know our land] which, in the various languages of Guinea and in Creole, talked about the Guinean people and ethnic groups, their cultural aspects, or the insularity and the droughts experienced in the Cape Verdean archipelago.[54] Furthermore, its programme content also included other anti-colonial circles, and was widely disseminated through national radio stations in Dakar, Conakry and Accra.[55]

In addition to *Rádio Libertação* broadcasts, the PAIGC's cultural services also published literary and musical works. As regards literature, one notable work was the 1964 book *Noti*, by Kaoberdiano Dambará, the poetic pseudonym of Felisberto Vieira Lopes, published by the Information and Propaganda Department of the PAIGC Central Committee. With an introduction by Ioti Kunta – the pseudonym of Jorge Querido, coordinator of the PAIGC Section in Portugal between 1959 and 1968 and a relevant cadre of the party, from which he parted ways in 1975 – *Noti* was the first book of poetry written entirely in the Cape Verdean language and in the variant of Santiago.[56] It is considered one of the most representative works of revolutionary and anti-colonial poetry associated with the liberation struggle of Cape Verde and Guinea, offering a pioneering dimension in its valorisation of the *badiu* – an expression often with negative connotations used to classify the black peasants of

30   *The Struggle as the Cradle of the Independent Nation*

Santiago – and its political and cultural aspects.[57] The poem *Batuku* is particularly illuminating:

> Tell me, Mr Dunda, what is *batuku*?
> Teach the youngest what you know.
> My son, I don't know what *batuku* is.
> We are born and here we find it
> We die and here we leave it.
> It's as distant as the sky,
> Deep as the sea,
> Hard as rock.
> It is our tradition, the joy of our people.
> Girls in the yard
> vigorous hips, intense *txabeta*.
> Their bodies ready to die.
> Resist. The soul calls me.
> Dozens and dozens buried in shallow graves,
> hundreds and hundreds dead in the *Assistência* disaster
> thousands upon thousands forced to work in São Tomé,
> burned in the lava of the volcano,
> the bodies die but the soul remains.
> The soul is the strength of *batuku*.
> In the suffering of famine,
> in the face of earthquakes,
> in the longing for the son who is far away,
> *batuku* is our soul.
> Feel it, my son.
> Anyone who loves us, loves *batuku*.
> *Batuku* is our soul![58]

The poem takes as its reference the *batuku*, a musical genre and type of dance common in Cape Verde at least since the 18th century. It is almost always performed by women (*batukaderas*) who play percussion, sing in an improvised way (*finason*) and dance with a characteristic movement of the hips.[59] Censored and despised during the colonial period, *batuku* came to be accepted, as with the poem by Kaoberdiano Dambará reproduced above, as an authentic – and muzzled – expression of Cape Verdean identity: one is born and dies in its presence. By mentioning *batuku*, the author evoked the cultural alienation to which the Cape Verdeans were subjected and the suffering they had gone through over the years. These experiences were particularly explicit in the mention of those who were "sold" and sent to the plantations in São Tomé and Príncipe, and Angola, and in the evocation of the events that became known as the "Assistência Disaster".

The name is a reference to what happened on 20 February, 1949, when after prolonged droughts and major food shortages, hundreds of people

The Struggle as the Cradle of the Independent Nation 31

from all over the island of Santiago gathered near the assistance canteen building in the city of Praia where meals were being distributed. That day, around lunchtime, a wall of the building collapsed, and an estimated 300 people were killed. The "Assistência Disaster", as an epitome of the chronical neglect in the Portuguese colonial administration of the islands, becomes the milestone that divides the history of famines in Cape Verde into a "before" and "after".[60] It is this chain of violence that is denounced in *Batuku*.

Besides *Noti* and other literary publications, the party's cultural division also released at least three LPs, two of them on the Morabeza Records label, owned by João Silva (Djunga de Biluca), a Cape Verdean emigrant, coordinator of the PAIGC cell in the Netherlands and co-creator of the magazine *Nôs Vida* [Our life].[61] The back covers of these records were openly revolutionary, identifying their songs as weapons of combat. *Poesia cabo-verdiana. Protesto e Luta* [Cape Verdean Poetry. Protest and Struggle] (1970) is a collection of several political and cultural poems by, among others, Kaoberdiano Dambará, Ovídio Martins and Onésimo Silveira;[62] *Korda Skrabu! Unidade Guiné-Cabo Verde* [Awaken, Slave! Guinea-Cape Verde Union] (1973), by Kaoguiamo (its initials referring to the common struggle of Cape Verde, Guinea, Angola and Mozambique), released shortly after Cabral's assassination, conveys the message of struggle and unity advocated by the PAIGC and *Música cabo-verdiana. Protesto e Luta* [Cape Verdean Music. Protest and Struggle] (1974) denounced colonial repression and announced actions taken as part of the anti-colonial struggle by the PAIGC.[63]

Music had specific strategic purposes. With the armed struggle taking place outside the archipelago, revolutionary songs aimed to produce "a connection between the cultural autonomy experienced in Cape Verdeans' daily lives, in which music played a major role, and a desire or plan for political autonomy, two dimensions mismatched for much of the population of Cape Verde at the time nationalists were entering the islands".[64] It was for the purposes of political mobilisation and recognition of Cape Verdean oral traditions that, for example, three weeks before the proclamation of independence, the Ministry of Education and Culture in the transitional government organised a soirée dedicated to *batuku*.[65]

The struggle as a mnemonic device was thereby celebrated with particular intensity after the Carnation Revolution and after the return of several of the liberation movement militants to the islands. Through a gesture of "cultural nationalism",[66] music appears as a vehicle to spread political messages associated with notions such as the resistance of Cape Verdeans, oppression and violence under Portuguese colonialism, or the struggle of the PAIGC and its fighters.[67] Renato Cardoso, composer and one of the young militants who had returned

32 *The Struggle as the Cradle of the Independent Nation*

from Lisbon, said the following about this moment in the archipelago's history:

> Music played a very important role in those early days of mobilisation [following the 25 April] [...]. For a long time, it served as a facilitating factor for rallies with the population, as a mobilising factor in emigrant circles, and as an immediate reason for meetings between students. In these meetings, through very politicised songs, we would have a political debate around the struggle for independence.[68]

Music and other arts continued to be used for similar purposes after 1975 by the post-colonial State. After independence, artistic expression operated as a kind of extension of the struggle, which now found room to establish a consistent cultural front, with the PAIGC developing a policy of encouragement and protection of artists mostly known for their revolutionary lyrics.[69] Through the Directorate General of Culture, they were recorded on disc, broadcast on the radio and performed in concert at the party's rallies and political campaigns.[70] Various musical events were also promoted with the support of party structures, such as the Abel Djassi Pioneers, the Amílcar Cabral African Youth and the Cape Verdean Women's Organisation. It is in this context that cultural practices (and musical ones, especially) were politically activated as a valuable instrument in the dissemination of the struggle's past. This is how one of the most emblematic Cape Verdean bands, *Os Tubarões*, sings it, for example, in two tracks from their first LP, *Pépé Lopi*, from 1976, entitled "*Labanta Braço*"[71] and "*Cabral ca mori*"[72] from which we provide two excerpts here:

> Raise your arm, celebrate your freedom (x4) / Shout, independent people! Celebrate, liberated people! (x2) / 5th July means freedom / 5th July is an open road to happiness / Shout, 'Long live the war' / Honour the fighters of our land / Shout 'Long live Cabral' / Honour the fighters of our land.[73]

> Oh, Cape Verde, your hour has come / just as your brothers in Africa have celebrated. / Our independence, children, we already have / to be free, free from anyone. / Cabral is not dead, Cabral is the cry that moved the world / Cabral is not dead, Cabral is the cry in my breast / Cabral is not dead, Cabral is freedom. / Honour the memory of the people's hero. / Of the PAIGC, the party of the struggle, / In the *finason* we cannot forget it, / as well as all our brothers who gave their blood / for the freedom and justice of our people.[74]

Cape Verdean cultural expression was also a part of the process of safeguarding national identity, as reaffirmed by Pedro Pires when he presented the government's programme for the second Legislature, and

The Struggle as the Cradle of the Independent Nation   33

announced that efforts would continue to prevent the dilution of cultural identity and the alienation of Cape Verde's people.[75] They would also be used in education and in consolidating the rapprochement with Africa. This involved elevating expressions of popular music considered more "African", which had previously been devalued by local elites (who had dismissed them as inferior and less significant in shaping Cape Verdean society) and repressed by the colonial authorities.[76] The latter saw them as destabilising the "institutionalised order" by empowering the manifestation of particular views and behaviours sanctioned by the Catholic Church.[77]

Along with initiatives to revive an Africanness that was thought to be lost or confined to the interior of Santiago, reworking, stylisation and modernisation of popular music was also encouraged. It was hoped that this would contribute to the progressive affirmation and development of these local cultural genres, which was not unrelated to the influence of the Cape Verdean diaspora.[78] In terms of Cape Verde's post-colonial State cultural policies, these were often enhanced through incentives for musicians to form groups and make records, or be invited to perform at public events. These encouraged the *funaná*, *batuku* or *tabanka* to break out of the rural confines of Santiago's interior and "go up to the Plateau", the symbolic location in the country's capital associated with the elite, to communicate new ways of belonging to the nation and celebrating its anti-colonial heritage.[79] One of the most significant examples of this movement happened during the Praia-80 festival, a successor to the first event held in Praia in 1977, during the third Congress of the PAIGC, which had brought together seven musical groups and was repeated in 1979.[80]

As part of the official commemorations of the fifth anniversary of Cape Verde's independence, the Praia-80 Festival, organised by the Information and Propaganda Sub-Commission, became one of the highlights of the official programme for the 5 July 1980 festivities. The event was organised into three distinct phases during the first half of the year, and initially included popular dances and performances by electronic groups from Santiago Island only, some associated with party organisations such as Djarama, from FARP, and Abel Djassi, from the Pioneers, plus a group from Guinea-Bissau, Super Mama Djombo. The second phase included performances by local groups from almost all of the Cape Verde islands and the third and final phase, planned for the week of 5 July, featured a show with the bands selected in the previous stages, which would be combined with Cape Verdean groups from the diaspora.[81]

According to David Hopffer Almada, President of the Organising Committee and then Minister of Justice, it was this festival – a "historic event" in his view – that brought the "soul of the people", previously confined to small rural circles of peasants in Santiago's interior, to the city.[82] It was also at Praia-80 that one of the bands most central to the

34 *The Struggle as the Cradle of the Independent Nation*

renewal of this musical genre, *Bulimundo*, opened the way for *funaná* to be recognised at home and then internationally. Founded in 1978 by Carlos Alberto Martins ("Catchás"), who had recently returned from a few years in Europe (he had studied in Portugal and fled to France, thus avoiding compulsory military service and fighting in the war), *Bulimundo*'s performances and records are considered the great revolution of *funaná*, modernising it by adding electronic instruments and amplifiers. The then leader of *Bulimundo*, who died prematurely in a car accident in 1988, said in an interview with *Voz di Povo* that the group was "a child of independence": "with the new Cape Verdean reality, it became necessary to work on what was ours. So, when I returned to the country, I noticed that there was a huge space to fill in the spectrum of Cape Verdean traditional music".[83] From this perspective, it was getting independence that provided the chance to revitalise and change the status of *funaná*.[84] In these years, several Cape Verdean cultural groups eventually became known internationally, and serve as cultural representatives of Cape Verde abroad.[85]

In a similar vein, the theatre group *Korda Kaoberdi* [Wake Up Cape Verde], created at Santiago Island in 1975 and directed by Kwame Kondé (pseudonym of Francisco Gomes Fragoso), also became established. Its name, according to João Branco, alludes to the immediate objectives of the group: to reclaim the cultural traditions of Santiago which had been repressed during the colonial period.[86] Its first play *Preto Toma Tom* (1976) was structured around revolutionary poems, among others by Amílcar Cabral, Ovídio Martins, Kaoberdiano Dambará and Kwame Kondé, and the rhythms of *batuku* and *tabanka*.[87] In 1980, its most famous, explicitly anti-colonial play, premiered in Praia city. *Rai di Tabanka* [King of Tabanka], was announced on the cover of *Voz di Povo* as the "apotheosis of *tabanca*"[88] and the following year, the play was presented in Porto, Portugal, at *FITEI – Festival Internacional de Teatro de Expressão Ibérica (International Festival of Iberian Expression Theatre)*.

Accompanied by the ritual of the *tabanka*, with a group of drummers on stage, the show tells the story, in the first person, of an enslaved African in his struggle for freedom.[89] João Branco reports, however, that despite the success of the play in the capital and abroad, it was poorly received in Mindelo, São Vicente, in 1982. In his opinion, and also based on interviews and reports from the time, Branco believes that the rejection of the play had to do with the rivalries that existed between the two islands, as well as with the association it makes between Cape Verde's cultural heritage and the more African cultural manifestations of a single island, Santiago: "by advocating a Cape Verdean culture that foregoes the European element, [*Rei da Tabanka*] ignores or rejects its importance in the socio-cultural formation of the Creole ethos".[90] The process of cultural reconciliation with Africa was giving increasingly explicit signs of not being consensual in the Cape Verdean islands.

The end of the union with Guinea-Bissau and its impacts

Although the project of unity with Guinea-Bissau, with the PAIGC as the binational party, was taken on board after the independence, the process never advanced beyond its initial stages, that is, it remained fundamentally at the level of organisation and discussion.[91] Even so, this project – one of the central points in Amílcar Cabral's thinking and a source of strength for the liberation movement – remained the great divisive issue among various sectors of Cape Verdean society and even among some PAIGC militants, right from the days of the anti-colonial struggle.[92] It was not a consensual issue in Guinean society either, for different reasons.

Unlike the Cape Verdeans who had participated in the war in Guinea, most of whom had formal schooling, a large number of Guinean combatants were peasants who came from rural areas. This led to tensions and differences in status during the struggle – the former mainly occupied leading positions, while the latter stayed at the war front.[93] These tensions then resurfaced, at various points in the post-independence period, over who had access to positions of power and public administration in Guinea-Bissau. Within the binational union framework advocated by the PAIGC, many of these positions were occupied by Cape Verdeans and Guineans from the city, with positions considered subordinate to citizens from rural areas. This generated various resentments among the latter, who had played a central role during the struggle.[94]

Thus, according to Leopoldo Amado, the armed struggle would have generated a violence that, in Guinea, took also root as a difficult heritage.[95] The tensions between Cape Verdeans and Guineans, the ethnic resentments and power struggles between the military and politicians, and their confluence with economic, social and institutional factors culminated in the coup d'état of 14 November, 1980, led by then Prime Minister Nino Vieira, one of the PAIGC's most important commanders.[96] In the immediate aftermath of the coup, Luís Cabral – Amílcar Cabral's brother – was deposed as President of the Republic and arrested along with several party leaders. With no generalised clashes, three deaths were recorded during the events (one of them accidental, according to the report prepared by a delegation of the Amílcar Cabral Information and Documentation Centre - CIDAC, sent from Lisbon to Bissau).[97] Control of the Guinean State now passed to a newly formed Council of the Revolution, presided over by Nino Vieira.

Initially, Nino Vieira stated over the radio that the intention of the coup was to expel "the colonisers" from Guinea-Bissau, referring to the Cape Verdeans who had remained there. During a later phase of the coup, self-designated the "Readjustment Movement", the intention to continue the policy of Cabral and the party was reaffirmed, highlighting the need to revitalise unity, but on equal terms for both parties.[98]

36   *The Struggle as the Cradle of the Independent Nation*

In his 1980 year-end speech, "Let's build Cabral's Homeland", Nino Vieira invoked the following reasons for the military coup: 1) to recover the values and objectives outlined in the struggle by Amílcar Cabral; 2) to put an end to Luís Cabral's anti-democratic stance and the economic decisions that the head of State had made, which, by underestimating investment in agriculture, were leading the country into a catastrophic situation; 3) to respond to the dramatic situation in which many of the former combatants found themselves and to the growing displeasure within the FARP because of what they perceived as deviations from power; 4) to satisfy the needs of the population afflicted by famine; 5) to recover the dignity of the people, and put an end to the inequality that they considered to exist between Guineans and Cape Verdeans; 6) to denounce the shootings of hundreds of Guineans who had served in the African Commandos – an elite troop of the Portuguese colonial army – or who were political opponents of Luís Cabral; and, finally, 7) to fight the asymmetry between Cape Verde and Guinea-Bissau as evidenced in the discrepancies contained in the wording of the two countries' constitutions, approved a few days earlier (notably, and contrary to what happened in the Cape Verdean constitution, the absence of an express reference to the president being a Guinean citizen; the concentration of power in the head of State with the consequent removal of the Prime Minister's duties and, finally, the introduction of the death penalty).[99]

In Cape Verde, the ruling authorities held an emergency meeting the day after the coup and quickly condemned the event.[100] The November editions of *Voz di Povo* were almost entirely dedicated to the events and the reactions of the main rulers, who refuted the accusations made against Cape Verdeans by the Council of the Revolution, considering that they revealed a certain anti-Cape Verdean perspective in Bissau.[101] During that month and the following one, Aristides Pereira and Nino Vieira exchanged messages and official emissaries until the final breakdown in communication on 16 December, 1980, when the Cape Verdean Head of State and Secretary-General of the Party wrote to Nino Vieira demarcating the Cape Verdean wing of what was going on in Guinea and stressing the consequences that this would have for the unification project and the survival of the PAIGC itself.[102]

In the archipelago, among party members with many years of experience in that country during the struggle, such as Agnelo Dantas and Pedro Pires, the coup was looked on with astonishment and dismay.

> I think there was shock. Not shock because the unity didn't happen, but because of the violence that occurred. Because in relation to unity, things were cold. 'Guinea-Cape Verde unity', you could see it in speeches. In reality, you couldn't see anything concrete. So, in that respect, I didn't mind much. What did matter to me was that Nino Vieira took advantage of the small frictions between Guineans and Cape Verdeans to conjure them up as one of the reasons for the

The Struggle as the Cradle of the Independent Nation   37

coup. That shocked me because it was false. That's why in relation to unification I was always reticent.[103]

The coup in Guinea, in terms of Africa, I think was a surprise, but it was also a disappointment. [...]. I think the impact was different for different people. There are those people who will have been disillusioned, those who will have been disappointed, but there are those who may have been happy, let's be honest, who said: 'At last! That burden of the unity with Guinea won't bother us anymore!' [...]. If you ask me what my reaction was, I say this: that it was surprise, incomprehension, but above all it was repudiation, rejection. Why? Because of the arguments and justifications presented which, to me, are all false [...]. I was tasked with making the rupture speech. I don't know if I was the one who was more offended or if I tasked myself with the justification of the rupture. But I took charge of the rupture speech [...]. In very simple language: a divorce is preferable to a bad marriage [laughter].[104]

The final rupture came at a meeting of the CNCV on 20 January 1981, on the anniversary of Cabral's death, when the creation of the African Party for the Independence of Cape Verde (PAICV) was publicly and officially announced. On that occasion, Aristides Pereira stated that the coup against the State of Guinea represented a coup against the Party and that the "painful experience of 14 November" is proof that the "principle of unity, one of the foundations of the Party as a bi-national organisation, has been rejected".[105] In the final speech delivered by Pedro Pires, the then Deputy Secretary-General of the Party and Prime Minister of Cape Verde emphasised the historical lineage of the new national party: "the PAICV is the child born of the PAIGC, its direct heir, the legitimate heir to its principles, its ideology, its history and its struggle. [...]. We are children of this struggle, we were formed in the struggle".[106]

The creation of the PAICV and the breaking of unity with Guinea-Bissau produced political, social and mnemonic changes in Cape Verde, driven in part by a feeling of fragility or vulnerability inherited from the end of the PAIGC in the archipelago, where, in certain islands, it always had difficulties in fully taking root, as several disputes had shown, among them the so-called "crisis of the Trotskyist ministers"; the creation of the Independent and Democratic Cape Verdean Union (UCID), a Christian-democratic party formed in 1977 by Cape Verdean emigrants in the diaspora; the student protests in Mindelo; or protests against Agrarian Reform in 1981, events which will be discussed in the next chapter.[107]

Recalibrating memory

Accompanying the changes and pressured by protests that followed in the early 1980s, the PAICV gradually began to develop a political, cultural and social response to the distinctive stage that the country was experiencing. At its Second Congress in 1983, the Party announced the goal

38 *The Struggle as the Cradle of the Independent Nation*

of encouraging the broader involvement of the population in collective decisions, and of seeking "power with popular participation".[108] While in the first five years of independence the focus was on state-building, now the party explicitly stated its goal of boosting social organisations and popular participation through mass organisations, trade unions and cooperatives, or local institutions of power such as neighbourhood committees and area courts.[109]

At the same time, there were changes in the composition of the government and leadership positions, in which ex-combatants occupied a less hegemonic space, and new party cadres were recruited to government positions and, more broadly, also to join the State bureaucracy. While, in 1977, of the 14 main posts in the executive, 10 were occupied by prominent PAIGC officials during the war, with the government reshuffle of 1983, there was a slight change, with the 7 secretaries of State, the highest posts after the ministries, being occupied by party cadres who had not been involved in the struggle.[110]

The new cadres benefited from more widespread access to education and higher training through the granting of scholarships to study abroad.[111] These opportunities created by the independent State emerged in the wake and deepening of a policy of welfare, organised around the spectre of famines and indebted to the actions of the refounded late-colonial authorities from 1968 onwards, as Correia e Silva argues.[112] Nevertheless, according to the same author, until 1985 little changed in the selection process for leaders who were chosen from among the most prominent militants in the PAICV, since this was one of the ways in which the regime sought to maintain its hegemony.[113]

From 1985, with the beginning of the third Legislature, and until 1990, the regime went through a phase of liberalisation at various levels, seeking to adapt its institutions more visibly to the dynamics that were intensifying in Cape Verde society. In an attempt to broaden its bases of support, the PAICV then took a series of gradual measures that Correia e Silva calls "authoritarian decompression" which included a "growing parliamentarisation of political life", a greater hybridisation of the party with other social and cultural organisations and less control over the political space, including the possibility of running candidates for deputies from "citizens' groups".[114]

One of the most symptomatic examples of the PAICV's reactions to the need for change is the holding, in 1986, of a symposium as part of the 50th anniversary of the magazine *Claridade*, and the establishment of a literary award with the same name. The generation of Cape Verdean intellectuals of the 1930s associated with this publication defended the importance of the archipelago's socio-cultural elements – language, folklore, lifestyle – as part of the claim for a regional place for Cape Verde within the Portuguese nation.[115] As Baltasar Lopes da Silva, one of its most prominent figures, wrote in a 1931 article, "let us therefore be

The Struggle as the Cradle of the Independent Nation   39

intransigently regionalist and intelligently Portuguese".[116] In this context, which *Claridade* sought simultaneously to decode and promote, the idea of Cape Verdean culture as a "regional manifestation of the universalistic tendency of the Lusitanian identity" and the search for the defining traits of an identity forged around insularity, migration, the sea, droughts, famines or the drama of the island man was vindicated.[117]

The sublimation of miscegenation, particularly amongst the first generation of *Claridade* authors, is a tribute to an imaginary of Luso-tropicalist assimilation and integration along the lines of what Gilberto Freyre had theorised for Brazil. Freyre's Luso-tropicalism constituted a theory of hybridity without violence, which shared the assumption of a harmonious relationship between coloniser and colonised and offers up the *mestiço* as the visible result of this process.[118] The adoption of Luso-tropicalism in Portugal occurred in the 1950s, when it replaced the more overtly racist arguments used to sustain the legitimacy of the "Portuguese Colonial Empire". At the same time, the theory was used to resist international pressures for the country to begin the decolonisation process. Thus it was that, at the invitation of Portuguese Overseas Minister Sarmento Rodrigues, Freyre made an official visit of about six months (between August 1951 and February 1952) to what were by now termed the "overseas provinces".[119] Following these trips, which included a visit to Cape Verde in October 1951, the Brazilian author published *Aventura e Rotina* [Adventure and Routine] and *Um Brasileiro em Terras Portuguesas* [A Brazilian in Portuguese Lands], both in 1953, in which he set out his reflections on the archipelago that deeply displeased the followers of *Claridade*, particularly Baltasar Lopes da Silva.

In 1956, Baltasar Lopes broadcast a series of six commentaries on *Rádio Barlavento* in response to Freyre's observations in which Freyre compared Cape Verdean society to that of the Antilles, as "islands in which the populations were predominantly African in colour, appearance and customs, with only a smattering of 'European' influence".[120] The perception that the Cape Verdean was more African than Portuguese was an opposite reading to Baltasar Lopes, who believed that African cultural heritages were not the "dominant force" in the islands, and called Freyre's social characterisation "absurd".[121] He went on to say that "the Messiah" had let them down.[122]

During the 1930s, the circulation of Gilberto Freyre's writings among the *Claridade* affiliates was evident, and the author was quoted in the very first issue of the magazine, in March 1936. A text by João Lopes describes the difference between the islands, the miscegenation process and – "as Gilberto Freyre says for Brazil" – the emergence of a "creative expression" derived from the combination of these elements. In Cape Verde, this

> great human freedom, arising from this uniquely Portuguese process, (manifested itself), unlike the Anglo-Saxon colonisers who, always

40 *The Struggle as the Cradle of the Independent Nation*

armed with the pious Protestant Bible, morally asphyxiated the poor black man, in the name of civilization, squeezing him between the pincers of the colour bar, and not allowing him to escape from this watertight compartment.[123]

Cape Verde was therefore the result of this singular Portuguese colonisation experience (or rather, of the encounter and creation of Creoleness), at the same time that this "encounter" took place in an unequal manner: it was the European element that would allow the black man to "escape" from the compartment in which he was enclosed. The attraction to the foundations of Luso-tropicalism in the first phase of *Claridade* occurs alongside a view of Africanness as spurious residue, evident in the definition of the *badiu* as "the other of Cape Verdean assimilation and miscegenation".[124] As defenders of the recognition of Cape Verdean singularity, these intellectuals ended up being involved in an "equivocal situation", in the words of José Vicente Lopes, that consisted in demanding equal rights within a colonial framework that, by nature, was unequal and discriminatory.[125]

A few years later – especially in the diaspora in Portugal, namely the *Casa de Estudantes do Império*, an institution created in 1944 by the Ministry of the Colonies which was to become one of the main anticolonial nucleuses in the metropolis – a group of young intellectuals committed to the struggle for independence emerged and proposed the rediscovery of Africa. This process signalled a change in the way Cape Verde was imagined: no longer as substantially different from other African peoples and close to the Portuguese, but united in an emancipatory destiny common to the colonised peoples of the continent. The group was mostly made up of assimilated people who, in the metropolis, experienced in their skin that a discourse of Cape Verdean exceptionalism was unworkable, and were painfully discovering themselves to be black and, therefore, brothers in Africanness.[126] That is why, in 1963, Cabral in referring to Cape Verde made a distinction between a conservative petty bourgeoisie and a "rebel petty bourgeoisie", made up mostly of young people, whose aspirations could be identified with the popular masses.[127]

It is in this context that Amílcar Cabral asserted that the men of *Claridade* had looked at the reality of the "land-martyr" from a "dream of evasion" and a "desire to want to leave", and offered as a counterpoint to this approach, which he criticised, one affirming – quoting the verse of the poet and friend Aguinaldo Fonseca – "another land within our land".[128] The landmark criticism of the *Claridoso* movement was, however, a text by Onésimo Silveira, published in 1963, in which he argues that Cape Verdean literature was "deeply wounded with inauthenticity" by the current escapist philosophy.[129] In a different sense, the author is part of a "new generation" for whom Cape Verde "is a case of African regionalism", and it is therefore up to art and literature to bring the common Cape Verdean man closer to this "African destiny".[130]

The Struggle as the Cradle of the Independent Nation   41

For these and other reasons, given the political and cultural processes and options we described above, there were no public and / or official celebrations honouring the *Claridade* movement in the first decade after independence. However, in the late 1980s, this situation changed. José Carlos Gomes dos Anjos speaks, in this regard, of an "intellectual reconciliation" carried out by the PAICV in order to provide a new key for interpreting the past, in which the opposition between the generations of *claridosos* and nationalists was no longer read in terms of antagonism, but as a path of continuity between a movement for cultural autonomy and a movement for political autonomy.[131] This is precisely what was stated at the 1986 symposium, leading *Voz di Povo* to make the headlines by proclaiming that "After 50 years – *Claridade* officially enters Cape Verde's History".[132]

At this meeting, Aristides Pereira recognised the role of culture in the formation of Cape Verdean identity, and attributed to the movement the creation and building of an independent national literary system "whose work must be appreciated and cherished until it reaches Amilcar Cabral".[133] Calling for this moment of homage to be made "a solemn occasion of communion for all the generations that, with their social and ideological praxis, have made their tribute to the emergence of a free and sovereign nation", the then president of the Republic emphasised the immense history of the Cape Verde nation, forged over several generations of intellectuals and different historical moments.[134] In this regard, Abílio Duarte, President of the Symposium and of the National Assembly of Cape Verde, also said the following words:

> I am aware that the various generations who are present at this Symposium and who will be in dialogue in the coming days have, over the years, done nothing but persistently, I might even say doggedly, sought mutual understanding. This is because we think that no generation alone can claim to own history. It is perhaps on this basis that many have called this symposium the Symposium of Concord.[135]

For the occasion, the Cape Verdean Book Institute, created in 1976, republished the nine issues of the magazine *Claridade* in a facsimile edition, but now with a retrospective statement by Baltasar Lopes added. Two years later, in 1988, in the same conciliatory vein, the First National Music Meeting was held in the city of Praia, organised by the Ministry of Information, Culture and Sports. The event, marked by intense debates, resulted in the recognition of all Cape Verdean music genres as equally important and worthy of preservation, from *funaná* and *batuku* to *morna*, *coladeira* or classical music.[136]

The hypothesis here is that it was an attempt by the PAICV to·pacify the regime's relationship with important sectors of society, particularly the elites, who understood these symbols to be part of the national

42   *The Struggle as the Cradle of the Independent Nation*

heritage.[137] Anjos considers there to be another reason to justify this movement, which in his opinion was particularly evident after the end of the union with Guinea-Bissau: the survival and permanence among the PAICV's own leadership (many of them educated politically and culturally at the Gil Eanes High School, where Baltasar Lopes da Silva had also taught), of the idea of a specific Cape Verde identity, based on the concept of Creoleness.[138]

Between two ruptures

During the First Republic (1975–1991), particularly in the first five years, the public narrative of the struggle as the cradle of the independent nation was produced and disseminated. This was mostly centred on the following axes: a) condemning the colonial system and valuing the history of Cape Verde's liberation; b) an attempt to bring the archipelago closer in political, identity and cultural terms to the African continent; and c) a symbolic grammar organised around values such as heroism, sacrifice and courage eventually elevated the combatants of the armed struggle, now political actors, to a hierarchical place of super-citizenship in Cape Verdean society.

Socialising the memories of the struggle, especially in a country where it did not occur in its armed dimension, was a decisive process in consolidating post-independence political hegemony. However, after the rupture of the unity project with Guinea, and with the growing opposition to the single-party regime from emigrant destinations, but also internally, the PAICV, sensing the tensions and disputes of legitimacy at stake, extended a certain flexibility, which had already come from the past, now to the field of culture. This movement was part of a larger gesture of reconciliation with a certain intellectual elite from which he was estranged. Roughly from 1985 on and in an exercise that always has as its ultimate goal to value the struggle and independence, this is how the party opted to also highlight the importance of the cultural movements that preceded the PAIGC in the process of nation-building.[139] In January 1989, Aristides Pereira, addressing Cape Verdean artists and writers, said the following:

> The presence here, at the dawning of this year 1989, of national artists and writers of various generations, besides representing a patriotic message of reciprocal trust between the intellectuals and the political leadership of the country, surely testifies to two very simple truths. The first truth, if you'll allow me an image, is that the country's tree will only grow and blossom from the common sowing, by the cultivation of all Cape Verdeans; the second truth is that your presence here is testimony to the importance that today, more than ever, culture and men of culture are recognised throughout the country.[140]

The Struggle as the Cradle of the Independent Nation 43

In essence, without minimising the process of the national liberation struggle and the role that Amilcar Cabral and the combatants at his side played in it, the aim was now to dispel the ghost of activities carried out in the revolutionary heat of independence, which did not really chime with the image of an institutionalised regime. And, additionally, to accommodate the support of social segments that would be – or were – disaffected to it. To a certain extent, these steps were a prelude to what would be intensified in the post-1991 period, although then acquiring a very different political dimension, as we will show in the next chapter.

Notes

1 All translations from Portuguese and Cape-Verdean languages are our responsibility, unless otherwise explicitly noted (for this purpose, see Bibliography and Acknowledgements).

2 *Tabanka* is a genre of Cape Verdean music, but it is also a wider cultural expression of the community, whose members help each other, socialise or get together in devotion to Catholic saints, and it has become a central institution in the organisation of social life in the peasant villages in the interior of Santiago and the popular areas of Praia. Cf. Wilson Trajano Filho, *Por uma Etnografia da Resistência: o caso das tabancas de Cabo Verde* (Brasília: Departamento de Antropologia da Universidade de Brasília, 2006).

3 Cf., for example, "Cabo Verde vive as suas primeiras horas de independência. A mais antiga colónia do mundo tornou-se independente", *Diário Popular*, no. 11684, July 1975 and "Cabo Verde: só a esperança não morreu de sede", *O Jornal*, no. 11, 11–17 July 1975.

4 *Boletim Oficial da República de Cabo Verde*, no. 1, 5 July 1975, 3.

5 *Boletim Oficial da República de Cabo Verde*, no. 1, 5 July 1975, 2.

6 The LOPE, which was designed to fill a constitutional vacuum, remained in force until 5 September 1980, the date on which the text of the first Political Constitution of the Republic of Cape Verde was ratified.

7 Cf. José Vicente Lopes, *Aristides Pereira. Minha Vida, Nossa História* (Praia: Spleen, 2012), 401–403.

8 See José Vicente Lopes (2013), *Cabo Verde. Os Bastidores da Independência* (Praia: Spleen Edições, 2013, 3rd ed.), 60–66, 107–110, 122, 321–322 and Cláudio Alves Furtado, "Cabo Verde e as quatro décadas da independência: dissonâncias, múltiplos discursos, reverberações e lutas por imposição de sentido à sua história recente", *Estudos Ibero-Americanos* 42, no. 3 (2016): 864.

9 Cf. Furtado, "Cabo Verde e as quatro décadas da independência", 864 and Lopes, *Cabo Verde*, 311–312.

10 Guinea-Cape Verde unity had been a contentious issue since the beginning of the struggle. Julião Soares Sousa states that most of the liberation movements, especially in Guinea, were opposed to it. In Senegal, more than a dozen movements made up of Guineans who had emigrated there advocated the independence of Guinea only (among them, the Union of the Peoples of Guinea – UPG; the Popular Union for the Liberation of Guinea – UPLG; and the National Front for the Liberation of Guinea – FNLG). In addition, there were three Cape Verdean movements, also in Dakar, opposed to the idea of unity advocated by Cabral: The Cape Verdean Democratic Union (UDC); the Movement for the Liberation of Cape

44 *The Struggle as the Cradle of the Independent Nation*

Verde Islands (MLICV) and the Union of the People of the Cape Verde Islands (UPICV). Cf. Julião Soares Sousa, *Amílcar Cabral. Vida e morte de um revolucionário africano (1924–1973)* (Lisboa: Vega, 2011), 252–254.

11 UDC, "Manifesto" and UDC, "Programa".

12 Furtado, "Cabo Verde e as quatro décadas da independência", 855–887.

13 This agreement, signed by the Portuguese government and the PAIGC, recognised the independence of Guinea-Bissau and the right to self-determination of Cape Verde. However, it demanded that a referendum be held to consult the people of Cape Verde, which the PAIGC refused. Aristides Pereira said that the refusal to organise the referendum at the time was a result of pressure from the OAU (Organisation of African Unity) and that they feared the effects of this gesture in other countries, such as Angola and Mozambique. He noted that the PAIGC's capacity to mobilise at the time did not lead them to fear the results. Nevertheless, the National Assembly election was assumed to serve as a form of popular consultation. Cf. Lopes, *Aristides Pereira*, 216–218 and 228–229.

14 The transitional government was sworn in on 30 December 1974. On this period see, for example, Lopes, *Cabo Verde*, 363–383; José Luís Hopffer de Almada, "Das tragédias históricas do povo caboverdiano e da saga da sua constituição e da sua consolidação como nação crioula soberana, segunda parte", *Buala*. 17 February 2012, http://www.buala.org/pt/a-ler/das-tragedias-historicas-do-povo-caboverdiano-e-da-saga-da-sua-constituicao-e-da-sua-consolida; Ângela Coutinho, "O processo de descolonização de Cabo Verde", in *O Adeus ao Império. 40 Anos de Descolonização Portuguesa*, eds. Fernando Rosas, Mário Machaqueiro, and Pedro Aires Oliveira (Lisboa: Vega, 2015), 125–140 and Furtado, "Cabo Verde e as quatro décadas da independência", 864–866.

15 Cf. Ângela Benoliel Coutinho, *Os Dirigentes do PAIGC. Da fundação à ruptura, 1956–1980* (Coimbra: Imprensa da Universidade de Coimbra, 2017), 266–267, 272–273.

16 The expression "Combatentes da Liberdade da Pátria" can be translated literally as "Combatants for the Liberation of the Homeland". However, for ease of reading, we have chosen to use only "Liberation Struggle combatant". For writing convenience, we will sometimes alternate between the terms "combatant" and "fighter" throughout the book.

17 "Mensagem de Aristides Pereira ao povo de Cabo Verde no dia da Proclamação da Independência". Fundação Mário Soares e Maria Barroso / Arquivo Amílcar Cabral.

18 António Carreira, *Migrações nas ilhas de Cabo Verde* (Praia: Instituto Cabo-verdiano do Livro, 1983, 2nd ed), 37–38. See also, Ilídio Amaral, "Cabo Verde: introdução geográfica", in *História Geral de Cabo Verde*, eds. Luís de Albuquerque and Maria Emília Madeira Santos (Lisboa / Praia: Instituto de Investigação Científica Tropical e Direcção-Geral do Património Cultural de Cabo Verde, 1991, vol. 1), 15.

19 After the abolition of slavery and exacerbated by high cocoa prices in the early twentieth century, São Tomé and Príncipe struggled with a shortage of local labour to work the large farms. In order to deal with the labour crisis and relieve Cape Verde demographically, the Portuguese authorities encouraged "guided emigration" until 1970, recruiting thousands of Cape Verdeans mostly to São Tomé and Príncipe and, in much smaller numbers, also to Angola and Mozambique. Cf. Carreira, *Migrações*, 148–153, 238–239.

20 Cf. Manuel Brito-Semedo, *A Construção da Identidade Nacional. Análise da Imprensa entre 1877 e 1975* (Praia: Instituto da Biblioteca Nacional e do Livro, 2006) and Inês Cruz, "Cabo Verde em tempo de censura: o

The Struggle as the Cradle of the Independent Nation   45

descaminho do jornalismo e a missão de denúncia da literatura", in *Literaturas Insulares: Leituras e Escritas de Cabo Verde e São Tomé e Príncipe*, eds. Margarida Calafate Ribeiro and Sílvio Renato Jorge (Porto: Afrontamento, 2011), 65–69. The relationship between journalism and literature in Cape Verde between 1926 and 1975 is analysed in more detail by Sandra Inês Cruz in "A quase-informação na literatura de Cabo Verde em tempo de censura (1926–1975)" (Master's diss. Universidade de Coimbra, 2009).

21 Sandra Inês Cruz, "A quase-informação na literatura de Cabo Verde em tempo de censura", in *Heranças pós-coloniais nas literaturas de língua portuguesa*, eds. Margarida Calafate Ribeiro and Phillip Rothwell (Porto: Afrontamento, 2019), 183–187 and José Vicente Lopes, *Cabo Verde. Um corpo que se recusa a morrer. 70 anos contra a fome, 1949–2019* (Praia: Spleen Edições, 2021), 333.

22 Lopes, *Cabo Verde. Um corpo que se recusa a morrer*, 207.

23 Amílcar Cabral, "A Guiné e as Ilhas de Cabo Verde face ao colonialismo português", in *Obras Escolhidas de Amílcar Cabral. Unidade e Luta, a arma da teoria*, ed. Mário de Andrade (Praia: Fundação Amílcar Cabral, 2013, vol. 1), 83–84. Very similar phrases also appear in a PAIGC text addressed to the Portuguese government in December 1960, cf. Amílcar Cabral, "Memorandum do PAIGC ao Governo português", in *Amílcar Cabral. Documentário (textos políticos e culturais)*, sel. António E. Duarte Silva (Lisboa: Edições Cotovia, 2008), 69 and in the lectures that Cabral gave in "Seminário de Quadros" em 1969. Cf. Amílcar Cabral, "Resistência Armada", in *Amílcar Cabral. Documentário (textos políticos e culturais)*, sel. António E. Duarte Silva (Lisboa: Edições Cotovia, 2008), 118–119. See also the PAIGC report presented to the UN Decolonization Committee on 29 March 1974: PAIGC, *Sobre a situação em Cabo Verde* (Lisboa: Livraria Sá da Costa, 1974).

24 Cf. Lopes, *Cabo Verde*; António Correia e Silva, "O Nascimento do Leviatã Crioulo: esboços de sociologia política", *Cadernos de Estudos Africanos* 1 (2001); Coutinho, *Os Dirigentes do PAIGC*; and Lopes, *Cabo Verde. Um corpo que se recusa a morrer*, 207–211.

25 "PEDRO PIRES auto-retrato", *A Semana*, no. 318, 19 September 1997.

26 Michael Rothberg, *Multidirectional Memory. Remembering the Holocaust in the Age of Decolonization* (Stanford: Stanford University Press, 2009), 3.

27 Rothberg, *Multidirectional Memory*, 15–16, 313.

28 Barros, drawing on biographers such as Patrick Chabal and Julião Soares Sousa, notes that while it is true that the revolt against the famines and socio-economic problems of the archipelago is present early on in the young Cabral, it is not possible to identify a desire for anti-colonial rupture until the early 1950s. See Victor Barros, "Between truth and inventions. How public commemorations recite the biography of Amílcar Cabral", in *The Politics of Biography in Africa. Borders, Margins, and Alternative Histories of Power*, ed. Anais Angelo (London / New York: Routledge, 2021), 97–117.

29 Lopes, *Cabo Verde. Um corpo que se recusa a morrer*, 253–312.

30 As examples of success in building the country, Pedro Pires mentions the remittances and savings sent and deposited by Cape Verdean emigrants to the islands to make them economically viable; the collaboration of civil servants for political viability; and voluntary work undertaken, particularly in the reforestation of the country, for ecological viability. Pedro Pires, interview, Praia, 18 January 2020. On the process of state-building, see Elisa Silva Andrade, "Cape Verde", in *A History of Postcolonial Lusophone Africa*, Patrick Chabal et al. (Indiana: Indiana University Press,

46 *The Struggle as the Cradle of the Independent Nation*

2002), 264–290; Lopes, *Cabo Verde,* 435–476; and Coutinho, *Os Dirigentes do PAIGC*, 205–211.

31 "Tal como a Luta de Libertação Nacional também a luta pela construção dum Estado viável tem os seus heróis e mártires" *Voz di Povo*, no. 405, 29 September 1984.

32 Cf. Coutinho, *Os Dirigentes do PAIGC*, 272–273 and Odair Barros-Varela, *Crítica da Razão Estatal. O Estado Moderno em África nas Relações Internacionais e Ciência Política. O caso de Cabo Verde* (Praia: Pedro Cardoso Livraria, 2017). For a study on the education in the liberated zones, see, for example, Sónia Vaz Borges, *Militant Education, Liberation Struggle, Consciousness: The PAIGC Education in Guinea Bissau 1963–1978* (Berlin: Peter Lang, 2019). About popular justice in independent Cape Verde, read Boaventura Sousa Santos, *A Justiça Popular em Cabo Verde* (Coimbra: Almedina, 2015).

33 Lopes, *Cabo Verde*, 390–391.

34 From 1969 on, Trotskyism had influence in Portugal in student circles, particularly in the universities of Lisbon, Coimbra, and Oporto, where some young Cape Verdeans became politicised, and it continued in the post-independence period. On the radical left in Portugal in those years, including the development of the Trotskyist current, see: Miguel Cardina, *O Essencial sobre A Esquerda Radical* (Coimbra: Angelus Novus, 2010). Some of them were linked to GRIS (Revolutionary Group of Socialist Intervention), which, according to Jorge Carlos Fonseca, were not officially connected to (any of) the Fourth International(s). Dissident activity in this group gave rise to the Cape Verdean Circles for Democracy. Cf. Jorge Carlos Fonseca, "Prefácio", in *Cabo Verde e Guiné-Bissau: da Democracia Revolucionária à Democracia Liberal*, Fafali Koudawo (Bissau: INEP, 2001), 54. See also Lopes, *Cabo Verde*, 501–536, 621–623.

35 Different explanatory causes, from different perspectives, can be found, for example, in: Jorge Querido, *Cabo Verde. Subsídios para a História da nossa Luta de Libertação* (Lisboa: Vega, 1989); Manuel Faustino, *Jorge Querido: subsídios sob suspeita* (Mindelo: Ilhéu Editora, 1990); Manuel Faustino, "'Criação, Expulsão e vingança dos trotskistas' ou a necessidade de clarificação de acontecimentos políticos de alguma importância", *Horizonte*, no. 54, 20 January 2000; Fonseca, "Prefácio", 9–65; Fafali Koudawo, *Cabo Verde e Guiné-Bissau. Da Democracia Revolucionária à Democracia Liberal* (Bissau: Instituto Nacional de Estudos e Pesquisa, 2001); Lopes, *Aristides Pereira*, 255; Lopes, *Cabo Verde, 469* and 572; and Euclides Fontes, *Uma história inacabada* (Praia: Pedro Cardoso Livraria, 2018), 423–457.

36 Fonseca, "Prefácio", 20, 54.

37 Cláudio Alves Furtado, *Génese e (Re)produção da Classe Dirigente em Cabo Verde* (Praia: Instituto Caboverdeano do Livro e do Disco, 1997), 149–150. On this subject, see also Lopes, *Cabo Verde*, 391 (although this has different numbers) and Almada, "Das tragédias históricas", *Buala*.

38 Lopes, *Cabo Verde*, 391.

39 Silva, "O Nascimento do Leviatã Crioulo", 62–63.

40 Cf. Crisanto Barros, "As elites político-administrativas cabo-verdianas: 1975–2008" (PhD's diss., Universidade de Cabo Verde and Université Catholique de Louvain-la-Neuve, 2012) and Crisanto Barros, "Elitizados, dinâmicas de transformação da moderna elite política administrativa cabo-verdiana", *Journal of Cape-Verdean Studies* 1, no. 1 (2015): 43–44.

41 Silva, "O Nascimento do Leviatã Crioulo", 53–68. On this subject, see also Furtado, *Génese e (Re)Produção*; Barros, "As elites"; and Barros-Varela, *Crítica da Razão Estatal*, 261–289.

The Struggle as the Cradle of the Independent Nation   47

42 Coutinho, *Os Dirigentes do PAIGC*, 59, 118–119, 92 and 261–262.

43 The *Liceu Gil Eanes*, named in 1937, was formerly the *Liceu Nacional de Cabo Verde*, created in 1917 in São Vicente, after the closure that year of the *Seminario-Liceu de São Nicolau* in Ribeira Brava, the first high school in Cape Verde, dating from 1856. Children from well-to-do families sent their children to study in Mindelo, as was the case with Amílcar Cabral. Others went to Mindelo on specific dates to take their exams. In 1960 the *Liceu Nacional da Praia* was opened in Praia, which became the *Liceu Adriano Moreira* from 1962 on (in reference to the then Minister of the Overseas Territories) and was renamed the *Liceu Domingos Ramos* in 1975 (in reference to a relevant Guinean combatant who died during PAIGC's armed struggle, in 1966). In 1956, a section of the *Liceu Gil Eanes* had already been located in Praia, which had more than 200 students. In the absence of formal educational establishments, tutors had an important social function in preparing students for the acquisition of formal schooling. Cf. Barros, "As elites", 247 and Coutinho, *Os Dirigentes do PAIGC*, 61–62 and 258.

44 Furtado, *Génese e (Re)produção*, 119.

45 See analysis by Ângela Coutinho, "Imaginando o combatente ideal do PAIGC: a construção dos heróis nacionais na imprensa do pós-independência na Guiné-Bissau e em Cabo Verde", in *Comunidades Imaginadas: Nação e Nacionalismos em África*, eds. Luís Reis Torgal, Fernando Tavares Pimenta, and Julião Soares Sousa (Coimbra: Imprensa da Universidade de Coimbra, 2008), 173–180.

46 The Amílcar Cabral Institute (IAC), inaugurated in 1985 was the result of a decision taken in August 1976 at a meeting of the PAIGC Superior Council of Struggle to set up a Party school, located on the island of Santiago, for the training and development of leading cadres. Cf. "Instituto Amílcar Cabral: pensar a realidade cabo-verdiana", *Tribuna*, no. 9 (41), 20 January 1989.

47 Cf. Coutinho, *Os Dirigentes do PAIGC*, 135–140.

48 "Sol, suor, o verde e o mar, / Séculos de dor e esperança; / Esta é a terra dos nossos avós! / Fruto das nossas mãos, / Da flor do nosso sangue: / Esta é a nossa pátria amada. / Viva a pátria gloriosa! / Floriu nos céus a bandeira da luta. / Avante, contra o jugo estrangeiro! / Nós vamos construir / Na pátria imortal / A paz e o progresso! (x2) / Ramos do mesmo tronco, / Olhos na mesma luz: / Esta é a força da nossa união! / Cantem o mar e a terra / A madrugada e o sol / Que a nossa luta fecundou. (...)". Cf. Law No. 4/76, of 19 April, on the composition of national symbols.

49 Cf. Sérgio Neto, "Insularidade, Idiossincrasias e Imaginação. Representações de Cabo Verde no pensamento colonial português", in *Comunidades Imaginadas. Nação e Nacionalismos em África*, eds. Luís Reis Torgal, Fernando Tavares Pimenta, and Julião Soares Sousa (Coimbra: Imprensa da Universidade de Coimbra, 2008), 181–192; and José Carlos Gomes dos Anjos, *Intelectuais, literatura e poder em Cabo Verde: lutas de definição da identidade nacional* (Praia: Instituto Nacional do Património Cultural, 2002).

50 Vasconcelos, "Espíritos Lusófonos numa ilha crioula", 182–183.

51 Amílcar Cabral, "O papel da cultura na luta pela independência", *Obras Escolhidas de Amílcar Cabral. A Arma da Teoria – Unidade e Luta* (Lisboa: Seara Nova, 1978, vol. 1, 2nd ed.), 234–247.

52 Cf. Celeste Fortes and Rita Rainho, "Início das emissões da Rádio Libertação, do PAIGC (1967)", in *As Voltas do Passado. A Guerra Colonial e as Lutas de Libertação*, eds. Miguel Cardina and Bruno Sena Martins (Lisboa: Tinta-da-china, 2018), 180.

48   The Struggle as the Cradle of the Independent Nation

53 Fortes and Rainho, "Início das emissões", 180.

54 Amélia Araújo, interview, Praia, 17 May 2019.

55 Araújo, interview.

56 Jorge Querido, "Recordando", *A Nação*, no. 658, 9 April 2020.

57 José Luís Hopffer Almada, "Cabo Verde. Orfandade literária e alegada (im)pertinência de uma poesia de negritude crioula (III)", *Buala*, 28 March 2013, https://www.buala.org/pt/a-ler/cabo-verde-orfandade-identitaria-e-alegada-im-pertinencia-de-uma-poesia-de-negritude-crioula-i and Manuel Brito-Semedo, 'Noti, oh mai', Kaoberdiano Dambará partiu para terra-longe", *Expresso das Ilhas*, no. 958, 8 April 2020.

58 "Nha fla-m, Nha Dunda, kus'e k'e batuku? / Nha nxina mininu kusa k'e ka sabe. / Nha fidju, batuku N ka se kusa. / Nu nase nu atxa-l. / Nu ta more nu ta dexa-l. / E lonji sima seu, / fundu sima mar, / rixu sima rotxa. / E usu-l tera, sabi nos genti. / Mosias na terreru / tornu finkadu, txabeta rapikadu, / Korpu ali N ta bai. / N ka bai. Aima ki txoma-m. / Nteradu duzia duzia na labada, / mortadjadu sen sen na pedra-l sistensia, / bendedu mil mil na Sul-a-Baxu, / kemadu na laba di burkan, / korpu ta matadu, aima ta fika. / Aima e forsa di batuku. / Na batuperiu-l fomi, / na sabi-l teremoti, / na sodadi-l fidju lonji, / batuku e nos aima. / Xinti-l, nha fidju. / Kenha ki kre-nu, kre batuku. / Batuku e nos aima!" (cited in Gláucia Nogueira, "Percurso do Batuku: do menosprezo a património imaterial", *Revista Brasileira de Estudos da Canção* 2, no. jul-dez (2012): 339–340). Translation from the original language to English by Diltino Ferreira.

59 Gláucia Nogueira, *Batuku de Cabo Verde. Percurso histórico-musical* (Praia: Pedro Cardoso Livraria, 2015).

60 Lopes, *Cabo Verde. Um corpo que se recusa a morrer*, 65–66.

61 The magazine, produced with the support of Cape Verdean students in Belgium – since many of the group in Rotterdam had no more than a fourth grade education – circulated among several countries, denouncing famines and colonial repression and announcing the PAIGC's actions. Cf. Djunga de Biluca, *De Ribeira Bote a Rotterdam* (Mindelo: Self-published, 2009), 127–129.

62 Cf. Rui Cidra, "Música, poder e diáspora. Uma etnografia e história entre Santiago, Cabo Verde e Portugal" (PhD's diss., Universidade Nova de Lisboa, 2011), 224.

63 This, as Rui Cidra indicates, with poems predominantly by Manuel Faustino (a prominent PAIGC militant in the clandestinity in Lisbon, who terminated his connection with the party in the post-independence period following the break-away of the Trotskyists). Cf. Cidra, "Música, poder e diáspora", 224.

64 Cidra, "Música, poder e diáspora", 216 and 237.

65 Gláucia Nogueira, "Batuku, Património Imaterial de Cabo Verde. Percurso histórico-musical" (Master's diss. Universidade de Cabo Verde, 2011), 72.

66 Cf. Cidra, from reflections by Thomas Turino, "Música, poder e diáspora", 237.

67 Carlos Filipe Gonçalves, "A música de Cabo Verde: da independência aos dias de hoje", in *Radiografia Crioula. Um diagnóstico político e social de Cabo Verde*, ed. Bruno Carriço Reis (Lisboa / Faro: Universidade Autónoma de Lisboa / Sílabas & Desafios), 210. See also Rui Cidra, *Funaná, Raça e Masculinidade. Uma trajetória colonial e pós-colonial* (Lousã: Outro Mundo Cooperativa Cultural, 2021).

68 Declarations to Televisão Nacional de Cabo Verde, transcribed in *Morna Balada*, by Manuel Brito-Semedo, and quoted in Carlos Filipe Gonçalves and Wladimir Monteiro, "Cabo Verde, 30 anos de música. 1975–2005", in *Cabo Verde. 30 anos de cultura*, ed. Filinto Correia e Silva (Praia: Instituto da Biblioteca Nacional e do Livro, 2005), 101.

The Struggle as the Cradle of the Independent Nation   49

69 For example, by arranging stays in countries such as Cuba as part of musical courses, granting visas to musicians for the purpose of recording records in Portugal, Holland and the USA, and organising initiatives to safeguard cultural heritage, such as the *batuku* contest *"Tradison na skóla"*, in 1986, announced in the 8 February 1986 issue of *Voz di Povo*. Cf., on this subject, Gláucia Nogueira, *Notícias que Fazem a História – A Música de Cabo Verde pela Imprensa ao longo do Século XX* (Praia: Edição de autor, 2007); Cidra, "Música, poder e diáspora", 231–232; Gonçalves, "A música de Cabo Verde", 203–215; and Coutinho, *Os Dirigentes do PAIGC*, 272.

70 Cidra, *Funaná, Raça e Masculinidade*, 231–232.

71 [Raise your arm], a composition by Alcides Brito, part of the group *Voz de Djassi*, from the island of Sal, eventually became an anthem to the struggle and independence, and to this day is associated with these events. Cf. César Monteiro, "Alcides Brito: o braço da liberdade", *Expresso das Ilhas*, no. 837, 13 December 2017.

72 [Cabral is not dead] by composer Daniel Rendall was inspired by the slogans often repeated, even today, on the occasion of the celebration of 5 July and 20 January. On this subject, see Chapter 4.

73 "Labanta brasu bu grita bu liberdadi" (x4) / Grita, povo indipendenti! Grita, povu libertadu! (x2) / 5 di julhu é sinónimu di liberdadi. 5 di julhu kaminhu abertu pa flisidadi (x2) / Grita: 'Viva Cabral' / onra combatenti di nos tera / Grita: 'Viva a guerra' / onra kombatenti di nos tera / Grita: 'Viva Cabral / onra kombatenti di nos tera / [...].

74 Oi Kabu Verdi, / bu ora dja txiga / Sima bos irmons d' Áfrika gritá / Indipendênsia, fidjus djá no ten / Pa nô ser livri, / livri di tudo algén. / Cabral ca mori, Cabral é grito ki digidi mundo / Cabral ca mori, Cabral é grito na nha peitu / Cabral ca mori, Cabral é liberdadi. / Onra memória di erói di povu. / Di PAIGC, partidu di luta / Na finasón no ka podi squece-l / Di tudo irmon erói ki da se sangi / Pa liberdadi e justisa di nos povu. / [...]. See also: Juliana Braz Dias, "Language and Music in Cape Verde: Processes of Identification and Differentiation", in *Creolization and Pidginization in Contexts of Postcolonial Diversity*, eds. Jacqueline Knorr and Wilson Trajano Filho (Leiden: Brill, 2018), 289–308.

75 Cf. Pedro Pires, *Programa do Governo, 1981–1985* (Praia: Grafedito, 1981).

76 José Luís Hopffer Almada, "Das tragédias históricas do povo cabo-verdiano e da saga da sua constituição como nação crioula afro-atlântica – uma incursão crítica aos legados teóricos Claridoso e Neo-Claridoso", in *Claridosidade. Edição Crítica*, eds. Filinto Elísio and Márcia Souto (Lisboa: Rosa de Porcelana, 2017), 87.

77 Cf. for example, José Maria Semedo and Maria Turino, *Cabo Verde: o ciclo ritual das festividades da tabanca* (Praia: Spleen Edições, 1997); Vasconcelos, "Espíritos Lusófonos numa ilha crioula", 149–190; Gláucia Nogueira, "Percurso do Batuku"; and Rui Cidra, "Politics of Memory, Ethics of Survival: The Songs and Narratives of the Cape Verdean Diaspora in São Tomé", *Ethnomusicology Forum* 24, no. 3 (2015): 304–328.

78 Cf. Almada, "Das tragédias históricas", 85–87 and Cidra, *Funaná, Raça e Masculinidade*, 211–271.

79 Cf., for example, "Funaná a maior conquista", *A Tribuna*, no. 29, December 1986 and supplement dedicated to Funaná in *Voz di Povo*, no. 897, 13 January 1990.

80 "Música, bailes e convívio com o Festival Praia-80. Os Tavares, Bana e os Apolos na Praia na semana do 5 de julho?", *Voz di Povo*, no. 227, 25 March to 1 April 1980.

81 "No quadro das comemorações do V Aniversário. Festival Praia-80 em março", *Voz di Povo*, no. 225, 5–12 March 1980.

50 *The Struggle as the Cradle of the Independent Nation*

82 David Hopffer Almada, interview, Praia, 17 January 2020.
83 "'Bulimundo' e a música tradicional cabo-verdiana", *Voz di Povo*, no. 226, 15–22 March 1980. See also, "Funaná, a maior conquista", *Tribuna*, no. 29, December 1986.
84 According to Olívio Pires, in an interview with the authors, *funaná* was "hived off" to Santiago before independence. After 5 July and with the support of the new State, it became possible, according to this liberation struggle combatant, to boost the wider recognition of this musical genre both on the other islands and internationally. Olívio Pires, interview, Mindelo, 23 May 2019. The same view is held by Rui Cidra in "Música, poder e diaspora" and *Funaná, Raça e Masculinidade*, 211–271.
85 See, for example, Lopes, *Cabo Verde*, 537–568.
86 João Branco, "Crioulização Cénica. Em busca de uma Identidade para o Teatro Cabo-verdiano" (PhD's diss., Universidade do Algarve, 2016), 103–104.
87 Kwame Kondé, *Escritos sobre Teatro* (Praia: Artiletra, 2010), 67–68.
88 "TEATRO – KORDA KAOBERDI na apoteose da Tabanca", *Voz di Povo*, no. 239, 20 September 1980.
89 Cf. Branco, "Crioulização Cénica", 109–110.
90 Branco, "Crioulização Cénica", 110.
91 Among the practical actions for the planning and realisation of the unity project, which was to be conducted in stages, were the holding of intergovernmental conferences; cooperation in the fields of mail and telecommunications and in transport, increasing sea and air links between the two countries; the creation in 1977 of the Unity Council, a common body for the two States, responsible for outlining the process for achieving this goal; and the exchange and formation of working groups in areas such as sports, agriculture, trade, industry and education.
92 Lopes, *Cabo Verde*, 595.
93 Ethnic dimensions were used strategically by both the colonial army and the liberation movement. For example, the colonial powers sought to establish alliances with the Fulas, and the PAIGC mobilised mainly the rural Balanta population to war, who were among those most affected by colonial violence. Cf. Joshua Forrest, *Lineages of state fragility: rural society in Guinea-Bissau* (Athens: Ohio University Press, 2009) and Marina Padrão Temudo, "From the margins of the State to the presidential palace: the Balanta case in Guinea-Bissau", *African Studies Review* 52, no. 2 (2009): 47–67.
94 Joshua Forrest, "Guinea-Bissau Since Independence: A Decade of Domestic Power Struggles", *Journal of Modern African Studies* 25, no. 1 (1987): 96 and Sílvia Roque, *Pós-Guerra? Percursos de violência nas margens das Relações Internacionais* (Coimbra: Almedina, 2016), 271.
95 Cf. Leopoldo Amado, "Guiné-Bissau: 30 Anos de Independência", *Africana Studia* 8 (2005): 121.
96 Cf. Forrest, "Guinea-Bissau Since Independence", 105 and Roque, *Pós-Guerra?*, 262.
97 Cf. Luís Moita and Carolina Quina, *Relatório sobre a situação atual na Guiné-Bissau* (Lisboa: CIDAC, 1980), 10, drawn up by Luís Moita and Carolina Quina after a stay in Bissau, with the agreement of the Council of the Revolution, and in Praia, Cape Verde, where they met with various leaders of the PAIGC. After this report, CIDAC decided to resume cooperation with Guinea-Bissau, which had been suspended since 14 November, but called for the release of political prisoners.
98 "Golpe de Estado é contrário aos princípios do partido", *Voz di Povo*, no. 251, 17 January 1981 and Lopes, *Cabo Verde*, 606.

The Struggle as the Cradle of the Independent Nation 51

99 Cf. João Bernardo Nino Vieira, *'Vamos contruir a Pátria de Cabral'. – Discurso do fim de ano proferido pelo Presidente do Conselho da Revolução Comandante João Bernardo Vieira* (Bissau: Edições Nô Pintcha, 1980–1981); Moita and Quina, *Relatório*, 3–4; and Koudawo, *Cabo Verde e Guiné-Bissau*.

100 "Golpe de Estado é contrário aos princípios do partido", *Voz di Povo*, no. 251, 17 January 1981.

101 See, for example: "O Secretário Geral do PAIGC falou à Nação sobre os acontecimentos de Bissau. Golpe aventureiro trai 'princípios' e compromete uma luta de dignidade", "A história do golpe", "O golpe é uma aventura de graves consequências" and "A verdade por si só é revolucionária", *Voz di Povo*, no. 244, 19 November 1980; "Assumir a história da luta, aprendê-la com objetividade e no seu verdadeiro contexto'- afirmou Pedro Pires no 'meeting' da Assomada", "Guiné-Bissau. Responsabilidade histórica ou rutura com a Luta", *Voz di Povo*, no. 245, 29 November 1980.

102 Lopes, *Cabo Verde*, 588–589.

103 Agnelo Dantas, interview, Praia, 20 May 2019.

104 Pires, interview.

105 PAICV, *I Congresso do PAICV* (Praia: Grafedito, 1981), 41–45.

106 PAICV, *I Congresso*, 61.

107 Koudawo, *Cabo Verde e Guiné-Bissau*, 92.

108 Departamento de Informação e Propaganda do PAICV, *A Participação Popular. Documentos do II Congresso* (Praia: Grafedito, 1984).

109 Departamento de Informação e Propaganda do PAICV, *A Participação Popular*, 7–11.

110 Cf. Furtado, *Gênese e (re)produção* and Anjos, *Intelectuais, Literatura e Poder em Cabo Verde*, 232.

111 According to Crisanto Barros, 3 out of 4 high-ranking public sector officials would have benefited from scholarships granted by the State in the first five years of independence. Cf. Barros, "Elitizados", 46–47.

112 According to António Correia e Silva, the reconfiguration of the State in Cape Verde changed profoundly in the 1960s. In a situation where the effects of the drought in the archipelago were getting worse, the colonial authorities, anticipating the intensification of anti-colonial claims, tried to prevent the occurrence of a new period of famine by implementing a series of welfare measures. Cf. Silva, "O Nascimento do Leviatã Crioulo", 59. On this subject, see also Barros, "Elitizados", 39–55 and Lopes, *Cabo Verde. Um Corpo que se recusa a morrer*, 234–235.

113 Silva, "O Nascimento do Leviatã Crioulo", 67.

114 Silva, "O Nascimento do Leviatã Crioulo", 65, 68.

115 Gabriel Fernandes, *Em Busca da Nação. Notas para uma reinterpretação do Cabo Verde crioulo* (Praia: Instituto da Biblioteca Nacional e do Livro, 2006), 149.

116 Baltasar Lopes da Silva, "Regionalismo e nativismo", *Notícias de Cabo Verde*, no. 1, 22 March 1931, cited by José Vicente Lopes, *Cabo Verde. As causas da independência* (Praia: Spleen, 2nd ed., 2012), 54. Baltasar Lopes da Silva studied Law and Romance Philology in Portugal, and then returned to Cape Verde, where he was a prominent teacher (and principal) at the Gil Eanes High School in Mindelo, having taught many of the PAIGC's future militants. He was also a prestigious writer and author of one of the most important Cape Verdean novels, *Chiquinho* (1947). The first excerpts of the work were published in the magazine *Claridade*, of which he was a co-founder.

117 Anjos, *Intelectuais, Literatura e Poder em Cabo Verde* and Victor Barros, "As «sombras» da Claridade. Entre o discurso de integração regional e

52 The Struggle as the Cradle of the Independent Nation

a retórica nacionalista", in *Comunidades Imaginadas. Nação e Nacionalismos em África,* eds. Luís Reis Torgal, Fernando Tavares Pimenta, and Julião Soares Sousa (Coimbra: Imprensa da Universidade de Coimbra, 2008), 193–217.

118 On Gilberto Freyre and Cape Verde, see Michel Cahen, "A mestiçagem colonialista ou a colonialidade de Gilberto Freyre na colonialidade do Brasil", *Portuguese Studies Review* 26, no. 1 (2018): 299–349. For critiques of Gilberto Freyre's theory and the ways in which Luso-tropicalism was appropriated by the *Estado Novo* regime, see Cláudia Castelo, *O modo português de estar no mundo. O luso-tropicalismo e a ideologia colonial portuguesa (1933–1961)* (Porto: Afrontamento, 1999) and Marcos Cardão, *Fado tropical. O luso-tropicalismo na cultura de massas (1960–1974)* (Lisboa: UNIPOP, 2015).

119 Yves Léonard, "O ultramar português", in *Hisória da Expansão Portuguesa* V, eds. Francisco Bethencourt and Kirti Chaudhuri (Lisboa: Círculo de Leitores, 1999), 39.

120 Baltasar Lopes da Silva. *Cabo Verde visto por Gilberto Freyre. Apontamentos lidos ao microfone da Rádio Barlavento* (Praia: Imprensa Nacional, 1956), 14.

121 Silva, *Cabo Verde visto por Gilberto Freyre*, 4.

122 Silva, *Cabo Verde visto por Gilberto Freyre*, 11.

123 João Lopes, "Apontamento", *Claridade*, no. 1, March 1936, 9. For a resume of Freyre's reception in Cape Verde see Castelo, *O modo português de estar no* mundo, 80–84.

124 Gabriel Fernandes, "Entre a Europeidade e a Africanidade: os marcos da colonização / descolonização no processo de funcionalização identitária em Cabo Verde" (Master's Diss. Universidade Federal de Santa Catarina. Florianópolis, 2002), 80. According to Fernandes, the expression *vadio* (tramp) – from which *badio* originated – is documented for the first time at the end of the 18th century as a reference to blacks recently freed from slavery who, lacking the resources to cope with their freedom, were unable to integrate into the new social order. See also Almada, "Das tragédias históricas", *Buala.*

125 Lopes, *Cabo Verde. As causas da independência*, 64.

126 Fernandes, "Entre a Europeidade e a Africanidade", 107–108.

127 Amílcar Cabral, "Breve Análise da estrutura social das Ilhas de Cabo Verde (1963)", in *Unidade e Luta. A arma da teoria* (Praia: Fundação Amílcar Cabral, 2013), 130.

128 Amílcar Cabral, "Apontamentos sobre a poesia cabo-verdiana", Boletim de Propaganda e Informação, no. 28, 1 January 1952, in *Unidade e Luta. A arma da teoria* (Praia: Fundação Amílcar Cabral, 2013), 25–29. Reference to the poem "Sonho [Dream]", in Aguinaldo Fonseca (1951), *Linha do Horizonte*. Casa de Estudantes do Império. Ovídio Martins was another of the names in this militant poetry, having published *Caminhada* in 1962, a book which was also issued by the *Casa de Estudantes do Império*. See also Lopes, *Cabo Verde*, 417–419.

129 Onésimo Silveira, *Consciencialização na literatura cabo-verdiana* (Lisboa: Casa de Estudantes do Império, 1963).

130 Silveira, *Consciencialização.*

131 Anjos, *Intelectuais, Literatura e Poder em Cabo Verde*, 154–155.

132 *Voz di Povo*, no. 595, 27 November 1986.

133 "Presidente Pereira inaugura Simpósio. Aos 50 anos – Claridade entra oficialmente na História de Cabo Verde", *Voz di Povo*, no. 595, 27 November 1986.

The Struggle as the Cradle of the Independent Nation 53

134 "Presidente Pereira inaugura Simpósio", *Voz di Povo*.
135 "RESCALDO DO 'SIMPÓSIO CLARIDADE'. Caçador de Heranças", *Voz di Povo*, no. 596, 3 December 1986.
136 Almada, "Das tragédias históricas", *Buala*.
137 In line with Almada, "Das tragédias históricas", *Buala*.
138 José Carlos Gomes dos Anjos, "A condição de mediador político-cultural em Cabo Verde: intelectuais e diferentes versões da identidade nacional", *Etnográfica* 7, no. 2 (2004): 292. This view is also advocated by Jorge Querido, *Um demorado olhar sobre Cabo Verde. O País, seu Percurso, suas Certezas e Ambiguidades* (Praia: Edição de Autor, 2013), 242–244.
139 Cf. Anjos, *Intelectuais, Literatura e Poder em Cabo Verde*, 211.
140 Aristides Pereira, "Resposta à saudação dos artistas e escritores", in *Aristides Pereira. Discursos de Mudança – de 30 de novembro de 1988 a 16 de janeiro de 1991*, ed. Iva Cabral (Praia: Alfa Comunicações, 2010), 47.

Bibliography

Almada, José Luís Hopffer. "Cabo Verde. Orfandade literária e alegada (im)pertinência de uma poesia de negritude crioula (III)". *Buala*, 28 March 2013. https://www.buala.org/pt/a-ler/cabo-verde-orfandade-identitaria-e-alegada-im-pertinencia-de-uma-poesia-de-negritude-crioula-i.

Almada, José Luís Hopffer. "Das tragédias históricas do povo cabo-verdiano e da saga da sua constituição e da sua consolidação como nação crioula soberana, segunda parte". *Buala*, 17 February 2012. http://www.buala.org/pt/a-ler/das-tragedias-historicas-do-povo-caboverdiano-e-da-saga-da-sua-constituicao-e-da-sua-consolida.

Almada, José Luís Hopffer. "Das tragédias históricas do povo cabo-verdiano e da saga da sua constituição como nação crioula afro-atlântica – uma incursão crítica aos legados teóricos Claridoso e Neo-Claridoso". In *Claridosidade. Edição Crítica*, edited by Filinto Elísio and Márcia Souto, 63–102. Lisboa: Rosa de Porcelana, 2017.

Amado, Leopoldo. "Guiné-Bissau: 30 Anos de Independência". *Africana Studia* 8 (2005): 109–135.

Amaral, Ilídio. "Cabo Verde: introdução geográfica". In *História Geral de Cabo Verde*, edited by Luís de Albuquerque and Maria Emília Madeira Santos, 1–22. Lisboa / Praia: Instituto de Investigação Científica Tropical e Direção-Geral do Património Cultural de Cabo Verde, vol. 1, 1991.

Andrade, Elisa Silva. "Cape Verde". In *A History of Postcolonial Lusophone Africa*, edited by Patrick Chabal, David Birmingham, Joshua Forrest, Malyn Newitt, Gerhard Seibert and Elisa Silva Andrade, 264–290. Indiana: Indiana University Press, 2002.

Anjos, José Carlos Gomes dos. "A condição de mediador político-cultural em Cabo Verde: intelectuais e diferentes versões da identidade nacional". *Etnográfica* 7, no. 2 (2004): 273–295.

Anjos, José Carlos Gomes dos. *Intelectuais, literatura e poder em Cabo Verde: lutas de definição da identidade nacional*. Praia: Instituto Nacional do Património Cultural, 2002.

Barros, Crisanto. "As elites político-administrativas cabo-verdianas: 1975–2008". PhD diss., Universidade de Cabo Verde and Université Catholique de Louvain-la-Neuve, 2012.

54 The Struggle as the Cradle of the Independent Nation

Barros, Crisanto. "Elitizados, dinâmicas de transformação da moderna elite política administrativa cabo-verdiana". *Journal of Cape-Verdean Studies* 1, no. 1 (2015): 39–55.

Barros, Victor. "As 'sombras' da Claridade. Entre o discurso de integração regional e a retórica nacionalista". In *Comunidades Imaginadas. Nação e Nacionalismos em África*, edited by Luís Reis Torgal, Fernando Tavares Pimenta and Julião Soares Sousa, 193–217. Coimbra: Imprensa da Universidade de Coimbra, 2008.

Barros, Victor. "Between truth and invention. How public commemorations recite the biography of Amílcar Cabral". In *The Politics of Biography in Africa. Borders, Margins, and Alternative Histories of Power*, edited by Anais Angelo, 97–117. London / New York: Routledge, 2021.

Barros-Varela, Odair. *Crítica da Razão Estatal. O Estado Moderno em África nas Relações Internacionais e Ciência Política*. Praia: Pedro Cardoso Livraria, 2017.

Biluca, Djunga de. *De Ribeira Bote a Rotterdam*. Mindelo: Edição de Autor, 2009.

Borges, Sónia Vaz. *Militant Education, Liberation Struggle, Consciousness: The PAIGC Education in Guinea Bissau 1963–1978*. Berlin: Peter Lang, 2019.

Branco, João. "Crioulização Cénica. Em busca de uma Identidade para o Teatro Cabo-verdiano". PhD's diss., Universidade do Algarve, 2016.

Braz Dias, Juliana. "Language and Music in Cape Verde: Processes of Identification and Differentiation". In *Creolization and Pidginization in Contexts of Postcolonial Diversity*, edited by Jacqueline Knörr and Wilson Trajano Filho, 289–308. Leiden: Brill, 2018.

Brito-Semedo, Manuel. *A Construção da Identidade Nacional. Análise da Imprensa entre 1877 e 1975*. Praia: Instituto da Biblioteca Nacional e do Livro, 2006.

Cabral, Amílcar. "A Guiné e as Ilhas de Cabo Verde face ao colonialismo português". In *Obras Escolhidas de Amílcar Cabral. Unidade e Luta. A Arma da Teoria*, edited by Mário de Andrade, 75–88. Praia: Fundação Amílcar Cabral, 2013.

Cabral, Amílcar. "Apontamentos sobre a poesia cabo-verdiana". In *Obras Escolhidas de Amílcar Cabral. Unidade e Luta. A Arma da Teoria*, edited by Mário de Andrade, 25–29. Praia: Fundação Amílcar Cabral, 2013.

Cabral, Amílcar. "Breve Análise da estrutura social das Ilhas de Cabo Verde (1963)". In *Obras Escolhidas de Amílcar Cabral. Unidade e Luta. A arma da teoria*, edited by Mário de Andrade, 127–130. Praia: Fundação Amílcar Cabral, 2013.

Cabral, Amílcar. "Memorandum do PAIGC ao Governo português". In *Amílcar Cabral. Documentário (textos políticos e culturais)*, edited by António E. Duarte Silva, 65–78. Lisboa: Edições Cotovia.

Cabral, Amílcar. "O papel da cultura na luta pela independência". In *Obras escolhidas de Amílcar Cabral. A Arma da Teoria – Unidade e Luta*, edited by Mário de Andrade, 234–247. Lisboa: Seara Nova, vol. 1, 2nd edition, 1978.

Cabral, Amílcar. "Resistência Armada". In *Amílcar Cabral. Documentário (textos políticos e culturais)*, selected by António E. Duarte Silva, 115–143. Lisboa: Edições Cotovia.

Cahen, Michel. "A mestiçagem colonialista ou a colonialidade de Gilberto Freyre na colonialidade do Brasil". *Portuguese Studies Review* 26, no. 1 (2018): 299–349.

Cardão, Marcos. *Fado tropical. O luso-tropicalismo na cultura de massas (1960–1974)*. Lisboa: UNIPOP, 2015.

Cardina, Miguel. *O Essencial sobre A Esquerda Radical*. Coimbra: Angelus Novus, 2010.

The Struggle as the Cradle of the Independent Nation 55

Carreira, António. *Migrações nas ilhas de Cabo Verde*. Praia: Instituto Cabo-verdiano do Livro, 2nd edition, 1983.

Castelo, Cláudia. *O modo português de estar no mundo. O luso-tropicalismo e a ideologia colonial portuguesa (1933–1961)*. Porto: Afrontamento, 1999.

Cidra, Rui. "Cabral, popular music and the debate on Cape Verdean creoleness". *Postcolonial Studies* 21, no. 4 (2018): 2–19.

Cidra, Rui. "Música, poder e diáspora. Uma etnografia e história entre Santiago, Cabo Verde e Portugal". PhD's diss., Universidade Nova de Lisboa, 2011.

Cidra, Rui. "Politics of memory, ethics of survival: The songs and narratives of the Cape Verdean Diaspora in São Tomé". *Ethnomusicology Forum* 24, no. 3 (2015): 304–328.

Cidra, Rui. *Funaná, Raça e Masculinidade. Uma trajetória colonial e pós-colonial*. Lousã: Outro Mundo Cooperativa Cultural, 2021.

Coutinho, Ângela Benoliel. "Imaginando o combatente ideal do PAIGC: a construção dos heróis nacionais na imprensa do pós-independência na Guiné-Bissau e em Cabo Verde". In *Comunidades Imaginadas: Nação e Nacionalismos em África*, edited by Luís Reis Torgal, Fernando Tavares Pimenta and Julião Soares Sousa, 173–180. Coimbra: Imprensa da Universidade de Coimbra, 2008.

Coutinho, Ângela Benoliel. "O processo de descolonização de Cabo Verde". In *O Adeus ao Império. 40 Anos de Descolonização Portuguesa*, edited by Fernando Rosas, Mário Machaqueiro and Pedro Aires de Oliveira, 125–140. Lisboa: Vega, 2015.

Coutinho, Ângela Benoliel. *Os Dirigentes do PAIGC. Da fundação à ruptura, 1956–1980*. Coimbra: Imprensa da Universidade de Coimbra, 2017.

Cruz, Inês. "Cabo Verde em tempo de censura: o descaminho do jornalismo e a missão de denúncia da literatura". In *Literaturas Insulares: Leituras e Escritas de Cabo Verde e São Tomé e Príncipe*, edited by Margarida Calafate Ribeiro and Sílvio Renato Jorge, 63–79. Porto: Afrontamento, 2011.

Cruz, Sandra Inês. "A quase-informação na literatura de Cabo Verde em tempo de censura (1926–1975)". Master Diss., Universidade de Coimbra, 2009.

Cruz, Sandra Inês. "A quase-informação na literatura de Cabo Verde em tempo de censura". In *Heranças pós-coloniais nas literaturas de língua portuguesa*, edited by Margarida Calafate Ribeiro and Philip Rothwell, 181–192. Porto: Afrontamento, 2019.

Departamento de Informação e Propaganda do PAICV. *A Participação Popular. Documentos do II Congresso*. Praia: Grafedito, 1984.

Faustino, Manuel. *Jorge Querido. Subsídios sob suspeita*. Mindelo: Ilhéu Editora, 1990.

Fernandes, Gabriel. "Entre a Europeidade e a Africanidade: os marcos da colonização / descolonização no processo de funcionalização identitária em Cabo Verde". Master Diss., Universidade Federal de Santa Catarina, 2002.

Fernandes, Gabriel. *Em Busca da Nação. Notas para uma reinterpretação do Cabo Verde crioulo*. Praia: Instituto da Biblioteca Nacional e do Livro, 2006.

Filho, Wilson Trajano. *Por uma Etnografia da Resistência: o caso das tabancas de Cabo Verde*. Brasília: Departamento de Antropologia da Universidade de Brasília, 2006.

Fonseca, Aguinaldo. *Linha do Horizonte*. Lisboa: Casa de Estudantes do Império, 1951.

56 The Struggle as the Cradle of the Independent Nation

Fonseca, Jorge Carlos. "Prefácio". In *Cabo Verde e Guiné-Bissau: da Democracia Revolucionária à Democracia Liberal*, edited by Fafali Koudawo, 9–65. Bissau: INEP, 2001.

Fontes, Euclides. *Uma história inacabada*. Praia: Pedro Cardoso Livraria, 2018.

Forrest, Joshua. *Lineages of state fragility: rural society in Guinea-Bissau*. Athens: Ohio University Press, 2009.

Fortes, Celeste and Rita Raínho. "Início das emissões da Rádio Libertação, do PAIGC (1967)". In *As Voltas do Passado. A Guerra Colonial e as Lutas de Libertação*, edited by Miguel Cardina and Bruno Sena Martins, 178–183. Lisboa: Tinta-da-china, 2018.

Furtado, Cláudio Alves. "Cabo Verde e as quatro décadas da independência: dissonâncias, múltiplos discursos, reverberações e lutas por imposição de sentido à sua história recente". *Estudos Ibero-Americanos* 42, no. 3 (2016): 855–887.

Furtado, Cláudio Alves. *Génese e (Re)produção da Classe Dirigente em Cabo Verde*. Praia: Instituto Caboverdeano do Livro e do Disco, 1997.

Gonçalves, Carlos and Wladimir Monteiro. "Cabo Verde, 30 anos de música. 1975–2005". In *Cabo Verde. 30 anos de cultura*, edited by Filinto Correia e Silva, 99–119. Praia: Instituto da Biblioteca Nacional e do Livro, 2005.

Gonçalves, Carlos Filipe. "A música de Cabo Verde: da independência aos dias de hoje". In *Radiografia Crioula. Um diagnóstico político e social de Cabo Verde*, edited by Bruno Carriço Reis, 203–229. Lisboa / Faro: Universidade Autónoma de Lisboa / Sílabas & Desafios, 2016.

Kondé, Kwame. *Escritos sobre Teatro*. Praia: Artiletra, 2010.

Koudawo, Fafali. *Cabo Verde e Guiné-Bissau. Da democracia revolucionária à democracia liberal*. Bissau: INEP, 2001.

Léonard, Yves. "O ultramar português". In *História da Expansão Portuguesa V*, edited by Francisco Bethencourt and Kirti Chaudhuri, 31–50. Lisboa: Círculo de Leitores, 1999.

Lopes, João. "Apontamento". *Claridade*, no. 1 (March 1936): 1–10.

Lopes, José Vicente. *Aristides Pereira. Minha Vida, Nossa História*. Praia: Spleen Edições, 2011.

Lopes, José Vicente. *Cabo Verde. As causas da independência*. Praia: Spleen Edições, 2nd edition, 2012.

Lopes, José Vicente. *Cabo Verde. Os Bastidores da Independência*. Praia: Spleen Edições, 3rd edition, 2013.

Lopes, José Vicente. *Cabo Verde. Um corpo que se recusa a morrer. 70 anos contra fome, 1949–2019*. Praia: Spleen Edições, 2021.

Melo, Victor Andrade and Rafael Fortes. "Identidade em Transição: Cabo Verde e a Taça Amílcar Cabral". *Afro-Ásia* 50 (2014): 11–44.

Moita, Luís and Carolina Quina. *Relatório sobre a situação atual na Guiné-Bissau*. Lisboa: CIDAC, 1980.

Neto, Sérgio. "Insularidade, Idiossincrasias e Imaginação. Representações de Cabo Verde no pensamento colonial português". In *Comunidades Imaginadas: Nação e Nacionalismos em África*, edited by Luís Reis Torgal, Fernando Tavares Pimenta and Julião Soares Sousa, 181–192. Coimbra: Imprensa da Universidade de Coimbra, 2008.

Nogueira, Gláucia. "Batuku, Património Imaterial de Cabo Verde. Percurso histórico-musical". Master diss., Universidade de Cabo Verde, 2011.

The Struggle as the Cradle of the Independent Nation 57

Nogueira, Gláucia. "Percurso do Batuku: do menosprezo a património imaterial". *Revista Brasileira de Estudos da Canção*, no. 2 (2012, jul-dez): 328–349.

Nogueira, Gláucia. *Batuku de Cabo Verde. Percurso histórico-musical.* Praia: Pedro Cardoso Livraria, 2015.

Nogueira, Gláucia. *Notícias que Fazem a História – A Música de Cabo Verde pela Imprensa ao longo do Século XX.* Praia: Edição de autor, 2007.

PAICV. *I Congresso do PAICV.* Praia: Grafedito, 1981.

PAIGC. *Sobre a situação em Cabo Verde.* Lisboa: Livraria Sá da Costa, 1974.

Pereira, Aristides. "Resposta à saudação dos artistas e escritores". In *Aristides Pereira. Discursos de Mudança – de 30 de novembro de 1988 a 16 de janeiro de 1991*, edited by Iva Cabral, 47–48. Praia: Alfa Comunicações, 2010.

Pires, Pedro. *Programa do Governo, 1981–1985.* Praia: Grafedito, 1981.

Querido, Jorge. *Cabo Verde. Subsídios para a História da nossa Luta de Libertação.* Lisboa: Vega, 1989.

Querido, Jorge. *Um demorado olhar sobre Cabo Verde. O País, seu Percurso, suas Certezas e Ambiguidades.* Praia: Edição de Autor, 2013.

Roque, Sílvia. *Pós-Guerra? Percursos de violência nas margens das Relações Internacionais.* Coimbra: Almedina, 2016.

Rothberg, Michael. *Multidirectional Memory. Remembering the Holocaust in the Age of Decolonization.* Stanford: Stanford University Press, 2009.

Santos, Boaventura Sousa. *A Justiça Popular em Cabo Verde.* Coimbra, Almedina, 2015.

Semedo, José Maria and Maria Turino. *Cabo Verde: o ciclo ritual das festividades da tabanca.* Praia: Spleen Edições, 1997.

Silva, António Correia e. "O Nascimento do Leviatã Crioulo: esboços de sociologia política". *Cadernos de Estudos Africanos* 1 (2001): 53–68.

Silva, Baltasar Lopes da. *Cabo Verde visto por Gilberto Freyre. Apontamentos lidos ao microfone da Rádio Barlavento.* Praia: Imprensa Nacional, 1956.

Silveira, Onésimo. *Consciencialização na literatura cabo-verdiana.* Lisboa: Casa de Estudantes do Império, 1963.

Sousa, Julião Soares. *Amílcar Cabral. Vida e morte de um revolucionário africano (1924–1973).* Lisboa: Vega, 2011.

Temudo, Marina Padrão. "From the margins of the State to the presidential palace: the Balanta case in Guinea-Bissau". *African Studies Review* 52, no. 2 (2009): 47–67.

Vasconcelos, João. "Espíritos Lusófonos numa ilha crioula: língua, poder e identidade em São Vicente de Cabo Verde". In *A persistência da história: Passado e Contemporaneidade em África*, edited by Clara Carvalho and João Pina Cabral, 149–190. Lisboa: Imprensa de Ciências Sociais, 2004.

Vieira, João Bernardo Nino. *'Vamos contruir a Pátria de Cabral'. – Discurso do fim de ano proferido pelo Presidente do Conselho da Revolução Comandante João Bernardo Vieira.* Bissau: Edições Nô Pintcha, 1980–1981.

Archive documents – Unpublished sources

Author Unknown. *"Amílcar Cabral Portrait".* n. d. Photograph. Folder: 07223.002.036. Fundação Mário Soares e Maria Barroso / Arquivo Mário Pinto de Andrade. http://hdl.handle.net/11002/fms_dc_85089.

58   The Struggle as the Cradle of the Independent Nation

Author Unknown. *"Ceremony to Proclaim the Independence of Cape Verde, in Praia"*. 1975. Photograph. Folder: 05248.000.053. Fundação Mário Soares e Maria Barroso / Arquivo Amílcar Cabral. http://hdl.handle.net/11002/fms_dc_43946.

Pereira, Aristides. *"Mensagem de Aristides Pereira ao povo de Cabo Verde no dia da Proclamação da Independência"*. 1975. Document. Fundação Mário Soares e Maria Barroso / Arquivo Amílcar Cabral. http://hdl.handle.net/11002/fms_dc_39812.

Polimeni, Bruna. *"Amílcar Cabral Portrait"*. 1971. Photograph. Folder 05221. 000.006. Fundação Mário Soares e Maria Barroso / Arquivo Amílcar Cabral. http://hdl.handle.net/11002/fms_dc_44276.

UDC. *"Manifesto"*. 1974. Document. Ephemera – Biblioteca e Arquivo de José Pacheco Pereira. https://ephemerajpp.com/2011/07/15/cabo-verde-uniao-democratica-de-cabo-verde-udc/.

Legislation

Boletim Oficial da República de Cabo Verde, no. 1, 5 July 1975.

Newspapers

Diário Popular, Expresso das Ilhas, Horizonte, O Jornal, A Nação, A Semana, Tribuna, Voz di Povo.

Interviews

Almada, David Hopffer. Audio-recorded interview with Miguel Cardina, Inês Nascimento Rodrigues and Bruno Sena Martins. Praia, 17 January 2020.

Araújo, Amélia. Audio-recorded interview with Miguel Cardina, Inês Nascimento Rodrigues and Bruno Sena Martins. Praia, 17 May 2019.

Dantas, Agnelo. Audio-recorded interview with Inês Nascimento Rodrigues and Bruno Sena Martins. Praia, 20 May 2019.

Pires, Olívio. Audio-recorded interview with Miguel Cardina and Inês Nascimento Rodrigues. Mindelo, 23 May 2019.

Pires, Pedro. Audio-recorded interview with Miguel Cardina, Inês Nascimento Rodrigues and Bruno Sena Martins. Praia, 18 January 2020.

2 THE STRUGGLE IN THE MNEMONIC TRANSITION

The defeat of real socialism and the global expansion of neoliberalism and multi-party systems led to vast changes in the world during the 1980s and 1990s. Eric Hobsbawm notes this by bringing the "short twentieth century" to a close there. The era had begun with the First World War and the spectre of revolution and communism, had ushered in violence and the unprecedented entry onto the stage of classes, peoples and regions of the planet hitherto subjugated, colonised or rendered invisible, and then ended with the collapse of "real socialism" and the triumphant affirmation of liberal capitalism.[1] Regardless of the adjectives applied to characterise this period of time – a "short century" as posited by Hobsbawm, or a "long century" as Giovanni Arrighi saw it, more focused on the dynamics in the world system and on an analysis of the construction of the North American consolidation from 1860 to 1990[2] – a change was clearly identifiable. The early 1990s brought this period to a close, with the rise of neoliberalism, the end of the USSR and the Eastern Bloc, and the spread of models of liberal democracy accompanied by privatisation, individualism as a social model and the reinforcement of structural dependencies, particularly in the Global South.

This global capitalist horizon – which the anti-colonial struggles, among others, had temporarily confronted – now reconfigured the coordinates from which the present, but also the future and the past, were read. To this extent, the end of the Cold War was both the end of a historical period and the beginning of the gradual construction of neoliberalism as the dominant matrix. Social imagination, common sense and interpretations of the past were now overlaid by a new hegemony of anti-totalitarianism, which generally tended to see the different processes of socialising experiences and emancipatory struggle as more or less intense mechanisms of political imposition and individual oppression, while at the same time advocating a teleologically guided combination of (liberal) capitalism and (multi-party) democracy.[3]

Unlike what happened in the 1980s with a considerable number of African States – which resorted to the World Bank and the International

DOI: 10.4324/9781003265535-3

60 *The Struggle in the Mnemonic Transition*

Monetary Fund, and as a result applied deregulation measures and liberalised the economy – Cape Verde had not been subject to any adjustment programme during that time, and even recorded significant levels of growth.[4] The country did, however, acquire specific characteristics particularly as regards the extension of the country's development model, dependent as it was on emigrants' remittances and foreign aid, and to the questioning of a State-centric model by a petty-bourgeoisie of business people and professionals that, to a large extent, had flourished during the First Republic.[5] Political and economic liberalisation, as well as their more immediate consequences, had clear impacts on how the liberation struggle, as a mnemonic device, underwent a process of devaluation, questioning and reconfiguration.

An extensive literature has already addressed the nature of political transition in Cape Verde, noting its causes, examining the role of political actors and seeking to delineate periods and comparisons with similar cases.[6] But the role of what we have called the "mnemonic transition" remains to be examined in detail.[7] This chapter therefore explores the formation of a new memorial landscape in Cape Verde in the 1990s, which occurred simultaneously to the political, constitutional and economic changes then taking place in the country. This new memoryscape, to a large extent composed by anti-anticolonial features, stands as an alternative to the public representations and memorial landscape produced in the aftermath of independence, determined by the valorisation of the armed liberation struggle unleashed against Portuguese colonialism.

This framework was not made through a strict and direct recovery of representations of the colonial times. It signals, more appropriately, the emergence of a mnemonic complex that at times is nourished by the retrieval of figures and facts prior to independence, understood as having been banned by the First Republic, and at others try to find new symbols and national references to globally reposition Cape Verde as a creole society *between* Africa and Europe. Both gestures are rooted in a search for an alternative of what was seen as the memorial heritage of the anti-colonial struggle and particularly of the historical experience of the armed struggle.

The term *memoryscape* has come into widespread use within Memory Studies, especially as a synonym for the analysis of museums, squares, statuary or commemorative plaques in a particular space. One of its initial definitions states that "memoryscapes comprise the organisation of specific objects in space, resulting from often successive projects which attempt to materialise memory by assembling iconographic forms".[8] Demonstrating the interpretative significance of thinking about memory in terms of its territorialisation and materiality, the concept is often used to emphasise the processes by which "social memory" comes to be defined and negotiated in conjunction with particular spatially situated objects, such as monuments and other concrete elements.[9]

The Struggle in the Mnemonic Transition 61

Other authors have highlighted its potential to evoke not only artefacts but also the stories, myths or rituals through which memory is expressed in certain physical and metaphorical spaces and / or times.[10] This is closer to how the term is conceptualised in this book. In other words, it refers not only to the materialisations of memory in clearly defined physical spaces, but to an integrated analysis between materiality, politics and social imaginary in the composition of memorial landscapes.[11] The focus here is on the role that State agents or Cape Verdean political elites assume in the creation of these memorial complexes, stimulating socio-political dynamics around the monuments, symbols and discursive devices of which they are composed and which give them cohesion, but also in the contestation, appropriation and interaction that groups, communities and social movements in the country have with them.

The political transition: causes and processes

The political transition in Cape Verde, concretised in 1991, was preceded by a process of liberalisation starting in the mid-1980s. It was within the PAICV itself, and in the context of the difficulties the country was facing at the time, that a development model based on "economic extroversion" was proposed. In seeking to capitalise on the geostrategic position of the archipelago, and recognising its dependence on the international division of labour, the third Congress, held in November 1988, stressed the importance of the private sector – namely foreign capital – and confirmed the country's interest in functioning as a platform for the sale of services, highlighting the comparative advantages of its geostrategic location within a liberalised world economy.[12]

At this same congress, the tension between sectors more committed to openness and those opposed to it also became evident. This led, for example, to the removal of the term "civil society" from the meeting's documents as initially proposed, which was significant for the openness that it intended to initiate. However, it was only a matter of time before certain steps became inevitable. Between February 1990 and January 1991, occurred the intensification of the path that would lead to the elections.[13] On 19 February 1990, the PAICV National Council considered it necessary to "face the reorganisation of the political system from a new perspective". It decided that, in the upcoming legislative elections, besides the PAICV, groups of organised citizens could participate, and proposed that the necessary steps be taken to repeal Article 4 of the Constitution, which enshrined the PAICV as the "leading political force in society and the State".[14]

According to Fafali Koudawo, the PAICV, which had initiated the economic reforms, "would have pursued them anyway". He saw the distinguishing factor now as being the clear assumption of neoliberal philosophy by the future new elites, noting how economic and political liberalisation appear intertwined in the process.[15] Correia e Silva speaks

62   *The Struggle in the Mnemonic Transition*

of a contradiction at the end of the First Republic. This "neither liberalises the economy to the point of allowing part of the petty bourgeoisie to convert its cultural capital into economic capital, nor maintains welfare to continue to give drought-stricken peasants the socioeconomic support measures they demand".[16] To these explanatory factors should be added the effects of what he calls the "Tocqueville paradox": it was the PAICV's success in government, especially in the field of education and the training of new cadres, that generated social demands that could not be met. He also notes the political impact of the wage problems in the FAIMO (Labour Intensive Work Fronts), which employed a third of the active Cape Verdean workforce and which, on the eve of the elections, had been promised a solution by the opposition.[17]

Fafali Koudawo also points to international pressure, the erosion of power – as revealed, for example, in the student demonstrations that took place in Mindelo in 1977 – and the role of a well-established Catholic Church as explanatory causes of the transition.[18] Functioning as a kind of permanent, consensual semi-opposition, the Catholic Church emerged as a protest structure of great importance in a society historically marked by its presence. The newspaper *Terra Nova*, published in Mindelo and directed by António Fidalgo de Barros, was a constant voice of criticism of the single party.[19] At specific moments, the Catholic Church spoke out, such as when it criticised agrarian reform in 1981 or when it protested government approval of decriminalising the voluntary interruption of pregnancy up to 12 weeks in 1986, a phenomenon that accentuated the fractures between the religious institution and the political regime.[20] When Pope John Paul II visited the archipelago in 1990, he criticised the latter initiative and made clear references to democracy and freedom.[21]

In that years, there were also disturbances on the island of Maio in 1989[22] and, lastly, the assassination of Renato Cardoso, Secretary of State for Public Administration on 26 September, in circumstances never entirely explained. He was close with the so-called Trotskyists but had remained in the party after the departure of most of the militants associated with this political faction.[23] Alongside internal protest, there was also an acute awareness that the rapid international transformations taking place at the end of the 1980s were instigating necessary changes in the archipelago. In January 1990, the President of the Republic, Aristides Pereira, noted that the "nature, breadth and speed" of the international changes occurring in 1989 "will not fail to affect the systems which, in the construction of democracy, favour a degree of effective participation by the people in decisions usually the preserve of parties". And he concluded:

> We must therefore assess whether Cape Verdean society remains willing to continue its experience, proven to be valid, of introducing improvements recommended by the Congress, or whether there are new political demands from society that cannot be met by the current system.[24]

The Struggle in the Mnemonic Transition   63

The elections were scheduled at short notice, which meant that the UCID (Independent and Democratic Cape Verdean Union), organised since 1977 and particularly active among Cape-Verdean migrants settled in Holland and USA, and the Union of the People of the Cape Verde Islands (UPICV), the small, historical collective with Maoist leanings led by José Leitão da Graça, were unable to meet the minimum requirements to be legally validated. For its part, the Movement for Democracy (MpD) was able to legalise and publicly establish itself in a few months. While at first the PAICV had planned on a longer transition period, the pressure and dialogue with civil society and with what would emerge in November 1990 as the "Movement for Democracy" led to a constitutional revision that altered the party regime and eliminated Article 4 of the Constitution which mentioned the PAICV as the leading political force in society and the State.

Thus, following the announcement of openness in February 1990, a group of independents and dissidents drew up a political declaration, dated March 1990, stating that the changes produced since the end of the 1980s had resulted from external and internal pressures and from dysfunctions in the system itself. It stated that, "it is not a matter of deepening the current political system, but simply of replacing it because it has become counter-productive and historically outdated. Therefore, contrary to the insistent claims of the PAICV, democracy in Cape Verde has to be CONSTRUCTED and not perfected, because, in fact, it has never existed among us".[25]

The MpD was able to capitalise on social discontent with the regime that the PAICV leadership had not fully understood. Its leader, Carlos Veiga, was a well-known figure from Plateau, the capital city's noble area, who owned a major law firm and held important positions during the single-party regime. Between 1975 and 1980 he was, first, Director General of Internal Affairs, and then Attorney General. He was, later, a Member of Parliament from the December 1985 elections onwards, as part of the participatory process of drawing up lists of candidates for Parliament implemented under the First Republic. In contrast, some of the leaders and founders of the MpD came from the nebulous Cape Verdean "Trotskyism", although in 1991 they had already abandoned these ideological tendencies, and now generally sought not a combination of democracy and socialism, but democracy and liberalism.

The strict cycle of political transition was thereby consolidated with the landslide victory of the Movement for Democracy in the legislative elections of 13 January 1991, which enabled it to secure more than two-thirds of the seats in the National Assembly. This was a necessary pre-condition for making changes to the Constitution, which came about in 1992. This was followed by victory in the presidential elections, held on 17 February 1991, with António Mascarenhas Monteiro, former President of the Supreme Court of Justice, backed by the MpD, winning by 72.6% over Aristides Pereira, the outgoing President and PAICV candidate. In December, the local elections cemented the MpD's hegemony.[26]

64 *The Struggle in the Mnemonic Transition*

The return of removed images

The political transition was accompanied by a corresponding "mnemonic transition". During these years, the dominant memoryscape was replaced by a new one, erasing the centrality of the anti-colonial legacy of the armed struggle expressed in the approximation to Africa and the appreciation of its protagonists, and actively reclaiming events and figures prior to independence. An emerging "democratic legitimacy" – as opposed to the "legitimacy of independence" and its relation to the armed struggle – now manifested itself. This was the result of the capacity of the new political power to impose new symbols and historical understandings, although the process has some antecedents in the 1980s.

One of the first actions of the new government was to bring back monuments from colonial times, namely statues and busts removed from public spaces in the wake of independence. In the early morning of 5 July 1975, hours before the ceremony referred to at the beginning of the previous chapter, the statue of Diogo Gomes, believed to have been one of the first Portuguese men to land on the island of Santiago in the 16th century, was removed from its central position in Plateau, where it had stood since its inauguration in 1958.[27] Also removed was the statue of the Portuguese navigator Diogo Afonso, in Mindelo, as well as busts of various political and cultural figures that had stood in the main squares of various islands. In the 1987 novel *Xaguate*, by Henrique Teixeira de Sousa,[28] there is a reference to the removal by the population of the bust of the former governor of Cape Verde, Alexandre Serpa Pinto[29] on the island of Fogo, justified by the revolutionary situation:

> You supported the wrenching off of Serpa Pinto's head?
> I wasn't here, or in Cape Verde. I was living in Angola. But, had you been there, you would not have prevented this from happening.
> No?
> No, because you must understand that when this was done, and so many other acts perpetrated by the people, it was a time of revenge, of settling accounts, made possible thanks to the 25th April revolution in Portugal. Trying to immediately prevent such acts would be like stopping Niagara Falls.[30]

Some years later, in 1994, in the novel *Entre Duas Bandeiras* [Between Two Flags], another character took a less sympathetic stance on the historical context in which the removal of busts associated with the colonial period took place. The book has several references to the removal of busts from public spaces at the dawn of independence. On the busts of Luís Vaz de Camões – a major figure in Portuguese literature, author of the 16th century epic poem *Os Lusíadas* – and of the 19th century

Portuguese liberal politician Marquês Sá da Bandeira, removed from Praça Nova in Mindelo, São Vicente, he notes:

> In the gardens of the Praça Nova, they were making a racket around the bust of Camões. Only the plinth was left. The head had been wrenched off and thrown into a corner. On the pedestal it read: "Free your slave Jau, you slaver".
>
> At the other end of the gardens, another crowd gathered around the bust of Sá da Bandeira. The marshal was also beheaded and posthumously baptised a slaver, perhaps because he had the idea of abolishing slavery when he was Minister for the Navy and Overseas.
>
> Gaudêncio didn't like what he saw. Palapinha was filled with anger. That didn't correspond to the historical truth. Camões had been a great poet and a great patriot. Sá da Bandeira had been a champion of the abolition of slavery in Africa.[31]

And about the writer and teacher José Lopes, he writes:

> When the city awoke, some transformations had taken place during the night in various parts of Mindelo. The bust of the poet José Lopes had been painted black. In life he was white, blond, with blue eyes. The plinth was covered from top to bottom with swastikas. This hurt his admirers and those who had been his friends, who remembered his impeccable character, his cultured breeding, his literary talent and his pedagogical gifts.[32]

It is important to note, however, that the movement to restore public statuary dating from colonial times had already begun in the mid-1980s, during the First Republic. In January 1985, the authorities re-established the bust of José Lopes to the city of Mindelo. As the newspaper *Voz di Povo* reported at the time: "the ceremony took place in the same square where, ten years ago, and in a troubled period of our history, hands led on by ill-informed people violated it in a gratuitous and thoughtless gesture, pulling the bust of the poet from its pedestal".[33] Shortly afterwards, the bust of Adriano Duarte Silva, Cape Verdean professor and jurist, who died in 1961 and was an MP representing the archipelago in Portugal's National Assembly, was also returned.[34] This process of reclaiming figures and movements disconnected from the heritage of the anticolonial struggle marked the beginning of the previously mentioned process of valuing figures from the *Claridade* movement.

In the post-1991 period, it was not only a matter of "making peace" and "acknowledging" important figures from Cape Verde's past but also of performing an act of "historical justice". This was, in effect, a gesture associated with the process of imaginary reconfiguration of the nation and its cultural origins. The active redemption of an intellectual heritage

66   *The Struggle in the Mnemonic Transition*

that predates the anti-colonial struggle became evident in the immediate aftermath of the victory in the legislative and presidential elections, with the announcement, in May 1991 by the new president António Mascarenhas Monteiro, of the creation of the Baltasar Lopes da Silva Foundation, in honour of the writer, teacher and one of the most prominent founders of the magazine *Claridade*.[35]

Political and cultural sensibilities such as the one expressed by Baltasar Lopes da Silva were based on claims of a mixed Cape Verdean identity, owing to the country's European and Atlantic roots which, in this sense, distinguished it from other African countries colonised by the Portuguese.[36] Moreover, with the new political cycle, new national epics, new heroes of the motherland and new symbols of the State were also introduced. In addition to Cape Verdean teachers, poets and writers, those who were now being reclaimed were also governors, navigators and figures closely associated with the history of the Portuguese presence and "Lusitanian" cultural identity, such as Luís Vaz de Camões.

Thus, in March 1991, fulfilling an MpD electoral promise, the statue of navigator Diogo Gomes returned to the city of Praia. Its return to the presidential palace on the eve of Mascarenhas Monteiro's inauguration was hailed on the cover of *Voz di Povo* as a "way out of clandestinity".[37] This symbolic action thus marks the prelude to the consolidation of a narrative on the origins of the nation which no longer presents the liberation struggle as its antecedent, but displaces and personifies it in the founding figure of the navigator Diogo Gomes, to a certain extent in a gesture romanticising the historical past and of a supposed "fraternal" relationship with Portugal. This association is supported by one of the individuals interviewed by the newspaper, identifying Diogo Gomes as being "the first Cape Verdean" and also as "the first political prisoner" of the single-party regime, now finally freed from the confinement and invisibility to which he had been condemned during the first 15 years of independence. Although it indicates that the repairs to the space already dated from the previous government, an article in *Voz di Povo* states that Diogo Gomes is "at the dawn of the second Republic, the first historical outcast to resume the place he occupied for years. Others will follow".[38]

In São Filipe, on the island of Fogo, the bust of Serpa Pinto also returned that year. When it was relocated, *Terra Nova* also used the semantics of "ostracism" to which some of the prestigious figures of Cape Verde's history had been consigned, and highlighted the case of three governors whose busts had been removed: Alexandre Serpa Pinto (1894–1897), João de Figueiredo (1943–1949) and Leão do Sacramento Monteiro (1963–1969). In the same newspaper, and showing the echoes of this process across borders, the words of Mário Soares, founder of the Portuguese Socialist Party (PS) and President of the Portuguese Republic at the time, are quoted. On the relocation of the monument

Figure 2.1 Statues of Diogo Afonso (Mindelo) and Diogo Gomes (Praia).
Source: Photographs by the authors.

to Diogo Gomes, he noted that the gesture would confirm that "history is never erased".[39] In the same decade, the statue of another Portuguese discoverer, Diogo Afonso, was replaced in Mindelo (see Figure 2.1).

In August 1992, the busts of Luís Vaz de Camões and the Marquês de Sá da Bandeira returned to the centre of Mindelo, on the island of São Vicente, taking their place in the Praça Nova (officially called Praça Amílcar Cabral) (Figure 2.2). The then mayor of the city, Onésimo Silveira, stressed at the unveiling ceremony that since Cape Verde now lived in a democracy, it was "only right that these statues be restored" as he considered them to be unique figures in Portuguese history who should also be honoured by Cape Verdeans. Their return was subject to a donation from the Portuguese government of the time.[40]

The movement to relocate statues and busts associated with Portugal or Cape Verde during colonial times was not, however, free from criticism, either at the time or in the years that followed. An opinion piece entitled "E Amílcar Cabral? E Jorge Barbosa? E Baltas?" [Baltazar Lopes da Silva], published on 15 September 1992, in the newspaper *Notícias*, argued that the country should exalt the great figures of Cape Verde culture, and show particular indignation at the return of the busts of Camões and Sá Bandeira. The author, considering that "Chiquinho, by Baltasar Lopes, is more important to me than the Lusíadas"[41], traces a path that brings Cabral closer to Cape Verdean writers who, in colonial times, portrayed the daily life and hardships of life in the archipelago.

Figure 2.2 Bust of Camões (Mindelo).
Source: Photographs by M. Cardina.

At the same time, there is also explicit criticism of the reclamation of figures such as Diogo Gomes or Craveiro Lopes. An example of this appears in the song "Dimokransa", by Kaká Barbosa – a Cape Verdean musician, singer and writer (1947–2020) – made famous later by the voice of the singer Mayra Andrade.[42] The song assumes a criticism of electoral promises and political demagogy. At the same time, the reclaiming of historical figures valued during the Portuguese colonial presence (Diogo Gomes and Craveiro Lopes) is compared with the neglect of figures associated with the specific cultural traditions of Cape Verde (particularly the island of Santiago). This is the case of Nha Nácia Gomi (or Inásia Gómi, born Maria Inácia Gomes Correia) (1925–2011), one of the popular icons of *batuku* and *finason*, a form of singing based on improvisation and popular wisdom.

> They forgot Pepé Lópi
> They rescued Diogo Gomes
> They resuscitated Craveiro Lopes
> They don't know Inásia Gómi.[43]

In addition to the restoration of busts and statues, in some cases toponymy changes were made, modifying the names of African leaders known in the post-independence period by the names they bore during colonial times. Krzysztof Górny and Ada Górna studied this process in detail, taking Plateau as a reference, where part of the streets and avenues were renamed in the post-independence period. After the 1990s, some of these names were reversed. According to their data, today, of the 35 roads in Plateau, 31 refer directly to the colonial era, generally evoking the names

The Struggle in the Mnemonic Transition   69

of statesmen, soldiers or governors. This aspect leads the authors to consider it to be a particularly singular phenomenon in the context of the Global South.[44] Another example of renaming is Bairro Craveiro Lopes, built in 1954 and renamed after 1975 as Bairro Kwame Nkrumah, which reverted to its original name in 1993, in reference to the Portuguese politician and military from the time of the dictatorship and colonialism. On the other hand, in the second largest city in the archipelago, Mindelo, on the island of São Vincente, the streets and squares have not tended to change their names in the 1990s, although some of them are popularly referred to by the names they had during colonial times.

A new paradigm of remembrance

The mnemonic transition drew a new memorial landscape. It challenged the symbology bequeathed by the liberation struggle and by independence from an emerging "democratic legitimacy", and produced a reimagining of Cape Verde and the legacies that historically formed it. In this memoryscape, the party-political legitimacy of the new rulers as "combatants for democracy" emerged. The MpD tended to be portrayed as the party that liberated not only the authoritarian political system previously in force in the country, but also the historical destinies of the Cape Verdean population, who were to a certain extent seen as having been forced for 15 years to give up their Creole identity in favour of an artificial adoption of Africanness.[45]

This narrative attributed responsibility to the MpD for giving Cape Verdeans back their full history, no longer centred on the liberation struggle as a defining experience of national identity, but restoring to the archipelago and its inhabitants the symbols of cultural, intellectual and historical heritage that were "banned" or "erased" by the PAIGC / CV at the dawn of independence, and also the freedom to feel and assert themselves as Cape Verdeans and not Africans.[46] As Nuno Manalvo states in his biography dedicated to former Prime Minister Carlos Veiga, "if the PAIGC was the party of independence, the MpD was the party of freedom and democracy".[47]

It also unleashed a series of public criticisms of the PAIGC / CV and, subsequently, of those fighters who had occupied political decision-making positions during the single-party regime. These activities materialised from the end of 1990 during the election campaign, and with greater frequency in the years immediately afterwards, in dozens of press articles and graffiti openly hostile to the party and the former Prime Minister, Pedro Pires, who even became the target of "symbolic funerals".[48] Literature, memoirs and essays has also played an important role in the revisionist process of repositioning memories of the past.

In those years, books were published that openly attacked the PAIGC / CV and its leaders. Among them, one 1992 book stands out because it

70 *The Struggle in the Mnemonic Transition*

led the new government to open an enquiry into the alleged acts of violence under the First Republic reported therein and the author's troubled relationship with the PAIGC. This was *A tortura em nome do partido único. O PAICV e a sua polícia política* [Torture in the name of the single-party. The PAICV and its political police], by Onésimo Silveira, an important former militant from the liberation movement, from which he had withdrawn.[49] Other important pieces of this period condemning the old regime include the reflections of Humberto Cardoso, a member of the Political Committee of the MpD and advisor to the Prime Minister Carlos Veiga at the time of the publication, in 1993, of *O Partido único em Cabo Verde: um assalto à esperança* [The Single-Party in Cape Verde: an assault on hope].[50] In another sense, but also critically evoking the First Republic, are two novels by Germano Almeida: *O Dia das Calças Roladas* [The Day of the Rolled-Up Trousers][51] about the opposition in Santo Antão to agrarian reform in August 1981, in which the agricultural landowners had a major influence; and *O Meu Poeta* [My Poet],[52] a satirical comment on the First Republic and the unfulfilled dreams of the struggle. Later, in 1998, Germano Almeida published *A Morte do Meu Poeta* [My Poet's Death], a text which satirises the rulers and political power of the multi-party regime.[53]

In the first years of the 1990s, by diminishing combatants and their sphere of influence, the aim was to weaken the political legitimacy they laid claim to by being involved in the liberation struggle. The liberation struggle – particularly its armed front – was now considered detached from the founding symbolism of the nation, thereby strengthening a different narrative of the origins of the archipelago. In this other reading of the past, Cape Verde's independence is generally seen as a historical inevitability, that is, not as a direct result of the liberation struggle but as the by-product of a generic international context.[54] At the same time, the idea of the existence of a Cape Verdean nation prior to 5 July 1975 was reinforced.

The public promotion of Cabral through the media, political speeches, songs and public ceremonies during the First Republic, as mentioned in the previous chapter, was followed during the years of mnemonic transition by what could be called a process of de-Cabralisation of national symbols: his image gradually disappeared from the notes and coins of the Cape Verdean escudo, the date of his birth was no longer celebrated as a public holiday and the national anthem with lyrics written by Cabral was replaced. The process of de-Cabralisation coexisted with a series of actions against the historical combatants who were political leaders, sometimes classified as corrupt and oppressive. During this phase, for example, a decree was passed obliging the PAICV to provide proof of how it had acquired its assets; Pedro Pires, the country's Prime Minister for 15 years, was charged in the "Africa Dossier" case – over funding by the Cape Verdean State of the newspaper *África* published in

The Struggle in the Mnemonic Transition   71

Portugal – from which he was later cleared; and during the presidential campaign, António Mascarenhas Monteiro suggested that the participation of Cape Verdeans in the armed struggle was unrepresentative and removed from the experience of the islands.[55]

It is within this framework that we can also include the changes in awarding the Medal of the Order of Amilcar Cabral, the highest honour granted by the Cape Verdean State.[56] Introduced in 1987, it was only awarded at the end of the First Republic. In the space of approximately one month, between 22 December 1990 and 19 January 1991, Aristides Pereira awarded the insignia to 47 Cape Verdean historical combatants, some posthumously. Those honoured, all men, had, for the most part, experience in the armed struggle in Guinea and were high ranks of the People's Revolutionary Armed Forces (FARP).[57] During the ten years of the presidency of António Mascarenhas Monteiro, the same decoration was awarded seven times and only to foreign political leaders.[58] These, however, were from countries with close historical ties to Cape Verde: the Senegalese President Abdou Diouf (1994), the Mozambican President Joaquim Chissano (1995), Cuban leader Fidel Castro (1998), the Timorese President and Prime Minister Xanana Gusmão (2000), and Portuguese leaders António Guterres, Jorge Sampaio and Mário Soares (all in 2000).

At the same time, it was also in 1991 that the Statute of the Liberation Struggle Combatant was extended, resulting in a considerable increase in requests for certification throughout the decade.[59] While, in the first years of independence, most of the combatants recognised were those who had taken up arms in Guinea, the changes introduced in the legislation during the 1990s made it possible to include, in a more explicit way, other forms of participation in the struggle for independence. There was no longer necessary to have been involved in the armed struggle or even joining the ranks of the PAIGC, and thereby diminished the symbolic power of the historical combatants and of the armed conflict itself in the history of the birth of the nation. This, and the process of diversification in the official recognition of actors in the struggle who until then had occupied a relatively subordinate role, such as former political prisoners or clandestine militants, will be discussed in detail in the following chapter.

The struggle as a whole, however, could not be entirely denied as national historical heritage, not only because of the recognition of the liberation process but also because the elites now in power were nourished on the symbolic capital of the struggle. In fact, a significant number of the founding members of MpD, the party that won the elections in 1991, consisted of a group of PAIGC dissidents in the post-independence period who had participated in the struggle, mainly in political activities carried out in Portugal and other Cape Verdean diasporas. In a dichotomous act of antagonism towards the historical leaders, they offered themselves up as doubly combatants.

72 *The Struggle in the Mnemonic Transition*

On one hand, they were combatants for the freedom of their country, because some of them had participated in the struggle for national independence, although generally from positions – clandestinely in Portugal or in the archipelago – that were not considered to be at the top of the hierarchy of combatants defined by the First Republic. In 1994, on the commemoration of 5 July, the parliamentary leader of MpD, Gualberto do Rosário, maintained that "the majority of the leaders of the MpD, in one way or another, participated in the process of Cape Verde's independence".[60]

On the other hand, and more importantly in this context, these militants also defined themselves as combatants for democracy, since they believed that the "true" liberation of the archipelago was not achieved until 1991, at their instigation and as a result of their pressure. Following the MpD's victory in the 13 January parliamentary elections, Jacinto Santos, the party's spokesman, declared that "the victory of the presidential candidate, António Mascarenhas Monteiro" represented "the victory of democracy in Cape Verde".[61] In a speech at the Institute for Social Studies in The Hague in 1993, Carlos Veiga said, as paraphrased by *Novo Jornal de Cabo Verde*, that "the PAIGC leaders, asserting for themselves a historic right won in the armed struggle in Guinea-Bissau, quickly transformed themselves into a caste and began to set up a State apparatus to guarantee them power indefinitely. To that end (...) they constructed a mythology of the armed struggle in which their role was praised to the point of proclaiming themselves the 'best sons' of the Cape Verdean people".[62]

The change in national symbols

Political change established a new paradigm in the remembrance of the struggle and of nation-building. Not only was new life breathed into the narrative of the exceptional and particular nature of the Cape Verdean identity, especially by drawing on the heritage left by the *Claridosos* in the 1930s and highlighting, among the elements of that Cape Verdean identity, those supposedly possessing a Portuguese dimension. A process was also created for substituting national symbols, through a commission created for the purpose in which the PAICV refused to participate.[63]

As a result of the competition officially launched on 15 April 1992, 24 anonymous proposals for a new national coat of arms were received by 15 June of the same year and evaluated. The winning proposal replaced the ears of corn, a shell, a book, a black star and the motto "Unity - Work - Progress" which had been included in the design of the previous coat of arms for 1) a blue equilateral triangle with a white torch, symbolising, according to the descriptive statement submitted to Parliament, "equal civil rights granted to the people by the democratic government" and "freedom won after years of sacrifice, torture and struggle against oppressors", and 2) a

The Struggle in the Mnemonic Transition 73

Figure 2.3 Coat of Arms before 1992 and after 1992.

blue circle with the words "Republic of Cape Verde" with three straight lines in the same colour, in a reference to the sea "that surrounds the islands", the "inspiration of poets" and "sustenance of the people" (Figure 2.3).[64]

The new flag, which was hoisted for the first time on 25 September 1992 – the same date on which the new Constitution, based on a draft prepared by Wladimir Brito, would be approved – was chosen from among 64 proposals received in the competition. It does not bear much resemblance to the flags of Guinea-Bissau and the PAIGC or any reference to the colours associated with Pan-Africanism, still present today in many flags of African countries.[65] And it incorporates a graphic and chromatic design very similar to the European Union (EU) flag (see Figure 2.4). The transformation is a clear sign of the new political, strategic and economic alliances that came to be formed in the country, with Portugal and Europe in general heading the list of Cape Verde's favoured partners.

Pedro Gregório Lopes, the designer responsible for the winning proposal for the new flag, was accused at the time of showing a certain anti-Africanism. He denies, however, that it was the EU flag that inspired him and explained that the ten equidistant yellow stars represent the ten

Figure 2.4 Cape Verde Flags: The Post-Independence Flag *and* the Current Flag Since 1992.

74 *The Struggle in the Mnemonic Transition*

islands that make up the archipelago, all of equal importance. He justified the presence of blue, which almost completely covers the new flag, with the fact that this is the colour that permeates the day-to-day life of Cape Verdeans, at sea and in the sky.[66]

The symbolism attributed to the various components of the new flag and arms of the Republic – primarily the centrality that the sea acquires – thus highlights, in a nod to the great Cape Verdean diaspora and potential international cooperation, the migratory tendencies of the Cape Verdean people and the geostrategic position of the country in Macaronesia (made up of the Azores, Madeira, the Canaries and Cape Verde). In turn, the erasing of the five-pointed black star and its replacement, in both cases, by yellow stars representing the ten islands of the archipelago, can be interpreted as a gesture of refocusing on Cape Verde and its specific circumstances and, at the same time, as a distancing from the need to affirm the African unity that the previous black star embodied. These gestures can thus be seen as part of a process of symbolic devaluation of the armed struggle and visual erasure of its heritage. During the First Republic, they often consisted of the rhetoric of geostrategic and cultural rapprochement with Africa, the rescue of artistic manifestations assumed to be of African origin, and the affirmation of Africanness that initially translated into the pursuit of unity with Guinea-Bissau, as mentioned in the previous chapter.

The change of flag was hotly contested and debated in Cape Verde, giving rise to intense exchanges of opinion in parliamentary debates and in the media between 1991 and 1992, especially between members and / or sympathisers of the MpD and PAICV. The latter argued that a change of regime should not mean a change of symbols, which are intended to be perennial in their role of creating stability, sovereignty and national unity, and seen as representative of the recognition of the historical ties that united the archipelago to Guinea-Bissau, whose common past should not be devalued.[67] One of the arguments of those in favour of changing the flag was precisely that it was a copy of the flags of Guinea-Bissau and / or the PAIGC, and not an autonomous national symbol representative of the reality of Cape Verde.[68]

Further to the change of flag, there were demonstrations against this decision in Santiago and São Vicente, the two largest islands in the archipelago, but also in the diaspora community in the USA. In July 1992, a poll conducted in Mindelo by the newspaper *Notícias* showed that this was a fractious issue among the city's population.[69] Around the same time, a petition with around 25,000 signatures from citizens was delivered to Parliament arguing for the retention of the country's original flag.[70] There was also a proposal for a popular referendum, presented by the PAICV, which was ultimately rejected by the MpD. Constitutional reasons were then invoked (e.g. referendums are not foreseen in the National Assembly procedures), as were financial reasons (highlighting

The Struggle in the Mnemonic Transition   75

the costs that such an action would entail for the State), and also the question of legitimacy. It was agreed that the election result of 13 January had rejected the PAICV with all its national symbols, and that the flag brought by the fighters "from Guinea" in no way reflected Cape Verde's circumstances, its values and its history.

This was stated, for example, by three MpD members of parliament in June 1992, listing, among others, arguments such as that "by rejecting the PAICV, the people also rejected the symbols of that party that were abusively imposed on the Cape Verdean nation";[71] that a new Constitution has the obligation to bring national symbols that, on one hand, in fact represent the Cape Verdean identity and, on the other hand, represent the identity of the entire Cape Verdean people and not just a part of it;[72] or that it was the "force of arms" that legitimised a national flag that imitated that of Guinea-Bissau and the PAIGC, which, in turn, was inspired by the flags of the French-speaking nations of West Africa, and recognised the support that these countries gave to that party during the struggle and not the historical and cultural path of Cape Verde.[73]

The major mnemonic changes introduced in 1992 generated clear divisions evident not only in parliamentary debates, but also in numerous press texts, some supportive, others satirical and critical, like the one by J.G., published in October of that year in *A Semana* newspaper. Entitled "The symbols of discord", this opinion chronicle makes the following points about the rupture:

> In Cape Verde, everything is changing: the names, the symbols, the colours, the heroes, etc. Only the people remain the same: Cape Verdeans. God dammit! One way to speed up the process would be to change the people. And it was not without great public jeering and heckling that the people attended the inauguration of the blue flag.
>
> Changing the names of streets, squares, gardens, flowerbeds, statues, etc., is a feature of the year 1992. But then, what more do the people want? What the democrat does, gets done.[74]

According to Cláudio Furtado, these mnemonic and cultural changes, particularly visible in the 1990s, are mostly the result of a metamorphosis of the ideological divisions that marked the first years of independence, although they represent a more obvious capacity for segmentation of Cape Verdean society, in his opinion.[75] The debates and arguments surrounding the replacement of the national flag were an example of this.

The change of the anthem, the same as Guinea-Bissau's, was, however, a more consensual decision in party-political terms, especially because of some protocol incidents after the unity project with that country had come to an end. Nevertheless, it was more difficult to accomplish because for years it was considered that no quality proposal had been submitted and therefore no winning alternative would be agreed upon in terms of

76 *The Struggle in the Mnemonic Transition*

a parliamentary vote.[76] Despite the official call for proposals in 1992, the selection of the new anthem was successively postponed, and became an increasingly intense and disputed matter.

In July of that year, the jury recommended the opening of a new competition, now to be held in two distinct phases: the first for the submission of lyrics for the anthem, and the second for proposed melodies to accompany the selected lyrics. Of the poems received by 7 October, the text "Peace and Labour", by Amílcar Spencer Lopes, President of the National Assembly, was approved. It was widely caricatured at the time for the antiquated and pompous expressions it contained. It ended up not getting a consensus within the MpD itself, and was rejected by the votes of seven of its members.[77]

After two unsuccessful competitions, the anthem "Hymn of Freedom", written by Amílcar Spencer Lopes and composed by Adalberto Higino Tavares da Silva, was put to a vote through a bill presented by the MpD parliamentary benches in 1995, and on that occasion rejected. The same text was only approved the following year, in May, after the party had again won the elections with a qualified majority.[78] They justified it in view of the urgency of finding an anthem in line with the values of Cape Verdean society, more than two decades after 5 July 1975.[79]

> Sing, brother
> sing, my brother
> that Freedom is an anthem
> and Man the certainty.
>
> With dignity, bury the seed
> in the dust of the bare island;
> on the cliff of life
> hope is as big as the sea
> that embraces us.
> Sentinel of seas and winds
> persevering
> between stars and the Atlantic
> intones the chant of freedom.
>
> Sing, brother
> sing, my brother
> that Freedom is an anthem
> and Man the certainty.[80]

With *Cântico da Liberdade* [Hymn of Freedom], officially launched on the eve of the 21st anniversary of independence, all allusions to the colonial past and mentions of the struggle have disappeared, replaced now by favoured references to the sea, the Atlantic, and freedom, words repeated in its opening and conclusion. The idea of "freedom" is, in this context, also equivalent to democracy, achievements symbolically extolled by the MpD as its party's heritage and that give a name to the national holiday of

The Struggle in the Mnemonic Transition 77

Figure 2.5 500 Escudos Banknote, Issued in 1989, with Amílcar Cabral's Image and 500 Escudos Banknote, Issued in 1992, with Baltasar Lopes da Silva's Image.

13 January, instituted in 1999 as the "Day of Freedom and Democracy", in honour of the date of the first multi-party elections.

As far as the currency (the *escudo*) is concerned, it has like other national symbols undergone a process of "de-Africanisation", as Márcia Rego previously suggested.[81] The banknotes and coins with Cabral and other African revolutionaries on were gradually withdrawn from circulation during the 1990s and replaced by local flora and fauna motifs and images of other personalities, illustrious figures from the islands, prior to the African nationalists, which then became the new pedestal of citizens to be decorated, more in line with the new values that were intended for the nation (Figure 2.5). Although Baltasar Lopes da Silva and Eugénio Tavares, men of the literate and mixed race elite included in the issue of the Cape Verdean escudo in 1992 and 1999, were voices critical of the subordinate place of the Cape Verdean in the archipelago, they did not fight for an anti-colonial message or for a defence of Africanness, but rather for an appreciation of the Creole nature of the Cape Verdean considered to be sustained mainly by elements of Portuguese origin.[82] The new choice of iconography on the national currency shows how the movement to erase the black component in Cape Verde went hand in hand with a devaluation of the anti-colonial legacies and the aforementioned de-Cabralisation of national symbols.

The mnemonic transition: reasons and circumstances

This chapter has set out an analysis of the memoryscape that, with some moments of discord, was affirmed in the 1990s and later became dominant, giving rise to a fracture relative to that of the memorial landscape of the struggle. A mnemonic transition was thus configured which can be accounted for by a number of factors. Firstly, the defeat of the PAICV in an international context in which liberation movements that had become single-party regimes were already being widely criticised. Secondly, the broad party-political hegemony achieved by the MpD, allowing it to amend the constitution and make changes in symbology and public space by availing itself of this legitimacy at the ballot box. Thirdly, the reactivation of a diffuse social and political field, where political opponents to the PAIGC / CV before and after independence, and movements and

78 *The Struggle in the Mnemonic Transition*

institutions such as the Catholic Church, were disposed to re-awaken the imagination of the nation and revive pre-existing tensions. Finally, these symbolic and political changes found a resonance in significant segments of the population, receptive to the enhanced and ambiguous identity that Cape Verde was establishing in its relationship with Portugal and its colonial heritage. The readiness to accept the mnemonic transition thus suggests that, in addition to the loss of legitimacy of the PAIGC / CV and the First Republic, the presence in Cape Verdean society of a colonial imaginary that was shaping the post-colonial representations of the nation was also at stake.

The activation of this memoryscape was a key part of the process of establishing a new post-1991 political and ideological hegemony. It would consolidate the social reproduction of the ruling class, mostly taken up by PAIGC dissidents and by a new technocratic generation, of an anti-totalitarian matrix, attuned to the global discourse on democracy.[83] The replacement of the "era of the combatants" by the "era of the cadres" – to use an expression of Anjos[84] – was accompanied by the rise of this new memorial landscape, which was anchored not only in anti-anticolonial elements such as the downgrading of the armed struggle and its historical figures but also in a symbolic re-reading of the nation, highlighting elements of cultural prestige and continuity with the archipelago's colonial past. A result of exogenous and endogenous influences and dynamics, the most evident examples were the replacement of colonial statues in the location where they were previously on display, the changing of national symbols, or the reversion of the toponymy to names that appeared before independence. While it is true that no transition of memoryscapes operates in a homogeneous or monolithic way, it did operate at varying intensities and generated social and political contestation.

Thus, although it was hegemonically consolidated during the 1990s, acting more intensely and consistently until roughly the beginning of the second mandate of the MpD in 1996, the validity of this memorial complex, especially in the years and decades that followed, was accompanied by the relative re-emergence of the memory of the struggle. This is evident – notwithstanding moments of tension, which will also be noted – in specific actions to historically revalue the figure of the combatant, as well as in the process of pluralising and recognising the actors and their distinct trajectories of participation in the national liberation struggle, as will be discussed in the following chapter.

Notes

1 Eric Hobsbawm, *The Age of Extremes. A History of the World 1914–1991* (New York: Vintage Books, 1994).
2 Giovanni Arrighi, *The Long Twentieth Century. Money, Power and the Origins of Our Times* (New York and London: Verso, 1994).
3 Some authors consider that the rise of neoliberalism, the defeat of emancipatory dreams and the "memory boom" from those years are interconnected.

The Struggle in the Mnemonic Transition   79

This is what historian Enzo Traverso has argued, noting how the eclipse of utopia and the idea of an alternative future corresponded to mechanisms of memorial obsession with the past, at the same time as the memory of revolutions, anti-fascism, or anti-colonialism was being replaced by the figure of the "victim". See Enzo Traverso, *Le Passé, mode d'emploi: Histoire, mémoire, politique* (Paris: La Fabrique, 2005). While it is true that invoking the idea of victim runs the risk of depoliticising the historical processes that underlie it, it is also true that strategic recourse to this notion has fuelled movements for historical justice for individuals and groups targeted by violence (see, for example, the Latin American case).

4 "At the end of the 1980s, known as the 'lost decade for Africa,' Cape Verde had grown its GDP at an average annual rate of 6%, or about twice as much as the CILSS (Inter-State Committee for Drought Control in the Sahel) states, six times higher than the PALOPs (Portuguese-speaking African Countries), and 12 times higher than the continental average. The Human Development Index on the archipelago [which includes life expectancy, literacy levels and purchasing power] was also significantly higher than the three sets of figures mentioned above". Cf. António Correia e Silva, "Cabo Verde: Desafios económicos e a estruturação do Estado. Do Estado-Providência (sem contribuintes) ao liberalismo sem empresários. O Ciclo da Iª República", paper presented at the *VIII Congresso Luso-Afro-Brasileiro de Ciências Sociais – A Questão Social no Novo Milénio*, Centro de Estudos Sociais da Universidade de Coimbra, 16–18, September 2004, 3, https://www.ces.uc.pt/lab2004/inscricao/pdfs/grupodiscussao5/AntonioLeaoSilva.pdf.

5 Silva, "Cabo Verde: Desafios económicos e a estruturação do Estado".

6 See, among others: Aristides Lima, *Reforma Política em Cabo Verde. Do Paternalismo à Modernização do Estado* (Praia: ed. de autor, 1991); Michel Cahen, "Arquipélagos da alternância; a vitória da oposição das ilhas de Cabo Verde e de São Tomé e Príncipe", *Revista Internacional de Estudos Africanos* no. 14/15 (1991): 113–154; António Correia e Silva, "O Processo Caboverdiano de Transição para a Democracia" (Master's diss., ISCTE, 1997); Fafali Koudawo, *Cabo Verde e Guiné-Bissau. Da democracia revolucionária à democracia liberal* (Bissau: INEP, 2001); Peter Meyns, "Cape Verde: An African Exception", *Journal of Democracy* 13, no. 3 (2002): 153–165; Roselma Évora, *Cabo Verde: A abertura política e a transição para a democracia* (Praia: Spleen Edições, 2004); Edalina Sanches, *Party Systems in Young Democracies. Varieties of Institutionalization in Sub-Saharan Africa* (London and New York: Routledge, 2018), 73–95.

7 An initial approach to this concept can be found in Miguel Cardina and Inês Nascimento Rodrigues, "The mnemonic transition: the rise of an anti-anticolonial memoryscape in Cape Verde", *Memory Studies* 14, no. 2 (2021): 380–394. The term "mnemonic transition" was previously used by Astrid Erll, but in a very different sense, with a focus on literature and exploring the relationship between memory and generational transformations. Cf. Astrid Erll, "Fictions of Generational Memory: Caryl Phillips's In the Falling Snow and Black British Writing in Times of Mnemonic Transition", in *Memory Unbound. Tracing the Dynamics of Memory Studies*, eds. Lucy Bond, Stef Craps and Pieter Vermeulen (New York: Berghahn Books, 2017), 109–130.

8 Cf. Tim Edensor, "National identity and the politics of memory: remembering Bruce and Wallace in symbolic space", *Environment and Planning* 29 (1997): 178.

9 Some examples of these studies are: Hamzah Muzaini, "Producing / consuming memoryscapes: The genesis / politics of Second World War commemoration in Singapore", *Geojournal* 66, no. 3 (2006): 211–222; Ferdinand

80 *The Struggle in the Mnemonic Transition*

De Jong, "Recycling Recognition. The Monument as *Objet Trouvé* of the Postcolony", *Journal of Material Culture* 13, no. 2 (2008): 195–214; Hamzah Muzaini and Brenda S. A. Yeoh, *Contested Memoryscapes. The Politics of Second World War Commemoration in Singapore* (London and New York: Routledge, 2016); Stephanie Kappler, "Sarajevo's ambivalent memoryscape: Spatial stories of peace and conflict", *Memory Studies* 10, no. 2 (2017): 130–143; and Sarah de Nardi *et al.*, *The Routledge Handbook of Memory and Place* (New York and London: Routledge, 2019), 118–169.

10 For example: Jennifer Cole, *Forget Colonialism? Sacrifice and the Art of Memory in Madagascar* (Berkeley and Los Angeles: University of California Press, 2001); Paul Basu, "Palimpsest Memoryscapes: Materializing and Mediating War and Peace in Sierra Leone", in *Reclaiming Heritage: Alternative Imaginaries of Memory in West Africa*, eds. Ferdinand De Jong and Michael Rowlands (Walnut Creek: Left Coast Press, 2007), 231–259; and Susann Ullberg, *Watermarks. Urban Flooding and Memoryscape in Argentina* (Stockholm: Acta Universitatis Stockholmiensis, 2013); Thomas Van de Putte, "Delineating Memoryscapes: Auschwitz versus Oświęcim", *Holocaust Studies* 27, no. 1 (2021): 91–105.

11 For writing convenience, we will use the terms "memoryscape" and "memorial landscape" interchangeably as synonyms in the sense defined here.

12 Koudawo, Cabo Verde e Guiné-Bissau, 94–95.

13 Aristides Lima considers this to be the second phase of the transition process. Lima, *Reforma Política em Cabo* Verde, 9.

14 "Resolução sobre Regime Político", Praia, 19 February 1990.

15 Koudawo, *Cabo Verde e Guiné-Bissau*, 159.

16 António Correia e Silva, "O Nascimento do Leviatã Crioulo: esboços de sociologia política", *Cadernos de Estudos Africanos* 1 (2001): 67.

17 Silva, "Cabo Verde: Desafios económicos e a estruturação do Estado".

18 Koudawo, *Cabo Verde e Guiné-Bissau*, 118–122.

19 On *Terra Nova*, see "40 anos de Terra Nova: o único jornal que enfrentou o partido único", *Expresso das Ilhas*, April 21, 2015, https://expressodasilhas. cv/exclusivo/2015/04/21/40-anos-de-terra-nova-o-unico-jornal-que-enfrentou-o-partido-unico/44433.

20 Cf. Cahen, "Arquipélagos da alternância", 142–143 and Koudawo, *Cabo Verde e Guiné-Bissau*, 118–127.

21 Aristides Pereira recalls the talks with John Paul II and his opposition to "political monolithism", although he also sees in that visit an alignment of the Pope with the aims of openness that the PAICV was pursuing. José Vicente Lopes, *Aristides Pereira. Minha Vida, Nossa História* (Praia: Spleen Edições, 2012), 352–353.

22 In the August of that year, after a man accused of theft was found hanged in a prison cell, a group of people attacked the police, who then had to be taken off the island and moved to Santiago. Cf. Cahen, "Arquipélagos da alternância", 143.

23 The murder of this promising PAICV cadre also contributed to the deterioration of the regime, mainly due to the insinuations that there were political reasons behind his death, an accusation that has survived until today in certain circles. Cf., for example, Humberto Cardoso (2011), "Opacidade de regime e morte de Renato Cardoso", emcima (blog), 1 December 2011. https://emcima.blogspot.com/2011/12/opacidade-de-regime-e-morte-de-renato.html?m=0. On this matter, see also *Tribuna*, no. 53(85), 16 to 30 November 1990; *Voz di Povo* no. 1191, 16 January 1992, Koudawo, *Cabo Verde e Guiné-Bissau*, 118–119 and José Vicente Lopes, *Aristides Pereira*, 346–347.

The Struggle in the Mnemonic Transition 81

24 "Os acontecimentos políticos que se verificaram no plano internacional impõem-nos uma reanálise do sistema político – Aristides Pereira", *Voz di Povo*, no. 896, 11 January 1990. See also the speech by Aristides Pereira at the opening of the 2nd Congress of the JAAC-CV, with excerpts reproduced in "As transformações no mundo. Cabo Verde e o render da guarda", *Tribuna*, no. 30(62), 1 to 15 December 1989.

25 MpD, Document (Praia, June 1990), 4 [accessed from the CIDAC archive].

26 Koudawo points to the "minimalist vision" – albeit "clear, concise and coherent" – which stipulated that the political transition should be accomplished in eleven months. He speaks however of a longer "democratic transition", which involved consolidating the political and economic changes established earlier. Cf. Koudawo, *Cabo Verde e Guiné-Bissau*, 82–84. Jorge Carlos Fonseca, in his preface to Koudawo's work, refers to the need to take into account the notion of "constitutional transition", since this was fundamental to operationalising the "democratic transition". Cf. Jorge Carlos Fonseca, "Prefácio" in *Cabo Verde e Guiné-Bissau. Da democracia revolucionária à democracia liberal*, Fafali Koudawo (Bissau: INEP, 2001), 47.

27 José Vicente Lopes, *Cabo Verde. Os bastidores da Independência* (Praia: Spleen Edições, 2013), 23. See also the critical analysis by Victor Barros, "A escrita da história da 'descoberta' de Cabo Verde. Fabulário cronográfico, história oficial ou fabricação do consentimento?", *Práticas da História. Journal on Theory, Historiography and Uses of the Past* 5 (2017): 75–113.

28 Born on the island of Fogo, Teixeira de Sousa (1919–2006) was a Cape Verdean doctor and writer who was linked to the neo-realist current and anti-fascist circles in Portugal while he was a student. He took part in the *claridoso* movement and was the author of several novels that were important in Cape Verdean literature, including *Ilhéu de Contenda*, made into a film by Leão Lopes, in 1995. He was Mayor of São Vicente from 1959 to 1965. After 1974, he was linked to the UDC and, shortly after, he settled in Portugal, where he died, aged 87, after being run over by a car.

29 In addition to being the governor of Cape Verde between 1894 and 1897, Alexandre Serpa Pinto was one of the so-called "explorers" of the African continent, leading reconnaissance expeditions and wars to "pacify" rebellions against the Portuguese colonial presence in Africa.

30 Henrique Teixeira de Sousa, *Xaguate* (Lisboa: Publicações Europa-América, 1987), 292–293. On these events, including the reference to Teixeira de Sousa's novels, see: Joaquim Saial, "Arte Pública Escultórica do período colonial em Cabo Verde", *Convocarte - Revista de Ciências da Arte* 3 (2016): 290–308.

31 Teixeira de Sousa, *Entre duas bandeiras* (Lisboa: Publicações Europa-América, 1994), 69.

32 Sousa, *Entre duas bandeiras*, 118.

33 On the cover: "Busto do poeta José Lopes foi reposto numa praceta da cidade do Mindelo", *Voz di Povo*, no. 429, 30 January 1985.

34 Saial, "Arte Pública", 290–308. See also *Terra Nova*, no. 172, July 1990.

35 Cf. José Luís Hopffer Almada, "Cabo Verde – Orfandade identitária e alegada (im) pertinência de uma poesia de negritude crioula (I)", *Buala*, 27 March 2013, https://www.buala.org/pt/a-ler/cabo-verde-orfandade-identitaria-e-alegada-im-pertinencia-de-uma-poesia-de-negritude-crioula-1.

36 Cf. José Vicente Lopes, *Cabo Verde. As causas da independência* (Praia: Spleen Edições, 2012), 17. On this subject, see also João Vasconcelos, "Espíritos Lusófonos numa ilha crioula: língua, poder e identidade em São

82 *The Struggle in the Mnemonic Transition*

Vicente de Cabo Verde" in *A persistência da história: Passado e Contemporaneidade em África*, eds. Clara Carvalho and João Pina Cabral (Lisboa: Imprensa de Ciências Sociais, 2004), 149–190 e Victor Barros, "As sombras da Claridade. Entre o discurso de integração regional e a retórica nacionalista", in *Comunidades Imaginadas. Nação e Nacionalismos em* África, eds. Luís Reis Torgal, Fernando Tavares Pimenta and Julião Soares Sousa (Coimbra: Imprensa da Universidade de Coimbra, 2008), 193–214.

37 "Diogo Gomes sai da clandestinidade", *Voz di Povo*, no. 1070, 26 March 1991.

38 "Diogo Gomes dai da clandestinidade", *Voz di Povo*, no. 1070, 26 March 1991.

39 Cf. *Terra Nova*, no. 184, julho 1991.

40 Cf. "Bustos de Camões e Sá da Bandeira repostos no Mindelo", *Voz di Povo*, no. 1281, 25 August 1992.

41 "E Amílcar Cabral? E Jorge Barbosa? E Nhô Baltas?", no. 63, *Notícias*, 15 September 1992.

42 Song from her début album, *Navega*, from 2007. On this and for other examples of cultural criticism of MpD actions in this phase, see José Luís Hopffer Almada, "Das tragédias históricas do povo cabo-verdiano e da saga da sua constituição e da sua consolidação como nação crioula soberana, segunda parte", *Buala*, 17 February 2012, http://www.buala.org/pt/a-ler/das-tragedias-historicas-do-povo-caboverdiano-e-da-saga-da-sua-constituicao-e-da-sua-consolida.

43 In the original by Kaká Barbosa: "Dja skesedu Pépé Lópi / Bá rabuskádu Nhu Diogo Gómi / Rasusitádu Nhu Kraveru Lópi / Ka ta konxedu Inásia Gómi".

44 Krzysztof Górny and Ada Górna, "After Decolonization: Changes in the Urban Landscape of Platô in Praia, Cape Verde", *Journal of UrbaMarian History* 45, no. 6 (2019): 1103–1130.

45 Cf., for example, Humberto Cardoso, *O Partido único em Cabo Verde: um assalto à esperança* (Praia: Imprensa Nacional de Cabo Verde, 1993) and interview given to the authors, Praia, 4 July 2019. In a text published in the weekly *Expresso das Ilhas* on 23 March 2005 on the subject of the archipelago's integration into the European Union, Gualberto do Rosário, former Prime Minister of Cape Verde and leader of the MpD, referred to "a possible mistake in 1975 which made Cape Verde a member of the OAU, ECOWAS and the CILSS", considering that "Cape Verde's past is one of integration into Europe from the very beginning of the nation, particularly through its ties with Portugal". Cf. "Integração de Cabo Verde na União Europeia é uma tese revolucionária", *Expresso das Ilhas*, no. 172, 23 March 2005. On 13 June 2007, Armindo Ferreira, former Minister of Infrastructure in the MpD government of the 1990s, wrote an article in the same newspaper, in which he considered that the "5 July was [...] an assault on power" that "was also based on the attempt to destroy one of the dearest values to the Cape Verdean people – its men of culture". He added that "the 5 July would not have been possible if the long work of construction, formation and exaltation of the Cape Verdean identity, of the shaping of its nationality, had not already been done. A task carried out in Cape Verde, by Cape Verdeans, led by their men of culture and knowledge", cf. "5 de Julho, Manjacos & Intelectuais", *Expresso das Ilhas*, no. 288, 13 June 2007.

46 Some examples of this narrative and semantics can be found in: "Especial Empossamento António Mascarenhas Monteiro. O regresso dos banidos. Estátua de Diogo Gomes retoma pedestal na Praia", *Voz di Povo*, no. 1068, 21 March 1991; "Diogo Gomes sai da clandestinidade", *Voz di Povo*,

The Struggle in the Mnemonic Transition   83

no. 1070, 26 March 1991; "O PAICV e a lei de Parkinson", *Voz di Povo*, no. 1108, 27 June 1991; "Independência foi bom, mas democracia foi muito melhor", *Novo Jornal de Cabo Verde*, no. 235, 29 December 1994; "Reafricanização dos espíritos: consequências", *Expresso das Ilhas*, no. 736, 6 January 2016.

47 Nuno Manalvo, *Carlos Veiga: Biografia Política – O Rosto da Mudança em Cabo Verde* (Lisboa: Alêtheia, 2009), 103.

48 This led the PAICV National Secretariat to issue a declaration repudiating these acts which also denounced the existence of phone calls, letters and anonymous pamphlets threatening its members. For photos of the graffiti, see *Tribuna*, no. 49(81), 16–30 September 1990; no. 52(83), 16–31 October 1990 and no. 54(86), 1–15 December 1990. To read the declaration, see *Tribuna*, no. 53(85), 16–30 November 1990. João Pereira Silva, one of PAICV leaders at the time, considers that a decisive element in the electoral defeat of the PAICV was the dissemination of fake news about the Swiss bank accounts of top PAICV leaders who had fought in Guinea. Cf. "O 19 de Fevereiro de 1990, a Mudança do Regime Político e a Instauração da Democracia Representativa em Cabo Verde", *Expresso das Ilhas*, no. 955, 18 March 2020.

49 Onésimo Silveira, *A tortura em nome do partido único. O PAICV e a sua polícia política* (Mindelo: Terra Nova and Ponto & Vírgula, 1992). On the investigation that the government requested from the Attorney General's Office for the episodes portrayed in Onésimo Silveira's book, cf. "Governo pede inquérito sobre factos relatados no livro 'A TORTURA EM NOME DO PARTIDO ÚNICO', *Voz di Povo*, no. 1142, 19 September 1991.

50 Cardoso, *O Partido único em Cabo Verde*, republished in 2015. Humberto Cardoso began his political career with the Cape Verde press at the newspaper *Terra Nova*, where he worked between 1988 and 1990. He was also a MpD member of parliament for the constituency of São Vicente from 1996. He is currently director of the weekly *Expresso das Ilhas*.

51 Germano Almeida, *O Dia das Calças Roladas* (Lisboa: Editorial Caminho, 1992).

52 Germano Almeida, *O Meu Poeta* (Lisboa: Editorial Caminho, 1990).

53 Germano Almeida, *A Morte do Meu Poeta* (Cabo Verde: Ilhéu Editora, 1998).

54 We will return to this aspect in Chapter 4.

55 Accused of having deserted from the PAIGC during the struggle, Mascarenhas stated that "if the struggle that a handful of Cape Verdeans made in Guinea-Bissau" had mattered, the people would not have "severely punished the PAICV" at the polls. "Sou um desertor especial", *Voz di Povo*, no. 1055, 16 February 1991.

56 Law no. 19/III/87, of 15 August, published in B. O. no. 33, pp. 523–526. The Order comprises three degrees, may be awarded to national or foreign citizens and is attributed to the Liberation Struggle Combatants and to those who are considered to have made a significant contribution to enriching the country.

57 For the names of those honoured and more information on this subject, see, among others, "Homenagem aos oficiais-comandantes das FARP. Reconhecimento da Nação pelos serviços prestados na luta pela Independência Nacional. Presidente da República condecora os combatentes com a 'Ordem Amílcar Cabral'", *Voz di Povo*, no. 1036, 29 December 1990, "Nação homenageia Combatentes da Liberdade", *Tribuna*, no. 57(89), 2 January 1991 and "Presidente Aristides Pereira condecora combatentes", *Voz di Povo*, no. 1043, 17 January 1991.

84 *The Struggle in the Mnemonic Transition*

58 According to the database of honours provided to us by the Presidency of the Republic of Cape Verde, during his two terms of office Mascarenhas Monteiro awarded other honorary titles (Order of the Dragon Tree, Jaime Mota Medal, Volcano Medal and Merit Medal) to more than seventy men and women, mostly figures associated with Cape Verde's cultural and intellectual life. On 5 July 1994, for example, Mascarenhas Monteiro decorated António Aurélio Gonçalves, António Carreira, Jorge Barbosa, Manuel Lopes and Gabriel Mariano, among other individuals. This decision generated internal debates, mainly driven by former political prisoners, particularly Pedro Martins, Osvaldo Azevedo, Lucílio Braga Tavares and Jorge Querido. The latter contests the moment chosen for the awarding of the medals, pointing out that on 5 July "decorating people who collaborated with Portuguese colonialism and fought against Cape Verdean independence is a contradiction in terms", adding: "not that the merits of these figures should not be recognised, far from it, but not on the occasion of the celebration of national independence, a date that will always be unequivocally linked to the former freedom fighters". On this subject, see "Condecorações de personalidades nacionais. Ex-presos políticos questionam", *Novo Jornal de Cabo Verde*, no. 160, 2 July 1994.

59 Law no. 15/IV/91, of 30 December.

60 Cf. "5 de julho. Foi há 19 anos", *Novo Jornal de Cabo Verde*, no. 161, 5 July 1994.

61 "Movimento para a Democracia. A hora das estratégias para a mudança", *Voz di Povo*, no. 1045, 22 January 1991.

62 "Carlos Veiga no Instituto de Estudos Sociais em Haia. Democracia pode funcionar em África", *Novo Jornal de Cabo Verde*, no. 10, 31 March 1993.

63 Resolution no. 7/IV/91, of 30 December. On the changes of the national symbols, see chapter 3 of Márcia Rego, *The Dialogic Nation of Cape Verde. Slavery, Language and Ideology* (New York and London: Lexington Books, 2015), 65–84.

64 *Atas da 2ª Sessão Legislativa Extraordinária, IV Legislatura, Reunião Plenária de 21 de julho de 1992.*

65 *Atas da 2ª Sessão Legislativa Extraordinária, IV Legislatura, Reunião Plenária de 21 de julho de 1992.*

66 Pedro Gregório Lopes, interview, Praia, 17 January 2019, where the designer states that "the predominant element we have is the blue of the sky and the blue of the sea" and that the Cape Verdeans' connection with "the sea is deep, similar to the Portuguese".

67 Cf. the speech made by Manuel Inocêncio (PAICV) in the parliamentary session of 8 June, 1992, where he states that "The flag was not imposed by force. It is the result of a historical process [...]. It is the flag of independence, the flag of the creation of the Republic of Cape Verde. And no event in the life of a country can annul a historical event with the value that is its independence". See *Atas da 3ª Sessão Ordinária, IV Legislatura, Sessão Plenária de 8 de junho de 1992.*

68 Cf. arguments made at the plenary session on 8 June 1992, cf. *Atas da 3ª Sessão Ordinária, IV Legislatura, Sessão Plenária de 8 de junho de 1992.*

69 According to the results reported by *Notícias*, 52% of Mindelo voters agreed with the flag change, 46% disagreed, and 2% were indifferent: "Eleitorado mindelense está dividido na questão da mudança da bandeira. O Arrear da Bandeira", *Notícias*, no. 60, 20 July 1992.

70 Cf. "Bandeira em causa", *A Semana*, no. 58, 12 June 1992, which includes the following excerpt from the manifesto of the "For the Independence Flag" movement: "The flag we have is the one that galvanised a whole people,

The Struggle in the Mnemonic Transition 85

embodying and symbolising the birth of our Republic and constituting a national achievement and not that of any political force. A national symbol is above all a point of collective convergence. Herein lies its strength: in its adoption by the national community as something that represents it, that is, symbolises it. This is why nowhere in the world do symbols change according to regimes and governments. The latter come and go while the former remain - because the Nation which they represent remains". See also *Atas da 2ª Sessão Legislativa Extraordinária, IV Legislatura, Reunião Plenária de 22 de julho de 1992*.

71 Speech by MP Alberto Ferreira Fortes, cf. *Atas da 3ª Sessão Ordinária, IV Legislatura, junho de 1992*.

72 Speech by MP Manuel Roque Silva Júnior, cf. *Atas da 3ª Sessão Ordinária, IV Legislatura, junho de 1992*.

73 Speech by MP Teófilo Silva, cf. *Atas da 3ª Sessão Ordinária, IV Legislatura, junho de 1992*. See also *Atas da 3ª Sessão Ordinária, IV Legislatura, Sessão Plenária de 8 de junho de 1992, Atas da 2ª Sessão Legislativa Extraordinária, IV Legislatura, Reunião Plenária de 21 de julho de 1992* and "Proposta de referendo para símbolos nacionais chumbada pela bancada do MpD", *Voz di Povo*, no. 9 June 1991.

74 *A Semana*, no. 74, 2 October 1992.

75 Cláudio Furtado, "Cabo Verde e as quatro décadas da independência: dissonâncias, múltiplos discursos, reverberações e lutas por imposição de sentido à sua história recente" *Estudos Ibero-Americanos* 42, no. 3 (2016): 883.

76 Cf. "Constituição Nova. Hino Antigo", *A Semana*, no. 63, 17 July 1992. See also *Atas da 2ª Sessão Legislativa Extraordinária, IV Legislatura, Reunião Plenária de 21 de julho de 1992*. In 1992, other anthem proposals were submitted by António Caldeira Marques, leader of the UCID, an opposition party, and by Vasco Martins, one of Cape Verde's great musicians - see "A propósito do novo hino nacional", *A Semana*, no. 78, 30 October 1992.

77 Words to "Peace and Labour": "Come brother, bring your will / Champions of the same cause / United in the same intent / Let us celebrate Liberty. / Forget the iron that stayed your hand / Pity those who gagged your speech / Come quickly, come boldly / There are other pastures, other zephyrs. / With dignity promote peace / With fearlessness, plough and make / The world has fallen at your feet / The dawn awaits in your hands" [Vem irmão, traz o teu querer / Paladinos da mesma causa / Unidos na mesma vontade / Celebremos a Liberdade. / Olvida o ferro que te travou o gesto / Lamenta a quem te amordaçou o verbo / Vem depressa, vem lesto / Há outras lavras, outros zéfiros. / Com dignidade promove a paz / Com destemor, desbrava e faz / O mundo quedou a teus pés / A alvorada aguarda em tuas mãos]. On this subject, see for example, "Aprovada letra do novo hino nacional. Amílcar Spencer Lopes é o autor", *Voz di Povo*, no. 1302, 15 October 1992; Vadinho Velho, "Vem irmão", *Voz di Povo*, no. 1306, 24 October 1992 and "Sete deputados ventoinhas ajudam a chumbar o hino. Chumbadela", *Notícias*, no. 69, 30 December 1992.

78 In the general elections held in December 1995, the MpD managed to roughly maintain its vote: 61.3% and 50 MPs, against the PAICV's 29.8% (and 21 MPs). Due to a split in the MpD, the Democratic Convergence Party got 6.7% of the vote, and elected 1 MP. On the national anthem, see: "Cântico da Liberdade no Parlamento", "OE e hino na ordem do dia" and "Cântico da Liberdade novamente", *Novo Jornal de Cabo Verde*, no. 382, 8 May 1996.

86   *The Struggle in the Mnemonic Transition*

79 On the same occasion, recognising the need for change, a proposal was also presented by the PAICV, "Hino d' Amanhã", which was rejected by MPs in favour of the MpD's suggestion. On this subject, see also "Cântico da Liberdade' é o novo hino nacional", *Novo Jornal de Cabo Verde*, no. 387, 30 May 1996.

80 "Canta, irmão / canta, meu irmão / que a Liberdade é hino / e o Homem a certeza. / Com dignidade, enterra a semente / no pó da ilha nua; / no despenhadeiro da vida / a esperança é do tamanho do mar / que nos abraça. / Sentinela de mares e ventos / perseverante / entre estrelas e o Atlântico / entoa o cântico da liberdade. / Canta, irmão / canta, meu irmão / que a Liberdade é hino / e o Homem a certeza".

81 Rego, *The Dialogic Nation of Cape Verde*, 77.

82 See Vasconcelos, "Espíritos Lusófonos numa ilha crioula", 149–190 and Barros, "As 'sombras' da Claridade", 193–217.

83 Silva, "O Nascimento do Leviatã Crioulo", 53–68.

84 Anjos, "A condição de mediador político-cultural em Cabo Verde", 273–295.

Bibliography

Almada, José Luís Hopffer. "Cabo Verde – Orfandade identitária e alegada (im)pertinência de uma poesia de negritude crioula (I)". *Buala*, 27 March 2013. https://www.buala.org/pt/a-ler/cabo-verde-orfandade-identitaria-e-alegada-im-pertinencia-de-uma-poesia-de-negritude-crioula-1.

Almada, José Luís Hopffer. "Das tragédias históricas do povo cabo-verdiano e da saga da sua constituição e da sua consolidação como nação crioula soberana, segunda parte". *Buala*, 17 February 2012. http://www.buala.org/pt/a-ler/das-tragedias-historicas-do-povo-caboverdiano-e-da-saga-da-sua-constituicao-e-da-sua-consolida.

Almeida, Germano. *A Morte do Meu Poeta*. Cabo Verde: Ilhéu Editora, 1998.

Almeida, Germano. *O Dia das Calças Roladas*. Lisboa: Editorial Caminho, 1992.

Almeida, Germano. *O Meu Poeta*. Lisboa: Editorial Caminho, 1990.

Anjos, José Carlos Gomes dos. "A condição de mediador político-cultural em Cabo Verde: intelectuais e diferentes versões da identidade nacional". *Etnográfica* 7, no. 2 (2004): 273–295.

Arrighi, Giovanni. *The Long Twentieth Century. Money, Power and the Origins of Our Times*. New York and London: Verso, 1994.

Barros, Victor. "A escrita da história da 'descoberta' de Cabo Verde. Fabulário cronográfico, história oficial ou fabricação do consentimento?". *Práticas da História. Journal on Theory, Historiography and Uses of the Past* 5 (2017): 75–113.

Barros, Victor. "As sombras da Claridade. Entre o discurso de integração regional e a retórica nacionalista". In *Comunidades Imaginadas. Nação e Nacionalismos em África*, edited by Luís Reis Torgal, Fernando Tavares Pimenta and Julião Soares Sousa, 193–214. Coimbra: Imprensa da Universidade de Coimbra, 2008.

Basu, Paul. "Palimpsest Memoryscapes: Materializing and Mediating War and Peace in Sierra Leone". In *Reclaiming Heritage: Alternative Imaginaries of Memory in West Africa*, edited by Ferdinand De Jong and Michael Rowlands, 231–259. Walnut Creek: Left Coast Press, 2007.

Cahen, Michel. "Arquipélagos da alternância; a vitória da oposição das ilhas de Cabo Verde e de São Tomé e Príncipe". *Revista Internacional de Estudos Africanos* no. 14/15 (1991): 113–154.

The Struggle in the Mnemonic Transition   87

Cardina, Miguel and Inês Nascimento Rodrigues. "The mnemonic transition: the rise of an anti-anticolonial memoryscape in Cape Verde". *Memory Studies* 14, no. 2 (2021): 380–394.

Cardoso, Humberto. "Opacidade de regime e morte de Renato Cardoso". emCima (blog), 1 dezembro 2011. https://emcima.blogspot.com/2011/12/opacidade-de-regime-e-morte-de-renato.html?m=0.

Cardoso, Humberto. *O Partido único em Cabo Verde: um assalto à esperança*. Praia: Imprensa Nacional de Cabo Verde, 1993.

Cole, Jennifer. *Forget Colonialism? Sacrifice and the Art of Memory in Madagascar*. Berkeley and Los Angeles: University of California Press, 2001.

De Jong, Ferdinand. "Recycling Recognition. The Monument as *Objet Trouvé* of the Postcolony". *Journal of Material Culture* 13, no. 2 (2008): 195–214.

Edensor, Tim. "National identity and the politics of memory: remembering Bruce and Wallace in symbolic space". *Environment and Planning* 29 (1997): 175–194.

Erll, Astrid. "Fictions of generational memory: Caryl Phillips's in the falling snow and black British writing in times of mnemonic transition". In *Memory Unbound. Tracing the Dynamics of Memory Studies*, edited by Lucy Bond, Stef Craps and Pieter Vermeulen, 109–130. New York: Berghahn Books, 2017.

Évora, Roselma. *Cabo Verde: A abertura política e a transição para a democracia*. Praia: Spleen Edições, 2004.

Fernandes, Gabriel. *A diluição de África: uma interpretação da saga identitária cabo-verdiana no panorama (pós)colonial*. Florianópolis: UFSC, 2002.

Fonseca, Jorge Carlos. "Prefácio". In *Cabo Verde e Guiné-Bissau. Da democracia revolucionária à democracia liberal*, edited by Fafali Koudawo, 9–65. Bissau: INEP, 2001.

Furtado, Cláudio. "Cabo Verde e as quatro décadas da independência: dissonâncias, múltiplos discursos, reverberações e lutas por imposição de sentido à sua história recente". *Estudos Ibero-Americanos* 42, no. 3 (2016): 855–887.

Górny, Krzysztof and Ada Górna. "After decolonization: Changes in the urban landscape of Platô in Praia, Cape Verde". *Journal of Urban History* 45, no. 6 (2019): 1103–1130.

Hobsbawm, Eric. *The Age of Extremes. A History of the World 1914–1991*. New York: Vintage Books, 1994.

Kappler, Stephanie. "Sarajevo's ambivalent memoryscape: Spatial stories of peace and conflict". *Memory Studies* 10, no. 2 (2017): 130–143.

Koudawo, Fafali. *Cabo Verde e Guiné-Bissau. Da democracia revolucionária à democracia liberal*. Bissau: INEP, 2001.

Lima, Aristides. *Reforma Política em Cabo Verde. Do Paternalismo à Modernização do Estado*. Praia: ed. de autor, 1991.

Lopes, José Vicente. *Aristides Pereira. Minha Vida, Nossa História*. Praia: Spleen Edições, 2012.

Lopes, José Vicente. *Cabo Verde. As causas da independência*. Praia: Spleen Edições, 2nd edition, 2012.

Lopes, José Vicente. *Cabo Verde. Os bastidores da Independência*. Praia: Spleen Edições, 3rd edition, 2013.

Manalvo, Nuno. *Carlos Veiga: Biografia Política – O Rosto da Mudança em Cabo Verde*. Lisboa: Alêtheia, 2009.

Meyns, Peter. "Cape Verde: An African exception". *Journal of Democracy* 13, no. 3 (2002): 153–165.

88 *The Struggle in the Mnemonic Transition*

Muzaini, Hamzah and Brenda S. A. Yeoh. *Contested Memoryscapes. The Politics of Second World War Commemoration in Singapore*. London and New York: Routledge, 2016.

Muzaini, Hamzah. "Producing / consuming memoryscapes: The genesis / politics of Second World War commemoration in Singapore". *Geojournal* 66, no. 3 (2006): 211–222.

Nardi, Sarah de, Hilary Orange, Steven High and Eerika Koskinen-Koivisto, eds. *The Routledge Handbook of Memory and Place*. New York and London: Routledge, 2019.

Rego, Márcia. *The Dialogic Nation of Cape Verde. Slavery, Language and Ideology*. New York and London: Lexington Books, 2015.

Saial, Joaquim. "Arte Pública Escultórica do período colonial em Cabo Verde". *Convocarte - Revista de Ciências da Arte* 3 (2016): 290–308.

Sanches, Edalina. *Party Systems in Young Democracies. Varieties of Institutionalization in Sub-Saharan Africa*. London and New York: Routledge, 2018.

Silva, António Correia e. "Cabo Verde: Desafios económicos e a estruturação do Estado. Do Estado-Providência (sem contribuintes) ao liberalismo sem empresários. O Ciclo da Iª República", paper presented at *VIII Congresso Luso-Afro-Brasileiro de Ciências Sociais – A Questão Social no Novo Milénio*, 2004. https://www.ces.uc.pt/lab2004/inscricao/pdfs/grupodiscussao5/AntonioLeaoSilva.pdf.

Silva, António Correia e. "O Nascimento do Leviatã Crioulo: esboços de sociologia política". *Cadernos de Estudos Africanos* 1 (2001): 53–68.

Silva, António Correia e. "O Processo Caboverdiano de Transição para a Democracia". Master Diss., ISCTE, 1997.

Silveira, Onésimo. *A tortura em nome do partido único. O PAICV e a sua polícia política*. Mindelo: Terra Nova and Ponto & Vírgula, 1992.

Sousa, Henrique Teixeira de. *Entre duas bandeiras*. Lisboa: Publicações Europa-América, 1994.

Sousa, Henrique Teixeira de. *Xaguate*. Lisboa: Publicações Europa-América, 1987.

Traverso, Enzo. *Le Passé, mode d'emploi: Histoire, mémoire, politique*. Paris: La Fabrique, 2005.

Ullberg, Susann. *Watermarks. Urban Flooding and Memoryscape in Argentina*. Stockholm: Acta Universitatis Stockholmiensis, 2013.

Van de Putte, Thomas. "Delineating Memoryscapes: Auschwitz versus Oświęcim". *Holocaust Studies* 27, no. 1 (2021): 91–105.

Vasconcelos, João. "Espíritos Lusófonos numa ilha crioula: língua, poder e identidade em São Vicente de Cabo Verde". In *A persistência da história: Passado e Contemporaneidade em África*, edited by Clara Carvalho and João Pina Cabral, 149–190. Lisboa: Imprensa de Ciências Sociais, 2004.

Archive documents - Unpublished sources

Atas da 2ª Sessão Legislativa Extraordinária, IV Legislatura, Reunião Plenária de 21 de julho de 1992.

Atas da 2ª Sessão Legislativa Extraordinária, IV Legislatura, Reunião Plenária de 22 de julho de 1992.

Atas da 3ª Sessão Ordinária, IV Legislatura, junho de 1992.

Atas da 3ª Sessão Ordinária, IV Legislatura, Sessão Plenária de 8 de junho de 1992.

MpD. MpD – Documento Oficial. Document. CIDAC – Centro de Intervenção para o Desenvolvimento Amílcar Cabral.

Newspapers

Expresso das Ilhas, Notícias, Novo Jornal de Cabo Verde, A Semana, Terra Nova, Tribuna, Voz di Povo.

Interviews

Cardoso, Humberto. Audio-recorded interview with Miguel Cardina and Inês Nascimento Rodrigues. Praia, 4 July 2019.
Lopes, Pedro Gregório. Audio-recorded interview with Miguel Cardina and Inês Nascimento Rodrigues. Praia, 17 January 2019.

3 THE STRUGGLE AND THE IMAGE OF THE COMBATANT

In 1994, in the context of the mnemonic transition identified in the previous chapter, Gualberto do Rosário, the MpD parliamentary leader, referred to the liberation struggle combatants at one of the national independence celebrations. While understanding that the country had granted "dignified treatment to national heroes", he pointed, however, to what seemed to him to be a recent change in this process: while, during the single-party regime, they had been selectively overvalued, now a new phase was under way where the attitude was to praise "all Cape Verdeans" who had participated in building the country.[1] This statement is particularly significant, as it demonstrates how the concept of "combatant" has been subject to fluctuations in the discourse throughout Cape Verde's post-colonial history. Taking into consideration what was defined in the introduction as a "mnemonic device", we propose to reflect here on the political trajectory of this concept.

The issue of the statute of the Liberation Struggle Combatant (henceforth LSC) occupies a significant place in this case, since legislation is one of the means by which to intervene in the construction of history and public memories. In this chapter, we will consider the evolution and debates around the statute of the LSC, but also its connection with other public representations, highlighting the role these play in creating the imaginary of the "combatant", but also of the very idea of the "struggle" as a mnemonic device. The series of interpretative frameworks and symbolic spaces associated with the notion of "combatant" are actively and dynamically mobilised and disputed to this day in the archipelago, not only through the laws governing the figure of the LSC but also through (auto)biographical narratives, military honours and other memorial acts or products – speeches, public debates, currency, commemorative ceremonies, etc. – that comprise, test, expand and / or problematise it.

Initially, as we demonstrated in Chapter 1, a symbolic hierarchy emerges that highlights those who occupied top positions in the PAIGC during the struggle as the "the worthiest sons of the land" and attributes to these combatants a place of super-citizenship within the country. In the

DOI: 10.4324/9781003265535-4

The Struggle and the Image of the Combatant 91

1990s, especially during the first half, these combatants – who had held political decision-making positions during the single-party regime – were subjected to processes aimed at diluting the central relationship between participation in the armed struggle and political legitimacy, a movement we partially alluded to in Chapter 2. These and other circumstances in Cape Verde's journey have led to actions that broaden the recognition of the actors who participated in the struggle.

This process of pluralising the public and official recognition of the actors of the struggle who until then had occupied a relatively subordinate role, such as women, clandestine militants or former political prisoners, led to the re-emergence of debates around the figure of the combatant. This materialised over time in different ways: sometimes in specific moments of valuing and devaluing some of its segments, and sometimes in a more generalised search for consensus on the nation's history. We shall demonstrate how these rationales of mnemonic accommodation, which are not uncontroversial, manifest themselves not only in the political reframing of the struggle's past but also in the broadening of the category of combatant to subjects with very diverse anticolonial trajectories. Moreover, there has also been a growth in the use of the concept of hero in the archipelago, partly sustained by characteristics attributed to the combatant-like figure, ranging from those who opposed the First Republic to those who survived cyclical droughts and famines.

Constructing the liberation struggle combatant

The question that concerns us in this chapter is the following: How does the State conceptualise and design a figure – that of the combatant – which had a central legitimising place *in* and *for* the new independent nation? Part of the answer lies in how the category has been diachronically defined, produced and negotiated in Cape Verde through memory politics. In this case, as also happens in many other African countries which became independent after liberation struggles, one of the most relevant axes of ongoing memory policies consists in creating legislation that establishes a specific statute for LSCs and grants them a set of rights. This legal instrument is central to establishing the combatant as an important national figure in terms of symbolic value, that is, a prime witness of the past struggle, whose actions should be recognised and, therefore, worthy of protection and homage by the State, through the material and symbolic benefits that the law provides to grant them.

The first law to officially approve the statute of the LSC dates back to 1989.[2] Nevertheless, since 1980 the title had already been occasionally and formally recognised, mostly for historical figures in the armed struggle. Of the 32 names proposed until then, only two were not from the PAIGC's combat zones in Guinea and / or the movement's logistical, strategic and

92   *The Struggle and the Image of the Combatant*

political bases in neighbouring Guinea Conakry.[3] In the aforementioned statute, a combatant is considered to be "a Cape Verdean citizen who, between 19 September 1956 and 24 April 1974, actively and continuously fought for the National Liberation within the ranks of the African Party for the Independence of Guinea and Cape Verde (PAIGC)".[4] This phrasing has, however, proved to be problematic. On the one hand, because its scope was too narrow and on the other hand, because of the very process of recognising the statute, whose powers were attributed solely to the PAICV, the political heir of the PAIGC.

In a context such as that of the First Republic, where the credentials of the struggle had a symbolic and party-political aspect, the participation of combatants who had been at the war front and / or those who held positions in leading bodies of the liberation movement were generally more valued than other types of contribution to independence. Luís Fonseca, a former political prisoner who, in the post-independence period, became a PAIGC deputy in the National Assembly before embarking on a diplomatic career abroad, indicated some of the reasons why the distinction was made in this way.

> [During the First Republic] there was the recognition of the statute of the Liberation Struggle Combatant, in terms of small privileges that, in the end, were attributed and that were, practically speaking, based on the following: the time that the liberation struggle combatant had spent in the struggle counted double, but he had to prove that he had dedicated himself exclusively to the national liberation struggle. Because, obviously, a person who was here in Cape Verde during the clandestine struggle, as often happened, had a job, went about his business and also fought clandestinely, but we saw no reason for that person, who was paying his normal contributions, to then suddenly get to a certain time and decide it counted double. Their [political] activity had not harmed them. Our intention [with the statute] was, in a way, to compensate for the harm that people had suffered. Obviously, in my case, in Pedro [Martins]'s case, that we had spent [years] in jail, we considered it fair that those who had spent that time in jail ... that time be considered double.[5]

The representation of who should or should not benefit from the prerogatives covered by the statute ends up being expressed in the legal text, associated with a strict definition of those people who are to be considered combatants for independence. On the one hand, this statute was explicitly limited only to men and women who fought for the PAIGC – excluding militants who were not organically linked to the liberation movement or members of other political projects, such as the UPICV, for example. On the other hand, it favours activities undertaken in an "active and continuous" way. The wording of this criterion, which presupposes

The Struggle and the Image of the Combatant 93

exclusive dedication to the struggle, would potentially hinder the recognition process or even the eligibility of some of the militants who had dedicated themselves to clandestine actions, among others. In these cases, especially when these militants had not held prominent positions in the organisation or had not been taken prisoner, it became very difficult to get detailed evidence of their participation in the struggle or to fulfil the point that highlighted "continuous" militancy, since the nature of the clandestine struggle on an island, especially as a way of going more unnoticed in the eyes of the political police of the Portuguese dictatorship, the PIDE / DGS, meant that their political activities were limited and intermittent.

Thus, a significant number of the LSCs recognised in Cape Verde up to 1991 generally had a specific profile: they were men who had participated in the struggle, via the PAIGC, in positions of responsibility and / or command and as a result many of them had assumed important roles in the social and political geography of the archipelago in the early years of independence. The statute of the LSC approved in 1989 is, in this sense, a legislative text that recognises the symbolic importance of certain individuals in the nation's history by endowing them with conditions that honour their past of dedication and combat, but which, through the recognition processes instituted and the definition of who can or cannot be eligible as a combatant, ends up excluding other political trajectories consummated during the struggle. It is also a legal tool that values the armed struggle, endowing it with a foundational role in building the independent nation. And, thus, validates its main actors as legitimate representatives of the interests and concerns of the Cape Verdean people, especially for the role they played in defeating Portuguese colonialism.

The words spoken by Aristides Pereira, President of the Republic of Cape Verde, on the occasion of the proclamation of the Association of Liberation Struggle Combatants (ACOLP), on 14 April 1990 at the People's National Assembly, are along the same lines.[6] Pereira said then, in his speech, that "we are witnessing an act of great significance, which reminds us of the glorious pages of the struggle, the sacrifices and victories that we have left imprinted for all time on the history of the emancipation of the people".[7]

This speech came about within a context in which Cape Verde (and the world) was undergoing major changes, as we have seen in the previous chapter. Aristides Pereira's intervention reinforces the idea that these transformations should not mean "losing sight of the values" for which people had fought. He assumes that the creation of ACOLP will serve precisely this objective, that of preserving "the testimony and the experiences of those who took on the liberation of the country as a historical responsibility, to preserve and honour the memory of deceased combatants and national heroes".[8]

94 *The Struggle and the Image of the Combatant*

A little over a year after this speech, after the defeat of the PAICV at the polls, the law on the LSC statute was revised. With the opening to a multi-party system, there was a considerable expansion in the definition of its potential beneficiaries. This revised law helped expand the concept of combatant, by removing the date 24 April 1974 as the maximum time limit for considering militant activities for national liberation and by considering only "active" and not "continuous" forms of participation in the struggle.[9] Another of the significant changes concerns the process of recognising the statute, which was seen as excessively partisan, and whose powers of attribution were now not the responsibility of the PAICV, but were assigned to a State body.

The legal opening and the changes introduced in the specific legislation on the combatant during the 1990s made it possible, in line with the ongoing mnemonic transition, to diversify mobilisations and paths of participation in the struggle for independence. By no longer necessarily going through the armed struggle or joining the ranks of the PAIGC, the statute reflected the heterogeneity of the LSC group and the diversity of political experiences that shaped the national liberation struggle in Cape Verde. These ranged from the motivations for joining it to the different types of activities people would engaged in and periods of dedication to the cause, or even distinct relationships with the PAIGC cells and the party itself after independence. This is how some former PAIGC militants who until then, for a variety of reasons, had not applied for recognition under the statute, or were removed from the process, began to do so. The most iconic case, which remains unprecedented and is not covered in the legislation, occurred in 2004, when a collective request for recognition signed by 14 people was submitted to the Assembly, protesting against what the petitioners considered to be the excessively partisan nature of the procedures required for coming under the statute.[10]

With the pluralism introduced by the legislation, a series of memorial practices was activated at different levels of the State and civil society which targeted these same areas, with social, political and cultural impacts on the ways in which historical combatants were, in part, perceived. This process resulted in the mobilisation of conflicting representations, between legitimation and delegitimation, produced about them in the media, in literature, in official ceremonies and in draft laws. In them, "combatants" were no longer described only as liberators from colonialism, national heroes and symbolic anchors of the nation but also as "lords of the islands", "intolerant" and "autocratic", who were accorded a moral status that was seen by some as unfair and self-imposed.[11] Another interpretation, which emerges from one particular party-political sector, is that this statute was undeserved by historical combatants after independence. This is the opinion defended in 1994 by Celso Celestino, leader of UCID, a political organisation founded in 1977, which opposed the

The Struggle and the Image of the Combatant   95

PAIGC / CV and which today is the third largest Cape Verdean party in parliament:

> We all accepted independence, we all admired Amilcar Cabral to a greater or lesser extent and welcomed the heroes. But the subsequent behaviour saw their attitude and their heroism eclipsed by a series of behaviours [for which] they will have to make penance for a long time. So, the heroes have not been given due consideration, but to a large extent they are responsible for this.[12]

These simultaneously negative and ambivalent reactions to the figure of the combatant on the part of certain political-party sectors were mainly directed at the "Guinea group" – a designation often attributed in these years to PAIGC leaders who had spent several years in Guinea-Bissau or in Guinea Conakry, and often suggested their detachment from the actual situation in the islands. These processes benefited from the fact that the war was not experienced in the archipelago, that its experiences were not inscribed in the experiential memory of the majority of the population and, in part, also that the "mnemonic hegemony" of these combatants was, in a certain sense, fragile and context-dependent. Thus, in 1995, on the occasion of the commemoration of the 20th anniversary of national independence, ACOLP and its associates were excluded from the honours commission nominated to organise the celebrations. This generated a debate about the marginalisation to which they were being subjected to in the early 1990s.[13] Its inclusion on the commission, proposed by the PAICV, did not pass in the Assembly.

In the newspaper *A Semana* – generally considered to be a newspaper with PAICV sympathies[14] – it was reported that combatants and the association that represented them had been disregarded in the commemorations by not being reserved a prominent place, by being ignored in the honours and by the fact that, during Mascarenhas Monteiro's presidential speech, which began "with a heartfelt and profound 'thank you to Amilcar Cabral', the deputies of the majority, with the exception of three or four" did not join in the applause that followed this speech.[15] In the same edition of this newspaper, there was also a two-page report entitled "Liberation Struggle Combatants. The forgotten of History", where the main topic was the desecration of LSC graves. In the text, Álvaro Tavares, then president of ACOLP, confirmed the existence of several combatants living in very precarious situations, without due recognition from the State or funeral honours.[16]

In 1998, when a MpD bill was presented, an expression in its preamble caused controversy by classifying as a "heavy burden" the costs that the Cape Verde State would have with combatants. It argued that they put a bureaucratic burden on the Assembly with these recognition processes and represented a financial burden for the State of Cape Verde.[17]

96 *The Struggle and the Image of the Combatant*

ACOLP's president, Carlos Reis, acknowledged that the complexity of attributing the statute, especially in Cape Verde, "where participation in the struggle for national independence was felt on several fronts: in emigration, on the islands and in Guinea", made it more difficult to be certain about particular names and make decisions in accordance with the available data.[18] Eurico Monteiro[19] and other LSCs consulted on the same topic considered that the State's financial commitments to combatants were minimal.[20] The MpD, through the leadership of the party's parliamentary wing, considered that everything had been a misunderstanding and that there had been no intention to "offend or insult the LSC".[21] Following the protests, a new version of the bill was drafted where the expression was removed and the MpD proposed organising a ceremony in honour of the LSC on the occasion of its approval.

These events demonstrate the ambivalence with which the combatants were seen in the 1990s: firstly, there was an attitude of admiration for their deeds and for the dedication shown to the archipelago;[22] then there were attempts at exclusion or even direct attack aimed mainly at Amilcar Cabral and / or a specific segment of LSC – the combatants from the armed struggle who were relevant part of the political elite and ruled the country in the first 15 years of independence;[23] and finally, there were claims of abandonment and hostility inflicted by the State expressed by more vulnerable segments of combatants and by the management of the association that represented them, a feeling that was not unique to the 1990s.[24] ACOLP played an important role in being a useful mechanism for overcoming this last aspect, not only by setting up meetings between combatants and acting as an intermediary between them and the State – for the purposes of claiming rights, but also of conciliation – but also by organising regular meetings in honour of its members and Amilcar Cabral.[25] In this sense, Carlos Reis, current president of the association, considers that ACOLP does not carry out "party politics", but rather political work, preserving the memory and guaranteeing the dignity of those who fought for independence and their families.[26]

In addition to these expressions of the memory of the struggle and the experiences of the combatants mentioned above, other modes of memorialisation and public communication of that past were emerging in parallel. In the continuing discussions on the symbolic politics around the concept of the combatant, the 1990s saw the publication of (auto)biographical memories on the different kinds of participation in the liberation struggle. In effect, the struggle to produce and impose a national narrative and a historical memory of this past has been carried out less historiographically and more among its political and social players, through the publication of biographies, testimonies, essays or interviews that seek to establish what should be considered significant in the history of contemporary Cape Verde.[27] Initially, these publications emerged among sectors that until then were considered to have lower public visibility or recognition from the State. They were therefore

The Struggle and the Image of the Combatant 97

demanding that their particular type of combatant category – such as clandestine militants and political prisoners – be valued. Later, especially in the 2000s, works appeared which included some of the participants in the armed struggle and other political actors outside the PAIGC. Through these memorial products, the evocation of certain perspectives and experiences associated with the struggle was broadened and a more plural archive produced, thereby reconfiguring institutionalised narratives about the process that led to national independence.

Since the 1990s, therefore, there has been a battle not only for the memory of the struggle and the identity of the nation but also to define and systematise the events and figures considered worthy of inclusion in Cape Verde's history.[28] These disputes often took on a personal dimension, not unconnected to the small size of the islands and the close relationships and tendency to conflict that this situation potentially encouraged. Two researchers, Peter Meyns and Cláudio Furtado, suggest that the tone of the memoirs and most of the autobiographies published during the 1990s partly mimic the climate of political mistrust and personal friction in the political life of the archipelago.[29]

In 1989, Jorge Querido, who led the PAIGC clandestine activities in Portugal (where he was arrested three times) and in the islands (after his return in 1968), published *Cabo Verde. Subsídios para a História da nossa Luta de Libertação* [Cape Verde. Subsidies for the History of our Liberation Struggle], a book in which he criticises what he considers to have been the pernicious influence of Trotskyism among Cape Verdean students in Lisbon and Coimbra.[30] The following year, in direct dialogue with this text and its author, Manuel Faustino, one of the PAIGC dissidents in 1979, responded with *Jorge Querido: subsídios sob suspeita* [Jorge Querido: subsidies under suspicion].[31] In 1990, one of the most iconic statements on clandestine actions taken during the struggle in Cape Verde – *Testemunho de um Combatente* [A Combatant's Testimony] – was made by Pedro Martins, who was imprisoned in Tarrafal at the age of 17.[32]

Although there were Cape Verdeans incarcerated in other places, such as S. Nicolau (Angola) or in the PIDE / DGS prisons, Tarrafal acquired a particular symbolic place in the narratives of suffering associated with the anticolonial struggle (Figure 3.1). Located in the north of the Island of Santiago, in Cape Verde, Tarrafal Penal Colony was a particularly symbolic prison of the punishment system of the recently installed *Estado Novo* dictatorship (1933–1974). If the practice of deportation already had antecedents in Portugal, *Estado Novo* gave it new contours, "adding imprisonment to the deportation [procedure]" to an island.[33]

Created in 1936, Tarrafal was designed to house prominent oppositionists to the regime arriving from Portugal. Until 1954, when the camp was closed, the main detainees were Portuguese antifascists, including communist and anarchist leaders. In many cases, they remained in the camp without charges or indefinitely awaiting trial. Several of them died in these circumstances. In fact, the two main leaders of the Labour

Figure 3.1 Tarrafal Penal Camp, Nowadays Transformed into a Museum of Resistance.

Source: Photographs by Inês N. Rodrigues.

Movement lost their lives at Tarrafal: Bento Gonçalves (secretary-general of the Portuguese Communist Party from 1929 to 1935), as part of the communist movement, and Mário Castelhano, leader of the General Confederation of Labour, as part of the anarchist movement. During this period (1936–1954), 340 Portuguese political prisoners were deported to Tarrafal, 32 of whom ended up dying in the camp due to the harsh living conditions to which they were exposed. Also because of this, Tarrafal will become in Portugal a landmark in the memory of the political violence of *Estado Novo* and of the antifascist resistance.

The prison would be reopened in 1961, now with the official name of "Campo de Trabalho de Chão Bom". It emerged, at the time, as a penal device designed to house prisoners from the anticolonial movements, namely Angolans and Guineans. From 1968 onwards, Tarrafal also began to receive Cape Verdeans (around 20 men). Of the prisoners placed in the camp, four deaths are recorded (two Angolans and two Guineans). In its second life, Tarrafal played a role in the context of the colonial wars fought between Portugal and African liberation movements, being closed on 1 May 1974.[34]

In Martins account of his years incarcerated in Tarrafal, and to a lesser degree in Jorge Querido's book, there is an explicit expression of the need to give visibility to clandestine activities in Cape Verde and to the place of Cape Verdean political prisoners in the history of the liberation struggle.[35] The way in which these works, among others that we will refer to later, contribute to constructing, complexifying and disseminating the image of the combatant says a lot about the narratives of the struggle and the hierarchies of value attributed to that past. During the first stage of the nation's independence, the figure of the combatant was more directly and outwardly linked with the notion of armed struggle. However, as the years progressed and the legal and symbolic representations of the LSC evolved and became more pluralised, the notion of "struggle" began, in the law, to encompass anti-colonial activities in broader terms. In spite of

The Struggle and the Image of the Combatant 99

all the possible differences between them, there is a shared understanding not only of the central place of the liberation struggle in the history of the archipelago but also of those who participated in it in very different ways.

Public recognition and political disputes

In 2000/2001, a new political cycle began in Cape Verde, with the consecutive victory of the PAICV first in the local elections, then in the legislative and presidential elections.[36] This marked the return of Pedro Pires to central governance positions, now as President of the Republic, a role he held until 2011. His presidency, between 2001 and 2011, played an important function in updating the representations of the image of the combatant, as well as in the public reconfiguration of the place of institutions such as the ACOLP (the Association of the Liberation Struggle Combatants, where a mural in its honour adorns its outer walls, as Figure 3.2 shows) and the Amílcar Cabral Foundation.

Figure 3.2 Mural in Honour of Pedro Pires at ACOLP.
Source: Photograph by Inês N. Rodrigues.

100   *The Struggle and the Image of the Combatant*

As Pires himself stated in 2012:

> My candidacy for the Presidency of the Republic was based on being able to rescue the national liberation struggle, its principles and its symbols, bearing in mind what had happened during the previous ten years [of the MpD government]. My victory in the elections is proof that the people also attach importance to these principles.[37]

One of the first acts during his mandate was to recognise the participation of Cape Verdean women in the struggle, an experience which, until then, had rarely been acknowledged in the way it had been for other political actors. In 2004, on the occasion of the celebration of 29 years of national independence, Pedro Pires honoured the women who participated in the struggle for national independence by awarding eight of them the Order of Amílcar Cabral. According to the then President of the Republic, this was an attempt to "repair the omission found at the 1990 honouring of a significant number of Liberation Struggle Combatants which was held without the inclusion of a single woman".[38] The following year, in 2005, on the same occasion, among the dozens of LSCs honoured, there were also many women.

The official validation of these experiences has been accompanied by other public memory products and practices. In 2010, Paula Fortes, a nurse at the PAIGC Pilot School, published a collection of texts about her life.[39] Five years later, in 2015, the project "Memories for the Future: Highlighting Women's Experiences on Independence" began, coordinated by Celeste Fortes and Rita Rainho at the University of Cape Verde, and which resulted, among others, in the documentary "Canhão de Boca" ("Mouth Cannon"). This fictionally reproduced a programme with Amélia Araújo, the most iconic female speaker on the PAIGC radio station – *Rádio Libertação* – responsible for Portuguese language broadcasts. Later that year, Amélia Araújo was also decorated by the Cape Verde Government, which hailed her as a "voice recognised and admired by the populations and peoples of Guinea and Cape Verde, who had in radio the only means of finding out about the actions of the armed struggle" and the public functions she took on in Cape Verde after independence, "lending all her experience and professionalism to the development of the country".[40]

There have also been numerous interviews with Cape Verdean women combatants in the country's media, which testify to their heroism and where they are praised for their dedication, courage and fighting spirit. This demonstrates how the imaginary of the combatant has diversified to include, for example, the role played by women combatants in terms of communication, but also in whole range of areas, from logistics, education, diplomacy and health to the military and strategic dimensions.[41] These works have thereby helped to uncover the very diverse contributions of Cape Verdean women in the struggle as political subjects and

The Struggle and the Image of the Combatant   101

fighters in their own right, in a process that is both one of recognition and valorisation.[42] Despite this, according to data from the National Assembly provided to us in early 2018, until that date only about 15% of the 457 beneficiaries of the statute of LSC in Cape Verde were women (and for some of these it was not in recognition of activities performed, but as widows of male combatants).

Another of the most visible public actions for recognising the importance of the struggle's past – broadly speaking – is that of State honours. Unlike his predecessor, who awarded the Order of Amilcar Cabral only seven times to prominent foreign political figures – as mentioned in the previous chapter – Pedro Pires has honoured 186 individuals with this decoration, most of whom were Cape-Verdean citizens. Of those honoured, there is one common criterion that stands out – the connection to the liberation struggle – thus making this an act of inclusion. During Pedro Pires' presidency, the Order of Amílcar Cabral therefore served to distinguish the different types of LSC, from fighters in the armed struggle to clandestine activists and political prisoners, leaders of other political organisations (such as the UPICV), PAIGC dissidents and / or members formerly associated with the "Trotskyist" group, such as Manuel Faustino, Sérgio Centeio, Jorge Carlos Fonseca and Érico Veríssimo, as well as various women involved in the anti-colonial struggle.

During his two terms in office, foreign heads of State, journalists, academics and activists who were noted for their support of or participation in liberation movements were also honoured with the same decorations. These included, for example: Ahmed Ben Bella, first Algerian President; António Agostinho Neto, first President of Angola and Mário Pinto de Andrade, founder of the MPLA;[43] Alda Espírito Santo, nationalist, politician and writer from São Tomé and Príncipe; António Almeida Santos, Portuguese politician who was one of the leaders of the decolonisation processes; Marcelino dos Santos, Mozambican nationalist and founder of FRELIMO; Augusta Conchiglia, Basil Davidson, Bruna Polimeni, Dina Forti, Oleg Ignatiev and Lars Rudebeck, reporters and academics who visited the liberated zones and followed the struggles in Angola, Mozambique and Guinea; and Óscar Oramas, member of the UN Decolonization Committee and one of the great defenders of the anti-colonial liberation movement, who met Amílcar Cabral and followed the struggle of the PAIGC very closely. Through this gesture, the official place of the liberation struggle and its participants in the history of the nation was reaffirmed.

Major changes in the legislation occurred, however, only in 2014, the year preceding the commemoration of the 40th anniversary of independence. Law no. 59/VIII/2014, of 18 March, broadens the scope of application of the LSC statute to include former political prisoners with a definition that is different from the more general one applied to LSCs, equating them in terms of symbolic and legal value. The statute now

102 *The Struggle and the Image of the Combatant*

provides for the attribution of a pension or pension supplement to beneficiaries who are not covered by any type of social security system that guarantees retirement or retirement income. In addition to the more pronounced retributive understanding that the statute now explicitly presents, symbolic and mnemonic issues are also not overlooked.

The ACOLP and the Cape Verdean Association of Ex-Political Prisoners are declared in the text as the institutions representing the individual and collective interests of the combatants. They became directly involved in the procedures for recognising the statute, as well as in the process for granting a pension or pension supplement to its beneficiaries. A few months after the introduction of these new legal dimensions to the law, the statute of Commanding Officers was established, a position which, for political and historical reasons, has hierarchical supremacy over any military rank created in the post-independence period. Long claimed by some LSCs, it mostly serves to symbolically distinguish commanders involved in the liberation struggle from senior non-combatant officers, that is, career military personnel, who are not eligible for this position. The category of Commanding Officer is therefore directly related to the memory politics of the struggle, that is, with the recognition of a past of sacrifice, courage and dedication of exceptional value considered worthy of dignifying and rewarding.

The granting of symbolic elements and other types of incentives, including pensions, can, in this and other cases, be seen as a party-political mechanism for reproducing cycles of power, reinforcing certain public policies and narratives about the war and maintaining the exceptional status of certain figures or groups. The State, using its powers as a financier, legislator and legitimiser[44] thus ends up, through changes introduced in legislation that stimulate or neglect certain figures or decisions, or that support or discourage organisations like ACOLP or FAC, establishing itself as one of the main actors in the fluctuating process of producing imaginaries of the struggle and the regimes of memory associated with them.

The introduction of a monthly pension, in 2014, of 75,000 Cape Verde escudos (about 678 euros), as a guaranteed minimum for those LSCs who were not receiving any income or as a supplementary pension for those whose subsidies were less than this amount, once again strengthened criticism of the statute in certain social sectors. On the one hand, this payment creates a symbolic exception for combatants in the national narrative and alleviates those living in deprivation. On the other hand, these amounts can generate resentment and accusations of privilege in relation to the rest of the population.[45] It can also contribute to a sense of trivialising the image of the combatant, as Luís Fonseca, who was imprisoned in Tarrafal for seven years for his political militancy in the PAIGC, told us. According to Luís Fonseca, the introduction of the pension led to a very considerable increase in requests for recognition of the statute,

The Struggle and the Image of the Combatant 103

which helped trivialise not only the figure of the combatant but also the meaning of national independence itself.

> Hundreds of [recognition requests] began to appear only and exclusively because there was a pension attached. And we drew attention to this, [to] avoid people taking advantage of this and suddenly we had people who never thought they could be combatants. But then ... all of a sudden there was a whole bunch of people, some of whom, frankly, I wouldn't be surprised if they were informers for the PIDE, but they all turned up ... Now they are [combatants]. Only and exclusively because this chance of a pension came along, not out of patriotism or for having participated in anything. And then there are cases ... there's a pharmacy owner who appears as a pensioner ... there are landlords ... in short, because there's no-one checking up. And all this leads people to say: "Ah, those combatants ...". And this also leads to the image of the Liberation Struggle Combatant being diminished. I don't think the government was careful enough, it didn't take things into consideration and in short ... it let things drift. I am left with the question: was it intentional?[46]

Implicit in Luis Fonseca's statement is another question often discussed since the drafting of the first statute, relating to the nature of people's contribution in the struggle, and on which the law is either comprehensive or not very explicit: What is the minimum extent of suffering and dedication required for someone to be considered worthy of the title of LSC? Disagreements about the answers to this question have tended to generate tensions within the group of beneficiaries and among those who do not belong to it and believe they deserve it. But it also raises questions among some citizens who, without questioning the liberation struggle (and its result), react against what they consider to have been a process of PAIGC / CV "taking advantage" of this legacy.[47]

Carlos Reis, president of ACOLP, considers that the wave of requests submitted from 2014 onwards, following the approval of the pension, has raised these and other questions in the archipelago. The inevitable need to extend the concept of combatant to other types of contribution to the struggle was, according to Carlos Reis, a lengthy process which eventually resulted in excessive accessibility, leading many Cape Verdeans – including LSC – to question the beneficiaries of the law.[48] These tensions were not only related to the potential trivialisation of the Statute but were also associated with discussions around the veracity of participation in the struggle of the applicants and the rigour of the actual process of attributing the status. The decision, based on an opinion from ACOLP and the declaration of two witnesses who were recognised as combatants, was considered insufficient, partisan and prone to undue favouritism. This conviction was then reinforced by suspicions of fraud in some of the recognition processes, with reports emerging of cases in which applicants had paid 20,000 Cape Verde escudos (about 180 euros) for a document certifying their participation in the struggle for independence, in order to obtain the status and pension.[49]

The situation led to the implementation of a process for reassessing the names on the list of LSC approved by the Assembly, and ACOLP created an internal committee responsible for analysing the cases that raised doubts.[50] This reappraisal resulted in a report being sent to the National Assembly, recommending the removal of over one hundred names of LSCs from the list.[51] ACOLP ended up intervening crucially in preserving the authenticity and integrity of its members' image, protecting their status from being contaminated by cases perceived as illegitimate or subject of exploitation.

Carlos Reis stresses the "long-lasting legal evolution" experienced in Cape Verde for the combatant status to exist in its present form. Nowadays, ACOLP has associates who are linked with UCID and MpD, along with a larger number connected to PAICV: "it looks at citizens, at the evidence that they were combatants, regardless of which party they are associated with at the moment".[52] The "non-partisan" nature assumed by the organisation is visible in its premises, located in the nation's capital city.

On the inside walls of its headquarters, there is a mural in memoriam of the late LSCs, with photographs of each of them listed in chronological order of their death (see Figure 3.3). In the nearly 130 pictures presented,

Figure 3.3 In Memoriam: Mural to the Late Liberation Struggle Combatants at ACOLP.

Source: Photograph by Inês N. Rodrigues.

The Struggle and the Image of the Combatant   105

it is possible to find the faces of Amílcar Cabral and Aristides Pereira, two of the most representative figures of the PAIGC struggle, next to those of Onésimo Silveira (who fell out with the party after independence) or José Leitão da Graça (that never belonged to the liberation movement and which, within UPICV political framework, disagreed with the project of unity with Guinea-Bissau advocated by PAIGC). According to its president, these are recognition processes that take time and discussion, but ACOLP "fights for those in which they believe in, that have a right [to the status] and that express their willingness to obtain it", regardless of the specific circumstances – in the armed struggle, clandestinely, as political prisoners, or in PAIGC and UPICV – in which their political activities for the archipelago's independence occurred.

The diversification of the image of the "combatant"

In recent years, the notion of "combatant" has become openly more plural and acquired a broader meaning, particularly during the recent two presidencies of Jorge Carlos Fonseca (2011–2021). However, these processes were already showing signs of emerging, in a tenuous way, from the second half of the 1990s. The change in the public perception of the combatant and a certain mitigation of the processes of "decabralisation", although still ambiguous and intermittent in nature, was visible in 1995, shortly before the MpD repeated its victory in the legislative elections with a qualified majority in December. That same year, some of the speeches referring to the PAIGC / CV's historical combatants and leaders took on a less phlegmatic tone, a bust of Cabral was inaugurated in Santa Catarina, in Assomada, near the house where he grew up, and the construction of a memorial in his honour in the city of Praia was announced. This, however, was only completed in 2000 and will be dealt with in detail in the following chapter.[53]

In 1996, a statue to Cabral was erected at Sal international airport, which also bears the name of the historical leader of the PAIGC[54] and a monumental book of over 700 pages was published by the journalist José Vicente Lopes, *Cabo Verde. Os Bastidores da Independência* [Cape Verde. Independence Behind the Scenes], in which the author uses about one hundred interviews and a collection of sources from national and foreign archives to detail the complexity and diversity of experiences, interpretations and historical processes that led to self-determination and decolonisation of the archipelago. Because of its dimension, the book has been frequently mentioned in press releases and interviews since then. It is now in its third edition and is seen as the magnum opus on the struggle and early years of independence.[55]

The softening of aggressive criticism explicitly directed at the PAIGC / CV's historical combatants may have various explanations. On the one hand, the MpD consolidated itself as a legitimate political party on an equal footing with the PAICV, with whom it has alternated in power. As

106 *The Struggle and the Image of the Combatant*

a result, recourse to narratives about the liberation struggle – its visual icons, symbolic-mnemonic devices, protagonists – as sources of legitimising or delegitimising the opposition is losing the centrality it had until then occupied. On the other hand, the previous process of discrediting the segment of historical combatants created spaces where other actors in the struggle could assert themselves, and claim proper recognition of their role in the liberation process. At the same time, in recent years, we have also seen a general political impetus across the two largest parties, albeit for different purposes, to reach a consensus on national history, that is, to integrate and consider the role of different heritages in the formation of Cape Verde as a nation, arguing for an equal appreciation of both sides rather than placing them in competition.

It is with this sense of pluralisation, recognition and reconciliation in Cape Verde's more than 500-year journey that, in 2010, Manuel Veiga, the Ministry of Culture under the PAICV government led by José Maria Neves – the country's President since 2021 – announced the construction of a "Liberation Monument". Although it never came to pass, it was expected to create a space of "historical pilgrimage" and journey into the past struggles of the Cape Verde people. It was to refer to different milestones in the nation's history, from its discovery, colonisation, droughts, slavery, forced emigration, hunger and drought, to the fight against illiteracy, the armed struggle, independence, the reconstruction of the country and initiatives for development, progress and freedom.[56]

In an effort to accommodate the various national legacies – musical, political and literary – that are understood to be part of the archipelago's journey, the PAICV government brought a new series of banknotes into circulation, to pay tribute to great figures in Cape Verde's history and highlight the country's cultural and developmental aspects that, in different sectors of Cape Verde life, "harmonise with each other".[57] The 200-*escudos* banknote bear the head of the doctor and writer Henrique Teixeira de Sousa and the 500-*escudos* banknote that of the poet Jorge Barbosa, both associated with the *Claridade* movement, the latter note featuring extracts from the magazine. The 1,000-*escudos* banknote pays homage to *funaná* and one of its most emblematic composers, Codé di Dona; the 2,000-*escudos* banknote celebrates Cesária Évora, the most internationally acclaimed singer of *morna* and, finally, the 5,000-*escudos* banknote pays tribute to Aristides Pereira, Cape Verde's first president.[58]

Despite the conciliatory drive evident here, it is Jorge Carlos Fonseca, President of the Republic from 2011 to 2021 and whose candidacy was supported by the MpD, who has particularly insisted on this point. Besides being the great driving force behind the initiative known as "Republic Week", instituted since 2012 by the Presidency in conjunction with the Government and the Municipality of Praia, which combines two public holidays of significance in the political history of Cape Verde – 13 and 20 January – associated with the MPD and PAICV, respectively,

The Struggle and the Image of the Combatant 107

the former President of the Republic has on several occasions spoken out against what he considers to be a "selective appreciation" of the country's history.[59] The symbolic meeting that "Republic Week" encourages between the date of the first multi-party elections (Freedom and Democracy Day) and the date of the assassination of Amílcar Cabral (National Heroes' Day) reflects the way in which Fonseca's presidency understands the archipelago's journey: not in dispute, but in harmony, as the result of a collective effort. According to Jorge Carlos Fonseca, the dynamics of "Republic Week" therefore offers a clearly didactic objective:

> We symbolically wanted, and with some sense of pedagogy, to show Cape Verde society that the history of Cape Verde is a whole and should not be divided up by cyclical interests, or ideological or political options. The fact that Cape Verde has been independent is as important as the date on which democracy and freedom were won. [...]. So, this is the perspective that we are continuing. Basically, we are commemorating the entire history of the country. It is our history and we must accept it in its entirety, from the Discoveries, the period before independence, independence, democracy and history does not stop. We cannot have a selective view of what may interest one political activist or another. It is an integrated, symbolic and pedagogical vision of the whole that we want to emphasize with this Republic Week.[60]

Since December 2016, the two dates, 5 July (Independence Day) and 13 January (Freedom and Democracy Day), have been the subject of commemoration with special solemn sessions in the National Assembly.[61] The decision to combine the two dates met with a reaction from the PAICV leadership and led to the following statements from Jorge Carlos Fonseca:

> Progressively, 13 January was conceived and affirmed as a 'continuum' of 5 July, a missing piece in the dreams of many to take definitive form. The two glorious dates in our collective history are nothing more than two sides without which the struggle against colonialism would have remained incomplete.[62]

This gesture of equating the two dates and their significance for Cape Verde finds a correlation in the permanent discussion about notions of heroism that emerges in the celebration of these commemorations, especially in political speeches, in opinion articles published in the national media and in State award ceremonies. In this regard, Jorge Carlos Fonseca awarded 10 individuals with the Order of Amílcar Cabral, notably to some of the key figures of the 1991 political transition, such as Carlos Veiga. This gesture to enhance the profile of those honoured reflects a change in the symbolic concept of what it means to be a combatant and / or hero in Cape Verde. While, in the 1990s, the notion of combatant was

108 *The Struggle and the Image of the Combatant*

applied to those who undertook anticolonial activities, regardless of whether or not they participated in the armed struggle, more recently it has also been used to refer to those people who resisted Portuguese colonialism and the daily adversities of the archipelago before and beyond the context of the liberation struggle. They have sometimes been referred to as equivalent gestures. Jorge Carlos Fonseca's speech at a tribute to the LSCs on 20 January 2018 is an example of this.[63]

On this occasion, the President of the Republic highlighted "tenacity, courage and commitment" as the values praised by the nation on 20 January, the date that serves "as a temporal marker to honour as National Heroes all those who, known or anonymous, gave themselves to the cause of liberation". In the same speech, Jorge Carlos Fonseca stressed that the country was built internationally "as the expression of a hard-working people that throughout history" knew how to "face and overcome the most diverse difficulties". His message is that in the face of different challenges, in different contexts, what persists is the "tenacity, courage and commitment" of Cape Verdeans. He considers that "the struggle for the survival and empowerment" of its people "has been arduous, in the same way that it was very demanding for the combatants on the armed and political fronts, clandestine or not, [...] to confront the colonial regime and its allies".

Through this speech, in which he symbolically recognises the same heroic status for the LSC and the anonymous population in the struggle against the adversities faced by the archipelago, Jorge Carlos Fonseca reinforces his position of bipartisanship and harmonisation of Cape Verde's past. And, thus, the "national hero", celebrated on 20 January, shifts the spotlight away from the profiles of individuals with paths uniquely linked to the national liberation struggle or to military experience. By seeking the discursive features of the figure of the combatant and applying them to other actors, a narrative of the nation arises that brings the general idea of "combat" to the centre. This movement makes the anti-colonial fighters semantically and morally equivalent to the agents of the democratisation process and, abstractly, to the entire population that, over time, helped to overcome various obstacles – climatic, economic, political, ecological, etc. – that Cape Verde had to face. One of its objectives is to honour the whole of Cape Verde's past and not only the struggle in isolation.

The centrality of the lexicon associated with the combatant and the struggle had also been extended to other times and practices during the previous presidency, albeit for different purposes. Moving this lexicon away from the strict chronology of the liberation struggle, Pedro Pires stated the following in his inauguration speech on 22 March 2001:

> Throughout time, the Cape Verde people have always fought for their emancipation. In this collective struggle, it is right that we remember

The Struggle and the Image of the Combatant 109

the anonymous struggle of many men and women against injustice, hunger and domination, and refuse to accept them with fatalism as the natural condition of these islands. Among us today are thousands of men and women who every day reinvent the art of survival, "scraping together" life from almost nothing. To pave the way by force, blood and sweat seems to be our destiny and in this consists our civil and anonymous heroism.[64]

This gesture of public recognition is, for Pedro Pires, as he often mentions in speeches and interviews, one of the elements of "fully exercising" the "right to memory" that any people should enjoy.[65] In the opinion of the President of the Republic, as he expressed it in his speech commemorating the 30th anniversary of the 5 July, the passage of time has presented him "with the urgent need to give due attention to the actions carried out, at various times, by Cape Verdean patriots in support of independence and national dignity", in what he calls a *"reconciliation with our recent past"* (in italics in the original). In the words of Pedro Pires, this is one way, among others, of "remedying omissions that may have occurred before".[66]

The recourse to the symbolic field associated with the figure of the combatant to equate his / her narrative characteristics with other figures has also been used by critics of the First Republic to refer to their adversaries. These disputes over memory find a parallel in one of the most prominent cases of negotiating the perception of who is (or is not) a combatant and national hero and recognising the various causes for which it is valid to have fought on behalf of the nation – be they of a political, cultural or social nature. In 2019, a financial pension was introduced for Cape Verdeans who opposed the single-party regime in São Vicente and Santo Antão in 1977 and 1981 respectively by engaging in confrontations with the authorities.[67] The preamble to the aforementioned law, evoking the Universal Declaration of Human Rights of 1948 and the possibility of historical reconciliation, states that it is an imperative of justice for the State to make reparations for the abuses and arbitrary practices inflicted on Cape Verde citizens during the single-party regime, which were considered particularly serious in São Vicente and Santo Antão in the years mentioned. The right to a monthly pension, worth 75,000 Cape Verdean escudos (the equivalent of 678 euros), is then established for the beneficiaries of this law who are not covered by social security systems.[68]

This legally defined financial compensation is exactly the same amount as the pension awarded to LSCs. This can therefore be seen as a political gesture to establish a symbolic equivalence between these combatants and the victims of torture and ill-treatment. It also activates a strategy of party-political confrontation by using the image of the combatant as one of its drivers. In this way, opponents of the single-party regime, an opposition now officially legitimised as a sacrifice made for the development

110   *The Struggle and the Image of the Combatant*

of the nation, are no longer perceived only as victims, but also as fighters for freedom and democracy in the archipelago. Jorge Carlos Fonseca, commenting on the text of the law he promulgated, explicitly makes this comparison:

> We are today a democratic State and a State under the rule of law, but on the other hand, we also know that the construction of the post-independence State did not lead to a plural regime and liberal democracy, and so there was a whole process, a whole struggle by the people of Cape Verde for there to be political openness and for a constitutional State to be built, founded on freedoms. [...]. On one hand there is the representation of independence, of those who fought for independence, the heroes of independence, and on the other, those who fought against the single party, for democracy, for freedom, who were the heroes of freedom and democracy. I myself once expressed this, and used the expression, which was controversial despite being symbolic, that there were the liberation struggle combatants *for* the homeland, but that there were also the liberation struggle combatants *in* the homeland (our italics).[69]

This excerpt is particularly significant for the ways in which the political parties and their representatives have been mobilising and creating hierarchies and ideas of heroism, suffering and resistance, by taking some events out of their specific historical context. In doing so, a gesture is made to level out different events and, consequently, their importance and consequences for the history of the nation. This affects the way in which Cape Verdeans relate to and socialise different versions of national history and the past of the struggle in particular. This process is based on ideals of recognition, reciprocity and inclusion of the different memories and actors who have contributed to the production of a certain shared past – Cape Verde's past – and strategically distanced themselves from an openly dichotomous position.

Although, as we have seen, the State ends up acting as the great arbiter or decision-maker of what should or should not be valued about the past in public and in the official memory and history of the nation, through legislation and other memory products and practices referred to above, the dynamic factors, both internal and external – related to attracting capital, to an economy based mostly on tourism, to the action of associations and collectives and to specific international funding programmes – cannot be disregarded. For this constrains and affects the co-constitution of these mnemo-political decisions, in the sense of producing an image of Cape Verde "for the outside world" as a harmonious country, without resentments, comfortable with its past, safe, attractive in terms of investments, climate and beaches, with a warm-hearted Creole people full of *morabeza* – an epithet generally attributed to the

The Struggle and the Image of the Combatant 111

Cape Verdean and that highlights the quality of those who are delicate, hospitable, kind and gentle.

A composite memorial framework

Legislation and public representations of the "combatant" in Cape Verde have evolved hand in hand with political, social and economic changes in the country. Despite the different senses and meanings it has taken on, the concept of the "combatant" as a political category and, above all, the distinctive qualities associated with this figure, have remained central to Cape Verde's socio-political life. The source of legitimacy of the country's first government was initially based on the anti-colonial origins of the independent State and its key players. Later, especially after the process of opening up to a multi-party system in the 1990s and the significant defeat of the liberation party at the ballot box, the notion of combatant came to encompass not only a broader combination of the various forms of participation in the anti-colonial struggle but also appeared to be associated with those who faced what is considered to have been the autocratic and oppressive action of the single-party regimes.

In more recent years, the concept has acquired an even broader meaning, and seeks to consensualise the nation's various biographical milestones and what are seen as contributions to national history, particularly by those who resisted Portuguese colonialism and daily adversities before and beyond the liberation struggle. While, on the one hand, this establishes a narrative of the nation that brings the ideas of "struggle" and "combatant" to the centre, on the other, creating a semantic and moral equivalence between the anti-colonial combatants, the agents of the democratisation process and more vaguely, those who, over time, were resisting the actions of the coloniser, seems to displace the national narrative from the image of the liberation struggle and the figure of the LSC, thereby decontextualising and depoliticising it.

The ways in which these public representations determine and influence the construction of political subjectivities and the very notion of struggle and resistance is based on three key dimensions. The first, legal dimension corresponds to the right to official recognition and appreciation of the sacrifice and dedication demonstrated in services rendered to the homeland, both during the struggle and after independence. The second, the material and retributive dimension, corresponds to the right to social and financial protection. Finally, the third dimension, the symbolic, emphasises the values that the LSC embodies, on the one hand, while relying on these for other metaphorical categorisations (such as "victim", "combatant for democracy" or "anonymous hero"), which collide with that of the LSC – by opposition or convergence – and which have also come to be recognised as key figures of the nation.

112 *The Struggle and the Image of the Combatant*

These gestures of a legal, symbolic and discursive nature are in line with the attempt –already mentioned – to consensualise national history, both internally and externally, by accommodating diverse legacies, all perceived as fundamental units of a larger journey by the nation and as collective heritage that should be recognised. This memorial framework, often depoliticised, is constructed by combining historical – and apparently conflicting – elements from the archipelago's difficult past(s), a process we will explain in more detail in Chapter 4.

The type of narrative to which it gives rise, supported by exercises in mnemonic summation and inclusion, has been challenged in recent years by two antagonistic movements that demonstrate how public representations of Cape Verde's history and image are far more contested and complex than just the result of a fixed and dominant version of the past, however inclusive it attempts to be. We are referring in this case to a line of criticism that questions Cabral's place as the central figure of the archipelago, and another viewpoint that explicitly identifies itself as Cabralist. The first focuses on what it considers to be the mythification of Amílcar Cabral and a reconfiguration and distortion of history by certain political actors in power, which it believes to be based on a tacit agreement between government and party elites, so that everyone can be considered "prodigal sons of the land". The second considers that it is necessary to return to Amílcar Cabral and the heritage of the struggle to articulate the concerns of the present. These dynamics and processes of symbolic negotiation and contemporary social appropriation of Amílcar Cabral will be discussed in the next chapter.

Notes

1 Cf. "5 de julho. Foi há 19 anos", *Novo Jornal de Cabo Verde*, no. 161, 5 July 1994.
2 Law no. 46/III/89, of 13 July.
3 The reference to the title of Liberation Struggle Combatant before the official creation of its own Statute served, above all, specific purposes such as counting the time of service dedicated to the State for retirement purposes – see, by way of example, *Boletim Oficial da República de Cabo Verde,* no. 34, 21 August 1982, p. 462 and *Boletim Oficial da República de Cabo Verde*, no. 20, 18 August 1985, p. 316.
4 Furthermore, it may also cover not only those who left the PAIGC before 25 April, 1974, provided "by subsequent conduct", they did not disgrace the dignity of the combatant, but also, exceptionally, "foreigners and stateless persons who fought in a significant way for National Liberation".
5 Luís Fonseca, interview, Mindelo, 24 May 2019.
6 In 1987, about two years before the approval of the Statute and following a challenge from Aristides Pereira, about a hundred former combatants had gathered to lay the foundations of what would become the future Association of Liberation Struggle Combatants. Cf. "Associação de Antigos Combatentes da Liberdade da Pátria", *Voz di Povo*, no. 613, 4 February 1987.
7 Cf. "Combatentes da Liberdade da Pátria proclamam Associação", *Tribuna*, no. 39(71), 16 to 30 April 1990.

The Struggle and the Image of the Combatant   113

8   Cf. "Combatentes da Liberdade da Pátria proclamam Associação", *Tribuna*, no. 39(71), 16 to 30 April 1990. See also ACOLP's objectives and guidelines for its members in the statutes published in *Boletim Oficial da República de Cabo Verde*, no. 45, 10 November 1990, pp. 771–773.

9   Cf. Law no. 15/IV/91, of 30 December.

10   In an interview with the authors in Praia, on 7 July 2019, Manuel Faustino, one of the applicants, considered that this gesture helped enrich the statute. It separated it from the party and recognised that the struggle was broader than the understanding of the figure of the combatant up until then. This collective request, signed by some of the dissidents of the PAIGC in the 1970s, such as Manuel Faustino, was later approved (cf. Resolution no. 105/ VI/2004 in *Boletim Oficial da República de Cabo Verde*, no. 21, 19 July 2004, p. 531). Other names such as Jorge Carlos Fonseca and Luís Sousa Nobre Leite, who like Manuel Faustino had founded or participated in the first MpD government and split with it in 1993–94 for political and ideological reasons, were also part of this group. After the split, they created the Democratic Convergence Party (PCD) in 1994, led by Eurico Monteiro. In the 1995 legislative elections, the PCD obtained 6.7% of the vote and elected one deputy. In the subsequent elections, it always ran in coalition with small parties or, in 2006, supported the MpD lists. It was dissolved in 2007. Cf. Roselma Évora, *Cabo Verde: A abertura política e a transição para a democracia* (Praia: Spleen Edições, 2004) and Edalina Rodrigues Sanches, *Party Systems in Young Democracies. Varieties of Institutionalization in Sub-Saharan Africa* (London and New York: Routledge, 2018), 73–95.

11   Cf. for example, the following opinion pieces: "Acabar com o PAICV e fazer justiça", *Voz di Povo*, no. 1091, 18 May 1991; "O PAICV e a lei de Parkinson", *Voz di Povo*, no. 1108, 27 June 1991; "PAIGC / PAICV na agonia", *Voz di Povo*, no. 1216, 21 March 1992; "MpD – Modelo da Liberdade em Cabo Verde", *Novo Jornal de Cabo Verde*, no. 16, 21 April 1993; "Cabo Verde vive agora nova era histórica", *Novo Jornal de Cabo Verde*, no. 42, 21 July 1993.

12   Cf. "5 de julho. Foi há 19 anos", *Novo Jornal de Cabo Verde*, no. 161, 5 July 1994.

13   Cf. "Deputados aprovam leis do tabaco e dos 20 anos de independência. Depois da tempestade ... chega a bonança", *Novo Jornal de Cabo Verde*, no. 250, 11 February 1995 and text by S. Pinho Fonseca, in the column "Louvações ao Poder" (Praise to Power), addressed to the "Distinguished Liberation Struggle Combatants" (Exmos. Senhores Combatentes da Liberdade da Pátria), *Correio Quinze*, no. 3/94, 21 July 1995, among others.

14   Cf. Redy Wilson Lima, "A imprensa escrita e a cobertura dos conflitos entre gangues de rua em Cabo Verde", in *Media Freedom and Right to Information in Africa*, ed. Luca Bussotti, Miguel de Barros and Tilo Gratz, p. 110. Lisboa: Centro de Estudos Internacionais do Instituto Universitário de Lisboa, 2015. See also, Isabel Lopes Ferreira, "Mal-estar em tempo de transição. Jornalistas e governantes em Cabo Verde, 1991–1998", *Lusotopie* 11 (2004): 295–313.

15   "O discurso da recandidatura – Que mal fizeram os combatentes", *A Semana*, no. 214, 10 July 1995.

16   "Combatentes da Liberdade da Pátria. Os esquecidos da História", *A Semana*, no. 214, 10 July 1995.

17   "Parlamento. Combatentes sentem-se insultados pelo MpD", *A Semana*, no. 373, 16 October 1998.

114　*The Struggle and the Image of the Combatant*

18　"Combatentes sentem-se insultados pelo MpD", *A Semana*, no. 373, 16 October 1998.

19　Eurico Monteiro was a member of the PAIGC and became a dissident in 1979. He then joined the founding core of the MpD and, in 1994, after a split from the MpD, of the PCD (Democratic Convergence Party), which he led until 2006 when it was dissolved.

20　"Combatentes sentem-se insultados pelo MpD", *A Semana*, no. 373, 16 October 1998.

21　"Combatentes sentem-se insultados pelo MpD", *A Semana*, no. 373, 16 October 1998.

22　Cf. for example, Cláudio Furtado, "Heróis Nacionais e a construção do Estado-Nação", *A Semana*, no. 284, 13 January 1997 and Special supplement published by ACOLP / *A Semana* entitled "24 anos depois ... O sentido da História", *A Semana*, no. 285, 20 January 1997.

23　Cf. "Agostinho Lopes nos EUA. Amílcar Cabral não é o pai da independência", *A Semana*, no. 616, 4 June 2003.

24　For the celebration of "National Heroes' Day" on 20 January 2014, the then president of ACOLP stated that the Liberation Struggle Combatants complained, not of having been mistreated but of having been neglected by successive Cape Verde governments since independence. Cf. "Melhor homenagem a Cabral é reforçar democracia cabo-verdiana. No Dia dos Heróis Nacionais, PR pede 'desenvolvimento justo' do arquipélago", *RDP África*, 21 January 2014.

25　"Condecoração de personalidades nacionais. Ex-presos políticos questionam", *Novo Jornal de Cabo Verde*, no. 160, 2 July 1994; "«Cabral ca ta mori», confirma Assembleia Nacional. Incitamento ao estudo e pesquisa para avivar a memória coletiva", *Novo Jornal de Cabo Verde*, no. 450, 22 January 1997; "Simpósio Internacional. Repensar África à luz do pensamento de Cabral", *A Semana*, no. 643, 9 January 2004.

26　Carlos Reis, interview, Praia, 7 March 2018.

27　Cf. Cláudio Furtado, "Cabo Verde e as quatro décadas da independência: dissonâncias, múltiplos discursos, reverberações e lutas por imposição de sentido à sua história recente", *Estudos Ibero-Americanos* 42, no. 3 (2016): 879–882.

28　Furtado, "Cabo Verde e as quatro décadas da independência", 879–882.

29　Peter Meyns, "Cape Verde: An African exception", *Journal of Democracy* 13, no. 3 (2002): 153–165 and Furtado, "Cabo Verde e as quatro décadas da independência", 879–882.

30　Jorge Querido, *Cabo Verde. Subsídios para a História da nossa Luta de Libertação* (Lisboa: Vega, 1989).

31　Manuel Faustino, *Jorge Querido: subsídios sob suspeita* (Mindelo: Ilhéu Editora, 1990).

32　The book, published for the first time in 1990, was issued in a revised version in 1995 as *Testemunho de um Combatente*. Praia / Mindelo / Instituto Camões – Centro Cultural Português.

33　Victor Barros, *Campos de Concentração em Cabo Verde. As ilhas como espaços de deportação e de prisão do Estado Novo* (Coimbra: Imprensa da Universidade de Coimbra, 2009), 18.

34　On Tarrafal, see also, among others: *Tarrafal. Memórias do Campo da Morte Lenta*, directed by Diana Andringa, Lisbon and Praia: Fundação Mário Soares and Fundação Amílcar Cabral, 2010; Alfredo Caldeira, *Tarrafal: Memória do Campo de Concentração* (Praia, Lisboa and Vila Franca de Xira: Fundação Amílcar Cabral, Fundação Mário Soares, Museu do Neo-Realismo and Câmara Municipal de Vila Franca de Xira, 2010);

The Struggle and the Image of the Combatant   115

José Vicente Lopes, *Tarrafal – Chão Bom, memórias e verdades*, 2 volumes (Praia: Instituto da Investigação e do Património Culturais, 2010); Nélida Brito, "Libertação dos presos políticos do Campo do Tarrafal (Cabo Verde) (1974)". In Miguel Cardina and Bruno Sena Martins (org.), *As voltas do passado. A guerra colonial e as lutas de libertação*, 278–282 (Lisboa: Tinta-da-china, 2018); and Victor Barros, "O exílio colonial e os seus fantasmas (memórias, figurações e ausências)", *Revista de História das Ideias* 38 (2020), 155–179. For a comparative analysis of the symbolic place of Tarrafal and other political prisons in Cape Verde, see the work of Crisanto Barros and Jean Michel Chaumont, "Tracking Tarrafal's symbolic status and initiatives for its patrimonialisation in Cape Verde [unpublished].

35 For an approach on the testimonies of these clandestine militants, see José Augusto Pereira, "A luta de libertação nacional nas ilhas de Cabo Verde na encruzilhada da(s) memória(s)", *Lusotopie* 19 (2020): 76–100.

36 After two qualified majorities in 1991 and 1995, the MpD lost the legislative elections to the PAICV in the following three elections, in 2001, 2006 and 2011, with the executive of José Maria Neves taking over the government of the country for 15 years, with an absolute majority in the last two mandates; the presidential elections in 2001 and 2006, with the PAICV candidate, Pedro Pires, beating Carlos Veiga by 12 votes in the first case and 3342 in the second; and the municipal elections in 2000. In 2011, the MpD elected its presidential candidate, Jorge Carlos Fonseca and in 2016 it won the legislative elections, a change in power which led Cape Verde to be considered a two-party political system. In addition to an electoral model that, through the D'Hondt formula, favoured the two largest parties – the PAICV and MpD – the fact that both parties were associated with two of the most significant cycles in the history of the post-colonial nation, the attainment of independence and the opening-up to a multi-party system, also contributed to the bipartisanship of elections in Cape Verde. Cf. Edalina Rodrigues Sanches, "O processo de institucionalização do sistema de partidos cabo-verdiano", *Revista de Estudos Cabo-Verdianos* 4 (2012): 13–14. See, also, José Semedo, Crisanto Barros and Daniel Costa, *Estudo Sociológico sobre as Eleições Legislativas e Presidenciais de 2001 a 2006* (Praia: DGAE, 2007); Roselma Évora, "Poder Legislativo no Regime Democrático em Cabo Verde" (PhD diss., Instituto de Ciências Sociais da Universidade de Brasília, 2009); and Edalina Rodrigues Sanches and Gerhard Seibert, "Politics and economy in small African island states: comparing Cabo Verde and São Tomé and Príncipe", in *Handbook on the Politics of Small States,* ed. Godfrey Baldacchino and Anders Wivel (Cheltenham: Edward Elgar Publishing, 2020), 222–240. In 2022, the archipelago has a MpD government, led by Ulisses Correia e Silva, and the President of the Republic is José Maria Neves, supported by PAICV, who won the 2021 elections against Carlos Veiga.

37 "Pedro Pires – O exemplo da boa governação no continente Africano", *Nós Genti Cabo Verde*, January 1, 2012, http://nosgenti.com/o-exemplo-da-boa-governacao-no-continente-africano/.

38 Pedro Pires, *O meu compromisso com Cabo Verde. Volume I: 2001–2006* (Praia: Edição de Autor, 2012), 483.

39 Paula Fortes, *A minha passagem* (Praia: Fundação Amílcar Cabral, 2010).

40 Cf. Order no. 4/2015, 4 February, *Boletim Oficial da República de Cabo Verde,* no. 6, 13 February 2015, 116.

41 For some academic approaches to this topic, cf.: Patrícia Godinho Gomes, "Guinea-Bissau e isole di Capo Verde: partecipazione femminile alla lotta politica", in *Donna e Potere nel continente africano,* ed. Bianca Maria

116   *The Struggle and the Image of the Combatant*

Carcangiu (Torino: l'Harmattan, 2004), 92–244; Ângela Sofia Benoliel Coutinho, "Mulheres na 'sombra': as cabo-verdianas e a luta de libertação nacional", in *As Mulheres em Cabo Verde: Experiências e Perspetivas*, ed. Carmelita Silva and Celeste Fortes (Praia: Uni-CV, 2012), 39–48; Eurídice Furtado Monteiro, *Entre os Senhores das Ilhas e as Descontentes – Identidade, Classe e Género na Estruturação do Campo Político em Cabo Verde* (Praia: Uni-CV, 2015); Ângela Sofia Benoliel Coutinho, "The participation of Cape Verdean women in the national liberation movement of Cape Verde and Guinea-Bissau (1956–1974): the pioneers", *Africa in the World 02/2017* (Dakar: Rosa Luxembourg Stiftung West Africa, 2017); Ângela Sofia Benoliel Coutinho, "Militantes invisíveis: as cabo-verdianas e o movimento independentista (1956–1974)", *Revista de Estudos Feministas* 28, no. 1 (2020): 1–13.

42 Cf. Lia Kent and Naomi Kinsella, "A Luta Continua (The Struggle Continues)", *International Feminist Journal of Politics* 17, no. 3 (2015): 473–494.

43 Both were awarded posthumously.

44 Berber Bevernage and Nico Wouters, "Introduction", in *The Palgrave Handbook of State-Sponsored History after 1945*, ed. Berber Bevernage and Nico Wouters (London: Palgrave Macmillan, 2018), 6.

45 Cf. "Cabo Verde aprova aumento de salário mínimo no privado", *Radio France Internationale*, 7 January 2018, http://www.rfi.fr/pt/cabo-verde/20180107-cabo-verde-aprova-aumento-de-salario-minimo-no-privado [accessed 25 May 2020]. In December 2019, the Government announced that the minimum wage in the private sector would rise to PTE 15,000 in 2021. Cf. "Governo vai aumentar salário mínimo para 15 mil escudos até final deste mandato". Available at: https://www.governo.cv/governo-vai-aumentar-o-salario-minimo-em-15-mil-escudos-ate-final-deste-mandato/ [accessed 25 May 2020].

46 Luís Fonseca, interview.

47 Some of these questions are explored, in very different ways, in António Caldeira Marques, *Os Bazófios da Independência (com uma carta inédita de Baltazar Lopes da Silva)* (Lisboa: Edição de Autor, 1999); Nuno Manalvo, *Carlos Veiga: Biografia Política. O rosto da mudança em Cabo Verde* (Lisboa: Alêtheia, 2009); Djunga de Biluca, *De Ribeira Bote a Rotterdam* (S/l: Self-published, 2010); José Vicente Lopes, *Aristides Pereira. Minha Vida, Nossa História* (Praia: Spleen Edições, 2012); Jorge Querido, *Um demorado olhar sobre Cabo Verde. O País, seu Percurso, suas Certezas e Ambiguidades* (Praia: Self-published, 2013); Jorge Querido, *Tempos de um Tempo que Passou* (Praia: Acácia Editora, 2015); José Vicente Lopes, *Onésimo Silveira. Uma Vida, Um Mar de Histórias* (Praia: Spleen Edições, 2016); Euclides Fontes, *Uma história inacabada* (Praia: Livraria Pedro Cardoso, 2018). These works have helped to shed light on some of these disputes and mnemonic battles within the various types of LSC in the archipelago, not least because they take on the character of memorial and / or (auto)biographical records.

48 Carlos Reis, interview, Praia, 7 March 2018.

49 Cf. "Alta intensidade de combatentes da liberdade da pátria", *A Nação*, no. 394, 19 March 2015 and "Combatentes indignados – '20 contos por um certificado da ACOLP'", *A Nação*, no. 400, 30 April 2015.

50 Carlos Reis, interview.

51 Cf. "Estatuto dos Combatentes da Liberdade da Pátria – Nomes podem cair da lista", *A Nação*, no. 408, 25 June 2015. In 2017, on the basis of new evidence submitted by some petitioners targeted with an unfavourable

The Struggle and the Image of the Combatant   117

opinion by ACOLP, the institution re-examined these cases and, in some cases, issued a new opinion and backed the complaint.

52 Carlos Reis, interview, Praia, 9 February 2022.

53 Cf. "Inauguração do busto de Amílcar Cabral. Inauguração justa a um grande homem", *Novo Jornal de Cabo Verde*, no. 297, 5 July 1995 and "Memorial Amílcar Cabral no Taiti. Colocada a primeira pedra ... quem coloca agora a segunda", *A Semana*, no. 214, 10 July 1995.

54 Cf. "Domingos Luísa executa Estátua de Amílcar Cabral no Sal", *Novo Jornal de Cabo Verde*, no. 388, 6 June 1996.

55 See "Os bastidores da independência de Cabo Verde. Um contributo para a História do país", *Novo Jornal de Cabo Verde*, no. 449, 18 January 1997 and «"Cabo Verde Bastidores da Independência" lançado na Praia - Sede de História», *A Semana*, no. 285, 20 January 1997.

56 Cf. "Ministério da Cultura anuncia 'Monumento à Liberdade' na Praia", *A Semana*, no. 915, 8 January 2010.

57 Cf. *Boletim Oficial da República de Cabo Verde*, no. 69, 17 November 2014, 2096.

58 Cf. *Boletim Oficial da República de Cabo Verde*, no. 69, 17 November 2014, 2101.

59 Cf. "Presidente cabo-verdiano contra «valorização seletiva da história» do país", *África 21*, 21 January 2015. In 2019, Jorge Carlos Fonseca stressed that Cape Verde's landmark dates are national dates and belong to the people, the main protagonist of all struggles. Cf. "PR quer 20 de janeiro com ideias adequadas aos grandes momentos do País", *Santiago Magazine*, 20 January 2019.

60 Cf. "Jorge Carlos Fonseca: 'Somos um país com um processo democrático irreversível'", *Expresso das Ilhas*, no. 685, 14 January 2015.

61 Cf. Law No. 4/IX/2016, *Boletim Oficial da República de Cabo Verde*, no. 71, 23 December 2016, p. 2186, which amends Law No. 106/VIII/2016, *Boletim Oficial da República de Cabo Verde*, no. 4, 19 January 2016, p. 147, in which it was stipulated that the holidays of 5 July, 13 January and 20 January were "iconic commemorative dates, the subject of special solemn sessions".

62 Cf. "Celebração das primeiras eleições em Cabo Verde 'não é património privativo' de nenhum partido", *Observador*, 13 January 2017. This decision, according to the newspaper, created some discomfort for the PAICV's parliamentary leader, Janira Hopffer Almada, not only because of differences of opinion on the role of each party in the political opening, but also because, without undervaluing the importance of the 13 January, she insists against what she considers to be incomparable: "The dates are never the same and any attempt to make them compete may undermine the importance of each". In an interview in 2020 with the authors, the current president of the PAICV corroborated this statement, adding that bringing "into dispute historical dates does not ennoble any people or nation" and that 13 and 20 January should be treated by the State with the same dignity. Cf. Janira Hopffer Almada, interview, Praia, 21 January 2020.

63 Cf. "Discurso de o Presidente da República Jorge Carlos Fonseca, na Cerimónia de Homenagem aos Combatentes da Liberdade da Pátria". Available at: http://presidencia.cv/arquivo/1649.

64 Pires, *O meu compromisso com Cabo Verde*, 36.

65 Pires, *O meu compromisso com Cabo Verde*, 67.

66 Pires, *O meu compromisso com Cabo Verde*, 489–490.

67 Law no. 67/IX/2019, *Boletim Oficial da República de Cabo Verde*, no. 94, 6 September 2019.

118　*The Struggle and the Image of the Combatant*

68　A list of victims was approved up to July 2020, which included 51 beneficiaries of the pension or supplementary pension from São Vicente and Santo Antão. Cf. *Boletim Oficial da República de Cabo Verde*, no. 12, 31 January 2020, pp. 2–3 and *Boletim Oficial da República de Cabo Verde*, no. 81, 9 July 2020, p. 1642.

69　Cf. "Jorge Carlos Fonseca: 'Somos um país com um processo democrático irreversível'", *Expresso das Ilhas*, no. 685, 14 January 2015.

Bibliography

Barros, Crisanto and Jean Michel Chaumont. "Tracking Tarrafal's symbolic status and initiatives for its patrimonialisation in Cape Verde" [unpublished].

Barros, Victor. "O exílio colonial e os seus fantasmas (memórias, figurações e ausências)". *Revista de História das Ideias* 38 (2020): 155–179.

Barros, Victor. *Campos de Concentração em Cabo Verde: As ilhas como espaços de deportação e de prisão do Estado Novo*. Coimbra: Imprensa da Universidade de Coimbra, 2009.

Bevernage, Berber and Nico Wouters. "Introduction". In *The Palgrave Handbook of State-Sponsored History after 1945*, edited by Berber Bevernage and Nico Wouters, 1–36. London: Palgrave Macmillan, 2018.

Biluca, Djunga de. *De Ribeira Bote a Rotterdam*. Mindelo: Self-published, 2010.

Brito, Nélida. "Libertação dos presos políticos do Campo do Tarrafal (Cabo Verde) (1974)". In *As voltas do passado. A guerra colonial e as lutas de libertação*, edited by Miguel Cardina and Bruno Sena Martins, 278–282. Lisboa: Tinta-da-china, 2018.

Caldeira, Alfredo. *Tarrafal: Memória do Campo de Concentração*. Praia, Lisboa and Vila Franca de Xira: Fundação Amílcar Cabral, Fundação Mário Soares; Museu do Neo-Realismo and Câmara Municipal de Vila Franca de Xira, 2010.

Coutinho, Ângela Sofia Benoliel, "Militantes invisíveis: as cabo-verdianas e o movimento independentista (1956–1974)". *Revista de Estudos Feministas* 28, no. 1 (2020): 1–13.

Coutinho, Ângela Sofia Benoliel. "Mulheres na 'sombra': as cabo-verdianas e a luta de libertação nacional". In *As Mulheres em Cabo Verde: Experiências e Perspetivas*, edited by Carmelita Silva and Celeste Fortes, 39–48. Praia: Uni-CV, 2012.

Coutinho, Ângela Sofia Benoliel. "The participation of Cape Verdean women in the national liberation movement of Cape Verde and Guinea-Bissau (1956–1974): the pioneers". In *Africa in the World 02/2017*. Dakar: Rosa Luxembourg Stiftung West Africa, 2017.

Évora, Roselma. "*Poder Legislativo no Regime Democrático em Cabo Verde*". PhD diss., Instituto de Ciências Sociais da Universidade de Brasília, 2009.

Évora, Roselma. *Cabo Verde: A abertura política e a transição para a democracia*. Praia: Spleen Edições, 2004.

Faustino, Manuel. *Jorge Querido: subsídios sob suspeita*. Mindelo: Ilhéu Editora, 1990.

Ferreira, Isabel Lopes. "Mal-estar em tempo de transição. Jornalistas e governantes em Cabo Verde, 1991–1998". *Lusotopie* 11 (2004): 295–313.

Fontes, Euclides. *Uma história inacabada*. Praia: Livraria Pedro Cardoso, 2018.

Fortes, Paula. *A minha passagem*. Praia: Fundação Amílcar Cabral, 2010.

The Struggle and the Image of the Combatant 119

Furtado, Cláudio. "Cabo Verde e as quatro décadas da independência: dissonâncias, múltiplos discursos, reverberações e lutas por imposição de sentido à sua história recente". *Estudos Ibero-Americanos* 42, no. 3 (2016): 855–887.

Gomes, Patrícia Godinho. "Guinea-Bissau e isole di Capo Verde: partecipazione femminile alla lotta politica". In *Donna e Potere nel continente africano*, edited by Bianca Maria Carcangiu, 92–244. Torino: l'Harmattan, 2004.

Kent, Lia and Naomi Kinsella, "A Luta Continua (The Struggle Continues)". *International Feminist Journal of Politics* 17, no. 3 (2015): 473–494.

Lima, Redy Wilson. "A imprensa escrita e a cobertura dos conflitos entre gangues de rua em Cabo Verde". In *Media Freedom and Right to Information in Africa*, edited by Luca Bussotti, Miguel de Barros and Tilo Gratz, 99–123. Lisboa: Centro de Estudos Internacionais do Instituto Universitário de Lisboa, 2015.

Lopes José Vicente. *Aristides Pereira. Minha Vida, Nossa História*. Praia: Spleen Edições, 2012.

Lopes, José Vicente. *Onésimo Silveira. Uma Vida, Um Mar de Histórias*. Praia: Spleen Edições, 2016.

Lopes, José Vicente. *Tarrafal – Chão Bom, memórias e verdades*, 2 volumes. Praia: Instituto da Investigação e do Património Culturais, 2010.

Manalvo, Manalvo. *Carlos Veiga: Biografia Política. O rosto da mudança em Cabo Verde*. Lisboa: Alêtheia, 2009.

Marques, António Caldeira. *Os Bazófios da Independência (com uma carta inédita de Baltazar Lopes da Silva)*. Lisboa: Self-published, 1999.

Martins, Pedro. *Testemunho de um Combatente*. Praia, Mindelo: Instituto Camões – Centro Cultural Português, 1995.

Meyns, Peter. "Cape Verde: Na African Exception". *Journal of Democracy* 13, no. 3 (2002): 153–165.

Monteiro, Eurídice Furtado. *Entre os Senhores das Ilhas e as Descontentes – Identidade, Classe e Género na Estruturação do Campo Político em Cabo Verde*. Praia: Uni-CV, 2015.

Pereira, José Augusto. "A luta de libertação nacional nas ilhas de Cabo Verde na encruzilhada da(s) memória(s)". *Lusotopie* 19 (2020): 76–100.

Pires, Pedro. *O meu compromisso com Cabo Verde. Volume I: 2001–2006*. Praia: Self-published, 2012.

Querido, Jorge. *Cabo Verde. Subsídios para a História da nossa Luta de Libertação*. Lisboa: Vega, 1989.

Querido, Jorge. *Tempos de um Tempo que Passou*. Praia: Acácia Editora, 2015.

Querido, Jorge. *Um demorado olhar sobre Cabo Verde. O País, seu Percurso, suas Certezas e Ambiguidades*. Praia: Self-published, 2013.

Sanches, Edalina Rodrigues and Gerhard Seibert. "Politics and economy in small African island states: comparing Cape Verde and São Tomé and Príncipe". In *Handbook on the Politics of Small States*, edited by Godfrey Baldacchino and Anders Wivel, 222–240. Cheltenham: Edward Elgar Publishing.

Sanches, Edalina Rodrigues. "O processo de institucionalização do sistema de partidos cabo-verdiano". *Revista de Estudos Cabo-Verdianos* 4 (2012): 9–28.

Sanches, Edalina Rodrigues. *Party Systems in Young Democracies. Varieties of Institutionalization in Sub-Saharan Africa*. London and New York: Routledge, 2018.

Semedo, José, Crisanto Barros and Daniel Costa. *Estudo Sociológico sobre as Eleições Legislativas e Presidenciais de 2001 a 2006*. Praia: DGAE, 2007.

120   *The Struggle and the Image of the Combatant*

Legislation

Boletim Oficial da República de Cabo Verde, no. 34, 21 August 1982.
Boletim Oficial da República de Cabo Verde, no. 20, 18 August 1985.
Boletim Oficial da República de Cabo Verde, no. 45, 10 November 1990.
Boletim Oficial da República de Cabo Verde, no. 21, 19 July 2004.
Boletim Oficial da República de Cabo Verde, no. 69, 17 November 2014.
Boletim Oficial da República de Cabo Verde, no. 6, 13 February 2015.
Boletim Oficial da República de Cabo Verde, no. 4, 19 January 2016.
Boletim Oficial da República de Cabo Verde, no. 71, 23 December 2016.
Boletim Oficial da República de Cabo Verde, no. 94, 6 September 2019.
Boletim Oficial da República de Cabo Verde, no. 12, 31 January 2020.
Boletim Oficial da República de Cabo Verde, no. 81, 9 July 2020.

Newspapers

África 21, Correio Quinze, Expresso das Ilhas, A Nação, Nós Genti Cabo Verde, Novo Jornal de Cabo Verde, Observador, RDP Africa, Santiago Magazine, A Semana, Tribuna, Voz di Povo.

Interviews

Almada, Janira Hopffer. Audio-recorded interview with Miguel Cardina and Inês Nascimento Rodrigues. Praia, 21 January 2020.

Faustino, Manuel. Audio-recorded interview with Miguel Cardina and Inês Nascimento Rodrigues. Praia, 7 July 2019.

Fonseca, Luís. Audio-recorded interview with Miguel Cardina and Inês Nascimento Rodrigues. Mindelo, 24 May 2019.

Reis, Carlos. Audio-recorded interview with Miguel Cardina and Inês Nascimento Rodrigues, Praia, 7 March 2018.

Reis, Carlos. Video and áudio-recorded interview with Miguel Cardina, Inês Nascimento Rodrigues and Diana Andringa, Praia, 9 February 2022.

Film / Video

Andringa, Diana, dir. *Tarrafal: Memórias do Campo da morte Lenta.* 2010. Lisbon, PT and Praia, CV: Fundação Mário Soares and Fundação Amílcar Cabral.

4 THE STRUGGLE AND CABRAL'S AFTERLIVES

On 2 September 1976, the mortal remains of Amílcar Cabral were transferred by plane from the city of Conakry to Bissau. In *O Regresso de Cabral* [The Return of Cabral] – the first documentary made in independent Guinea – there is a series of images of the liberation struggle and excerpts of Cabral's speeches, as well as footage of the newly founded State receiving the body of the assassinated leader.[1] The camera pans across the tearful and perplexed faces of people watching the removal of the coffin from the plane and its journey. According to Sana Na N'Hada, one of the directors, the aim of the film was to mobilise the Guinean and Cape Verdean diaspora communities by showing that "Cabral had not disappeared just because he was dead".[2] Flora Gomes, another of the directors, recalled that the film was not shown again publicly following Nino Vieira's coup in 1980, which ended the unity between Guinea-Bissau and Cape Verde.[3] As for Amílcar Cabral's body, it remains buried to this day inside Amura Fort, the headquarters of the Guinean Armed Forces, where it is protected from contact with the population (Figure 4.1).[4]

The status of "national heroes" attained by the leaders of African liberation struggles has an inescapable centrality in nations forged from an anti-colonial struggle. Amílcar Cabral is a special case here, for a number of reasons already listed in Chapter 1. It is important to return to two of these aspects. Firstly, Cabral was assassinated months before Guinea's unilateral declaration of independence. The fact that he did not had the opportunity to witness the moment of independence or to direct the construction of the nation-state that followed increased his ability to function as a martyr-leader. Secondly, Cabral founded his struggle on the gesture of unity between Guinea and Cape Verde and is today, therefore, the object of a dual appropriation in both countries, distinct in its characteristics, but coincident in the shared definition, forged in the post-independence period as "father" of the nationality.

Anthropologist Katherine Verdery has already analysed the place of mausoleums, memorials and rites associated with the bodies of political leaders, in the context of the transitions that took place in Eastern

DOI: 10.4324/9781003265535-5

Figure 4.1 Mausoleum of Amílcar Cabral. Forte de Amura, Bissau (Guinea-Bissau).
Source: Photograph by M. Cardina.

Europe after the Fall of the Berlin Wall. In her view, these spaces are "excellent means of accumulating something essential to political transformation: symbolic capital", emanating a power of their own to support the foundations of the State. The transmutation of the physical body into a symbolic body allows the historical subject to be dissociated from the fluctuations of time and the vicissitudes of the State. At the same time, the very foundations of the political body of the nation fed back into the sovereignty that the leader's post-mortem materialisation continually institutes and actualises.[5]

It should be noted that in Cape Verde, the body of the nation is configured from a spectral body. The figure of Cabral is simultaneously a material absence, given that he is buried in Guinea, and a symbolic presence, due to his inevitable influence on the historical process that led to the independence of the archipelago. This same dual characteristic may indeed apply to the armed struggle: absent (from the archipelago) and present (in the historical causality that led to independence). In Cabral's case, he emerges as a national hero who, paradoxically, defined himself as both Cape Verdean (due to his parents' origins and his adolescent education) and Guinean (where he was born and later led the armed struggle), although his only formal nationality was that of colonial Portugal. But Cabral is also seen as a revolutionary whose recognition went beyond the borders of those two countries, as a result of the importance and success of his struggle and the political, intellectual and popular influence he gained internationally.

The Struggle and Cabral's Afterlives 123

In fact, Cabral's life and work have been the subject of hundreds of studies around the world.[6] Robert Young cites him, along with Franz Fanon, as one of the most prominent theorist-activists to have laid the foundations of post-colonial thought.[7] In a competition held in 2020, *BBC World Histories Magazine* invited 20 historians to draw up a list of the names of 20 political leaders they considered to have had the greatest positive impact on the world. Amílcar Cabral was one of the nominees, chosen by Hakim Adi, British Professor of the History of Africa and the African Diaspora at the University of Chichester, UK. The list was then put to a vote by the magazine's readers, in which over 5,000 people participated. Cabral collected about 25% of the votes, and was selected as the second greatest leader ever, after Maharaja Ranjit Singh, founder of the Sikh empire. Despite the nature of these contests, which are very likely to encourage block mobilisations around one candidate or another, Cabral's vote effectively demonstrates how he is able to gather expressions of support and appreciation outside Guinea and Cape Verde. African, North-American, Brazilian and Portuguese youth and intellectuals involved in anti-racist and / or socialist activisms have been repeatedly drawn to Cabral, as has the attention of academic sectors interested in reflecting on the (anti)colonial past.[8]

The previous chapter examined how there have been diachronic transformations in the way the figure of the "combatant" has been socially and legally constructed. In this final chapter, we will explore the changing interpretations of the struggle's past through the memorialisation – by homage, open attack or relative omission – of the PAIGC's historical leader, Amílcar Cabral. To this end, we have explored the way his figure has manifested itself in monuments, political speeches, popular evocations and public performances, assuming that his symbolic place constitutes a decisive mechanism for both valuing and devaluing the struggle as a singular mnemonic device.

Crossroads of memory

In January 1987, the newspaper *Voz di Povo* announced the construction of a complex dedicated to the memory of Amílcar Cabral in Praia. The future development was to be "a centre for homage, education and people's training" and would comprise a national museum, a library and an auditorium, in addition to a statue of Cabral.[9] About a year earlier, a visit by the President of Brazil, José Sarney, had opened the door to the support of the Brazilian State for the project. This was embodied, in May 1987, in the offer of an architectural project for a Historical and Cultural Centre designed by Oscar Niemeyer, who had briefly met Cabral in Algeria (see Figure 4.2). At first it was thought that the centre and a large statue should be built on the island of Santa Maria,[10] but the final location chosen was Taiti (Várzea), a more accessible part of the city, in order to allow more

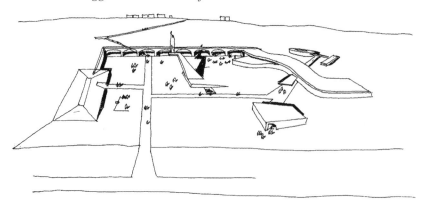

Figure 4.2 Cultural Centre in Cape Verde.
Source: Sketch by Oscar Niemeyer. © Óscar Niemeyer, AUTVIS, São Paulo/SPA, Lisboa, 2022.

interaction "between the population and the person honoured".[11] In fact, the project, of which only sketches are preserved today, was never built.

In 1992, the Minister of Culture and Communication, Leão Lopes, announced his intention to inaugurate a monument to Amílcar Cabral on 12 September 1994. It would, however, be different from the one designed by Niemeyer.[12] Despite this, it was not until three years later, in July 1995, that the ceremony to lay the first stone for this memorial took place. The event was beset by conflicts and violent acts amongst the people present. During the ceremony, one person appeared at the site wielding the country's first national flag and ended up being injured.[13] The work was only finally completed and inaugurated on 5 July 2000. It was the end of a process marked by various impasses and uncertainties, against a backdrop in which the country, as mentioned in Chapter 2, had witnessed also a certain degree of "de-Africanisation" and "de-Cabralisation" during the 1990s.

The memorial to Amílcar Cabral was the result of an offer from the People's Republic of China, as part of an infrastructure package that also involved the construction of the National Library and other public buildings in the vicinity. At its base, there is a small museum with photographs and biographical information about Cabral's life. On top of the pedestal is a bronze statue approximately three meters high (Figure 4.3). Cabral's statue falls short in some people's opinion, in that there is a distance between the Cabral represented in the monument and the Cabral of popular imagination. Despite sporting the famous *sumbia* on his head, it is often informally commented that Cabral, book in hand, does not appear with the expressions or clothing he used to wear during the times of the struggle. Instead he is shown wearing a heavy overcoat and strikes a rigid pose, considered to be in imitation of the statues of Asian political leaders.

The Struggle and Cabral's Afterlives 125

Figure 4.3 Amílcar Cabral Memorial, Praia.
Source: Photograph by M. Cardina.

While the representation of Cabral has generated some unease, the memorial complex itself has over the years, in a number of different ways, been overshadowed by various threats. In the first place, a sort of continuous sense of desecration has hung over it, due to the neglect to which it appears to has been subjected. In 2014, a piece published in the newspaper *A Nação* denounced the abandoned State of the memorial, littered with accumulated trash, pictures and doors torn off in the small museum, and the statue itself the target of graffiti.[14] The following year, a new issue further accentuated the debate about the undignified treatment of Cabral's figure. For some months, Praia municipal market was provisionally located next to the memorial by the city's council, to the annoyance of organisations such as ACOLP and criticism by high-profile figures such as Amílcar Cabral's daughter, historian Iva Cabral.[15] These

126 *The Struggle and Cabral's Afterlives*

disturbances were seen by certain sections of the population as gestures blocking the memorial's function as a symbolic repository of the nation's legitimacy produced by the liberation struggle. According to some opinions, this was a metaphor for the country's ingratitude toward the main architect of its independence. In an interview, Iva Cabral herself said:

> Cabral doesn't need a memorial. It's Cape Verdean society that needs a memorial. His memory is not that memorial. His memory is beyond that. And, sometimes, it's beyond Cape Verde! (...). And I think that this negotiating where the memorial should be, where the memorial is going, how it is going to be, I think it's humiliating. For me it's humiliating. I'd prefer to take it away. Have done with it. Let each one go to the library and read Cabral's writings. And have a photograph of Cabral at home, if they need one.[16]

Secondly, in 2018, the memorial was also threatened with relocation: the idea of setting up the US Embassy in a part of the city where a high school was located, implied moving the latter to the place where the memorial to Amílcar Cabral was. The alternative put forward was to place his statue on a nearby traffic island, a proposal that eventually generated controversy and fell through. Ultimately, the memorial was inaccessible until the middle of 2019, as it was subject to council works that dragged on over time and that, for example, prevented the annual laying of flowers near the statue on National Heroes Day in 2018. On 5 July 2019, the renovated location was inaugurated, and now has a playground, grassed areas and free Wi-Fi.

The discussion about the possible relocation of the monument was later at the origin of a debate involving criticisms of the way Cape Verde had dealt with the image of the independence leader – evidenced in the above excerpt by Iva Cabral – and the identification of possible alternative locations for the statue. Scholars and activists even argued that the monument should, in fact, occupy the central space where the bronze figure of Portuguese navigator Diogo Gomes stands. For instance, in June 2018, when there was still uncertainty about keeping the statue in the same place, Redy Wilson Lima advocated an "insurgent citizens" movement aiming to enhance the symbolism owed to Cabral and put him in Diogo Gomes' place.[17] In fact, as he emphasises, these symbolic and political asymmetries had already been mentioned in rap music, where the prominent place of Diogo Gomes next to the presidential palace, contemplating the vast ocean and the parliament, is contrasted with Cabral who stands below, looking towards the city cemetery.[18]

Such positions have become increasingly common among Cape Verdean youth: in June 2020, Gilson Varela Lopes, a young Cape Verdean living in Luxembourg, launched an online petition requesting the removal of the statue of the Portuguese navigator Diogo Gomes. The petition, which

The Struggle and Cabral's Afterlives 127

asked for the issue to be discussed in the National Assembly, ended up triggering some debate in the archipelago, especially among the political elites and certain politicised sectors of youth. The text argued that Diogo Gomes was "a navigator who also trafficked slaves in part-time" and made explicit connections with what had been happening recently in the international context – the questioning of colonialist and slave-owners statues which had intensified and broadened globally following the murder of George Floyd in the USA. Criticising the presence in public space of sculptural works and memorials associated with past slavery was fundamental, the text stated, "in a historical period of racial protest, where the suffering caused by these traders in black human beings stirs deep wounds of the lived trauma, discrimination and injustice that we still suffer". The petition ended by proposing that the figure of Diogo Gomes be replaced by a statue of Amílcar Cabral.[19]

Years before, the musician, writer and former Minister of Culture, Mário Lúcio Sousa, also sang about this confrontation in "Diogo e Cabral", from the 2008 album *Badyo*: "Diogo Gomes is up there / Beside the president's house / He lives among three continents / Cabral, / Down here being acclaimed / Diogo facing the parliament / Amílcar facing the cemetery / My God, what a mystery! / Is it nostalgia or forgetfulness?".[20] Very different between them, these protest gestures dispute the symbolic place that the statue of Diogo Gomes occupies. By placing both figures in comparative confrontation, they downgrade the place of Diogo Gomes, removing him from the unheeding silence that so often surrounds this type of public symbol. As Ann Rigney reminds us in a text on monuments and their public contestation, consensual alignment with a given way of erecting and materially preserving representations of the past can be the shortest path to amnesia since, "It is ironically a lack of unanimity that keeps some memory sites alive".[21]

The aforementioned petition launched by Gilson Varela Lopes led to the intervention of the Minister of Culture and Creative Industries, Abraão Vicente. The Minister stated that no statue would be removed, since each one of them had its own place in the history of Cape Verde. As an alternative to removal or "destruction of memory" he proposed an exercise of addition, to be materialised through the erection of monuments and statues in celebration of events or actors of the past that he considered remained forgotten in the memorial landscape of the archipelago.[22] For Abraão Vicente, history must be seen in a broader way; that is, the history of Cape Verde cannot be summarised only by two of its defining moments, independence and first multiparty elections, but must be broadened, since Cape Verde was born neither in 1975 nor in 1991: "it has been alive for centuries".[23]

Seen together – they are a few hundred meters apart on foot – the two statues mentioned above form part of the country's composite memory-scape, a hybrid space made up of symbols, monuments and images that underline the logic of aggregation of all that, even if apparently antagonistic, is perceived as belonging to Cape Verde's broader history. This rationale of integration triggers occasional conflicts of memory, but its major goal is to form a natural consensus around the past. The definition of this composite landscape is a product and a producer of different mnemonic representations and historical interpretations of the archipelago's journey. By conciliating narratives about its discovery and occupation, the colonial past, the struggle for independence, and the construction of a post-colonial Cape Verde, this composite memorial framework both mobilises gestures of evocation and of silence, thus rendering historically distinct elements compatible, as part of a national odyssey where everything has its place.

There are several examples of what could be defined as this conciliatory impulse. One of them, which is particularly illustrative, can be found on the covers of the textbooks for the 5th and 6th grade of History and Geography of Cape Verde, which have been used in schools in the archipelago since 2018 (Figure 4.4). On the 5th grade textbook, there is an image of a Caravel – a symbol of Portuguese maritime expansion – with the cross of Christ, a direct reference to Portugal as the remote origin of the Cape Verdean archipelago, and the word "Africa" written above the West African coast. On the 6th grade book, the images of Amílcar Cabral, the two flags of the country (the current and the first), a globe pointing to Africa and a copy of the magazine *Claridade* are represented.[24]

Figure 4.4 Trial textbooks for the History and Geography of Cape Verde, 5th and 6th grades, Ministry of Education.

The Struggle and Cabral's Afterlives 129

This initiative is anchored in a perception of the past with a relevant social presence, as well as in the conciliatory impulse exerted by important political and social sectors that is reflected in other areas of Cape Verde's political and socio-cultural life, which we have also reported on in the previous chapter. Pacifying and often depoliticised, this conciliatory drive comes clad in supposed neutrality, sometimes seeking national consensus (in conjunction with religious bodies, private companies, social movements and academia, to name just a few examples), sometimes seeking to project self-representations of the country – an archipelago of transits, diasporas and *morabeza* (affability) – deemed more attractive at the domestic and foreign level. Often, they are also the result of opportunities that, given the economic constraints that the archipelago is experiencing, are defined from the outside, via support from supranational entities (such as the European Union, the Economic Community of West African States, or the International Monetary Fund, for example); possibilities for funding, cooperation and improvement projects stimulated by private companies, foreign states and international organisations; or through the reproduction of the more global language of multiculturalism, heritage and human rights.[25]

It is worth noting how the challenge made to this memorial composition arises, above all, from contributions by young people who have direct or indirect connections with foreign countries (particularly Portugal, Holland, USA and Brazil) and provide updates to contemporary and transnational debates about racism, slavery, colonialism and their legacies in Cape Verde. It should also be noted that this movement, which connects to external realities and foreign actors, is complex and has also been activated to rewrite Cabral's image in the public space, partly because of the importance that Cabral increasingly assumes among certain sectors of Cape Verdean youth – we will explore this aspect in more detail below – but also due to his aforementioned international relevance.

It is in this context that we can also understand the reappearance of images of the struggle in the city of Praia in recent years. New avenues associated with the liberation struggle have helped lay down other symbolic geographies of the capital since 2017. Through the urban art strand of the community intervention programme *Xalabas di Kumunidadi* – run by the NGO África 70 and the *Pilorinhu* Association, and funded by the European Union – it is now possible to visit the Achada Grande Frente neighbourhood, outside the city's most noble district, and see public artworks evoking some of the great symbols of resistance and anti-colonial struggle. This is the case with the three murals that appeared there in 2019.

The first one illustrates the art of the *Rabelados*, a group from the interior of the island of Santiago that will be covered later (see Figure 4.5). Created by Sabino and Fico the graffiti, with drawings of the *Rabelados*, can not only be found on the walls of one of the schools but also on several

Figure 4.5 Mural by Rabelados, at Achada Grande Frente (Praia).
Source: Photograph by M. Cardina.

houses of Achada Grande Frente. Nearby is perhaps its greatest attraction in terms of urban art. This is the work of Vhils, a Portuguese artist who, in 2019, sculpted the face of Amílcar Cabral onto one of the walls of the neighbourhood's secondary school (see Figure 4.6). The face of the anti-colonial leader is accompanied by a third mural, of Titina Silá, a Guinean freedom fighter, by the Kenyan Bankslave. These murals create alternative spaces to the conciliatory narrative, in which the visual and symbolic presence of the liberation struggle and the anti-colonial matrix coexists with elements from the colonial period, supporting the assertion of a Cape Verdean Creole identity in which all these components

Figure 4.6 Mural of Amílcar Cabral, painted in 2019 by Portuguese artist Vhils, at Achada Grande Frente (Praia).
Source: Photograph by M. Cardina.

The Struggle and Cabral's Afterlives   131

are connected and have a place. In this case, these are representations that, on the contrary, affirm the centrality of the struggle and its figures, as well as the African matrix as the basis for the construction of an independent Cape Verde.

Questioning Cabral

In a text published in 2012, Abel Djassi Amado noted the existence of "three Cabrals" in contemporary Cape Verde: Cabral the fraud, Cabral the icon and Cabral the theorist and ideologue. The third, which he considers less well known, corresponds to Cabral's intellectual dimension, whose theses and concepts remain to be studied and deepened, despite the international recognition they attract. The second Cabral was the "iconic Cabral", the one with the most media coverage and "greatest visibility" in the archipelago and in the Cape Verdean diaspora, to be found in stylised reproductions of his image or in the recycling of his most iconic quotes on clothing, in the public space or on social networks. The first Cabral identified by Amado was around the narrative of "Cabral the fraud". According to the author, "for some sectors of society (including some sections of the island's intelligentsia), Cabral represents everything wrong that came to pass in the post-colonial period". They find a "direct causal relationship between Cabral and the evils and political mistakes committed by the single-party regime".[26]

The idea of Cabral as a "fraud" is part of a broader view that points to the negative heritage of the revolutionary, based on a broad set of considerations that aim to devalue him. From this perspective, articulated particularly by local intellectuals linked to the liberal and conservative right, Cabral was an overrated intellectual with adverse legacies still embedded in the history of the archipelago. They claim that Cabral's life story and political ideas were, to a large extent, alien to Cape Verde; they identify in him a dictatorial drive that came to the fore during the war and that would be continued and deepened had he the chance to assume the leadership in the post-independence period; and they question his prime position in the popular imagination and the symbolic apparatus of the State.

Representations such as those listed above emerged at various times. Starting in the early 1990s, the criticism of the single-party regime was accompanied by a reconsideration of Cabral, seen as the great inspiration behind the political model implemented in the islands after 1975. Thus, in recent years, along with Cabral's growing visibility inside and outside Cape Verde, there have also been negative assessments of his career and legacy expressed by some Cape Verdean politicians, journalists and intellectuals.

In 2014, Daniel dos Santos published *Amílcar Cabral: um Outro Olhar* [Amílcar Cabral: a Different View]. In this book, dos Santos seeks to highlight lesser known and appreciated aspects of Cabral's trajectory and the

132   *The Struggle and Cabral's Afterlives*

PAIGC's liberation struggle.[27] His public statements have also focused on denouncing what he considers to be Cabral's pernicious legacies. In 2018, in an interview given to the weekly *Expresso das Ilhas*, with the significant title "Cape Verde needs to free itself from the liberators", Daniel dos Santos considers that "from Amílcar Cabral's head came the ideological and political architecture for the format of the single-party State". Even though Cabral was assassinated about two years before Cape Verde's independence, he believes that "nothing would have been different" because the "totalitarian" nature of his ideas would have dominated it.[28]

In 2015, when the book *O Partido Único em Cabo Verde: um assalto à esperança* [The Single-Party in Cape Verde: an assault on hope] was republished, Humberto Cardoso critically notes that Cabral's designation as the "father of the nation" obscures the fact that the "nation already existed long before independence, with a culture and a clear identity" and that this association derived from the need to legitimise the PAIGC / CV.[29] In an interview with the authors, he notes what he perceives to be Cabral's historically undemocratic profile, while considering that "there is no possibility of consensus between the two parties around it [his figure]. For one simple reason: the PAICV will not allow it".[30] In his opinion, Cabral's presence was enforced "in schools and in the media" and was part of an effort to constantly legitimise the PAICV in order to have "ideological control over society". He also points out that "the democratic regime did not change the honours system", particularly the Order of Amílcar Cabral, which seems problematic to him, and he condemns the fact that a State ritual was created near his memorial on festive days such as 20 January or 5 July.[31]

In an editorial published in January 2020 in the weekly newspaper *Expresso das Ilhas*, of which he is the director, Humberto Cardoso also criticises the attempts, particularly under the presidency of Jorge Carlos Fonseca, to create a communion between the memory of independence and the memory of freedom, symbolised in the dates 13 January (the day of the first multiparty elections, in 1991) and 20 January (the date of Amílcar Cabral's death), an initiative we reported on in more detail in the previous chapter. In his view, the so-called "Republic Week" would be unable to resolve "the fractures of a republic still divided by the confrontation between the defence of the principles and values of liberal democracy, derived from respect for human dignity, and the attachment of a political clique to historical and revolutionary legitimacies".[32]

It was in the *Expresso das Ilhas* newspaper that, to a large extent, these positions critical of the figure of Cabral appeared. In 2015, António Jorge Delgado, architect and former Minister of Culture in the MpD government, published an opinion article in this weekly newspaper entitled "Whoever wants my part of 5 July is welcome to it". The writer is referring to Independence Day, which he regards as having been taken over by the imaginary of "those who came from Africa", welcomed "as liberators"

The Struggle and Cabral's Afterlives   133

but later turned "into real occupiers". In his opinion, the 5 July "marks the end of a colonial fascist regime of bad memory and the beginning of a substitute regime of the same type, although in other guises".[33] And he then goes on to take aim at Cabral:

> Cabral is primarily responsible for the fifteen years of single-party rule that we have had to endure in Cape Verde. The effort that has been made to confuse Cabral with Democracy is comical. From the theories, and especially from his practice, it is easy to demonstrate that Cabral would have been anything but a democrat.[34]

This same view was presented to the authors, this time about the Amílcar Cabral memorial.

> I was Minister of Culture and in that capacity the monument project was presented to me for my assessment and opinion. As far as I know, the idea of building this monument arose following a visit to China by the then President of the Republic of Cape Verde, António Mascarenhas Monteiro, as a way of highlighting the good relations between the two countries. (...) The statue reminds me of Mao Tse-Tung. In fact, to my mind, no other statue could better represent Amílcar Cabral, a confessed admirer and follower of Mao Tse-Tung. What would make no sense, unless I'm very much mistaken, would be to erect a monument reminiscent of Churchill, Dwight Eisenhower, Leopold Senghor or Nelson Mandela, for example.[35]

Following this critical line, Armindo Ferreira wrote in 2019 an opinion piece entitled "The Offensive of the 'Better Sons' and the Complicity of the 'Prodigal' and 'Adoptive Sons'". In this article, he cites the work of Daniel dos Santos to affirm what he sees as a contradiction between Cabral's life and work: although the author considers that Cabral never felt Cape Verdean, he was later "the nerve centre of the whole narrative, the backbone of the whole plot, the necessary and indispensable instrument for the credibility" of a national narrative in Cape Verde that sees the nation as emerging from the struggle.[36] In this regard, he also states:

> Portraits of Amílcar Cabral can still be found in various departments and, it is said, even in the palace. And the truth is that he does not appear on any line or page of our Constitution. In short: he is not a figure of the State, which is not to say that he doesn't belong to History... At this rate, with the manipulation, formatting and subordination of the educational system as well as a certain neglect or ignorance in parts of the media, it will not be long before we have a kind of "National Union" as a metaphor for a single party running our destinies.[37]

134 *The Struggle and Cabral's Afterlives*

This excerpt points to what is considered to be a broader gesture of complicity by large sections of Cape Verdean society and politics in constructing a narrative that has elevated Cabral to the position of the greatest personality of the nation. This complicity was seen has having been manifested itself, for example, in accepting Cabral's placement in the pantheon of State. This element has been particularly highlighted by the critical argument that sees Cabral as a negative heritage and a foreign body imposed on Cape Verdean society. His place in the symbolism of the State gave rise to a circumstantial polemic in 2019, when the MpD deputy, Emanuel Barbosa, published a text on the social network Facebook criticising the display of Cabral's paintings in public buildings.

More specifically, the deputy mentioned the case of the airport on the island of Boa Vista, where there is "a picture with the figure of the omnipresent Amílcar Cabral, next to the official photograph of the President of the Republic and a picture with Cize, the Queen of our *morna*". Unlike the presence of Cize – Cesária Évora (1941–2011), an internationally renowned Cape Verdean singer – Cabral's presence bothered Barbosa because considering him "a state figure is an exaggeration".[38] His views were the cause of heated controversy on social networks, and ended up spilling over into the newspapers and into the party-political space itself, with the MpD distancing itself from the statements of its deputy.[39]

In contrast, organisations such as ACOLP and the Amílcar Cabral Foundation (FAC), whose governing bodies include former combatants, have focused on valuing the legacy of the struggle and of Cabral. Formally created on 12 September 1984, the day of his birth 60 years before, the Amílcar Cabral Foundation aims to preserve and disseminate Cabral's thought and the history and memory of the liberation struggle. Having currently Pedro Pires as its president, FAC has been making Cabral more visible through publications, colloquia and visits to schools, as well as other initiatives, among which the integral printing of his works. It has a permanent museum on the liberation struggle since December 2015 on its premises, which is its most constant vehicle for public memorialisation. In 2018, FAC proposed to have the writings of Amílcar Cabral included in UNESCO's Memory of the World Register, a programme created to safeguard the documentary heritage of humanity.

The figure of Amílcar Cabral has also, very recently, been mobilised for pedagogical and recreational purposes in children's and youth literature. In 2019, two illustrated works have appeared with these aims. The first to be released was the book *A Turma do Cabralinho e o Búzio Mágico* [Cabralinho's Gang and the Magic Whelk], with text by Marilene Pereira and illustration by Coralie Tavares Silva, which is inspired by the famous Brazilian comic strip *A Turma da Mônica* [Monica's Gang]. It follows the adventures of a group of pre-teen friends, and makes implicit reference to five prominent fighters, three men and two women: Amílcar Cabral (Cabralinho), Aristides Pereira (Tide), Pedro Pires (Piduca), Lilica Boal

The Struggle and Cabral's Afterlives   135

(Lica) and Titina Silá (Titina).[40] In this story, the characters have different temperaments, but it is Cabralinho who, in effect, defines the solutions and punctuates the narrative with wisdom.

The figure of Amílcar Cabral as a moral reference for a children's audience also features in the book *Eu, Amílcar*, with text by Marilene Pereira and illustrations by Renato Athayde.[41] In this case, the book is aimed at schools, so it presents a short historical biography of the revolutionary, who provides a first-person account of the path he has taken since his birth. The liberation struggle and the independence of Guinea and Cape Verde emerge as the impulse behind the narrative and the actions that Cabral takes.

Alternative representations

The almost mythological content of Cabral's presence in the social imaginary predates his assassination and goes beyond the memorialisations linked to the State, the media and the political arena. Cláudio Furtado had already noted the presence of a "mythical memory" associated with the revolutionary, which meant that "in rural parts of Cape Verde during colonial times" it was common to "hear people say that Amílcar Cabral had appeared in such and such a place".[42] Pedro Martins, who was imprisoned at the age of 19 in Tarrafal for his clandestine political activities in Cape Verde, and where he remained until the political prisoners were released on 1 May 1974, remembers it this way:

> [Cabral] had achieved the magical and paternalistic stature of a demi-god, a defender of the people who, disguised as a priest, sister of charity, old man, etc., appeared all over Cape Verde to see with his own eyes the suffering of the people, in order to encourage them in the fight against Portuguese domination. Any unidentified stranger wandering the hills or valleys was often taken to be "Amílcar" once again passing through in disguise. This undercover work was not limited to Cape Verde, but also extended to São Tomé and Angola where he supposedly travelled to witness the suffering of the labourers. (...) The will of the people to free themselves from the yoke of exploitation, and their anxiety to have a leader near them who had already achieved enormous prestige and popularity but was hundreds of miles away from the islands, led [the people], in their simplicity, to make him into a mystical figure.[43]

Amílcar Cabral would thus appear as a longed-for presence, as a spectre who reveals himself to his people – especially the rural poor and those most subjected to violent exploitation – in unsuspected and diverse disguises, in direct proportion to the physical distance of his real self. His strength lies, therefore, in his capacity to transcend himself as a situated

136   *The Struggle and Cabral's Afterlives*

body and to appear in unheard-of places and circumstances to alleviate the suffering of the population. Pedro Pires notes that Cabral's mythological dimension lies precisely in his ubiquity. As he told us in an interview, "in the interior of Santiago they say that Cabral was there, and I have a lot of trouble convincing many people that he wasn't".[44]

One expression of this is the particular significance and appropriation that the figure of Amílcar Cabral has acquired with the *Rabelados*. As a community living in Santiago, mention of the *Rabelados* requires an exploration of the long history of domination in the country. In fact, from the time of the first occupation in the 15th century, social life on the island created a slave society made up of a white European minority and a black majority who were forcibly brought there. While the first elite on the island was dedicated to the slave trade and to commercial and maritime exploitation of the "rivers of Guinea", the endogenous elite that succeeded it was also supported by land exploration and production (which had been allocated to their ancestors by the king, and passed on to them anchored in an inheritance system – the *morgadio* – which sought to prevent it from being divided up, with the transmission of property to the first-born son on the death of the parent).[45] As the years went by and the Cidade Velha [Old Town] of Santiago lost importance in the transatlantic transportation of enslaved subjects, this human mass decreased, with some of them escaping, while at the same time the number of those freed by their masters, for good behaviour or due to blood ties, also increased.[46]

António Correia e Silva points out how escape was a "structural feature of slave society", with the presence of enslaved people in the mountains who "organised themselves into gangs, overshadowing the *pax senhorialis*" and who, "under certain circumstances, attacked agricultural properties and violently resisted attempts at capture by the authorities". He goes on to explain that in 1731 the island of Santiago was comprised of 16% slaves, while two thirds of the population were free men and women. He notes how "the society that existed for two centuries was already completely subverted", with the land being worked by a "free and family labour force" that was already autonomous (in terms of the type of crops grown, the nature and pace of agricultural tasks, etc.) and was different from a slave society, although subject to the harshness of living conditions and a strong dependence on the landowning fringe.[47]

From the refusal to be controlled and dominated, and also from the process of manumission (*alforria*), came the figure of the *badiu* (also spelled "badio", derived from the Portuguese word *vadio*, tramp), who eked out a subsistence lifestyle by wandering or by dedicating himself to hard work on the land. As a black man attached to the habits and customs of his ancestors originating from the west coast of Africa, the *badiu* remained on the margins of what were understood, in terms of colonial society, to be the appropriate rudiments of civilisation. A property system concentrated in the hands of large landowners generated several

The Struggle and Cabral's Afterlives   137

revolts caused by the misery in which the tenant farmers lived. These served to reinforce the perception of Santiago as an island marked by an adverse climate and occupied by a rebellious peasantry.[48]

In contrast, the emergence of the *Rabelados* must be compared with the situation of the Catholic Church at the time. In the mid-20th century, the actual lack of priests in the archipelago – the São Nicolau High School Seminary closed in 1917 and therefore ceased training pastors – meant that most religious services were carried out by members of the community or by former priests with far from orthodox practices and rites, such as the explicit rejection of sexual abstinence. In November 1941, five priests from the Congregation of the Holy Spirit and the new bishop of the diocese arrived in Santiago, responsible for renewing and returning discipline to existing religious practices. These priests wearing the "white cassock" – one of the changes established due to the harsh climate of the island, replacing the traditional black cassock used until then – were explicitly rejected in the rural areas of Santiago, for whom the new precepts brought by the missionaries clashed with their established religious practices and were seen as the work of the devil.

The tension became worse when, in 1961, the Portuguese State implemented a campaign to eradicate malaria and proposed to spray houses with DDT, collect blood from the population and introduce a BCG vaccination programme without any proper background work or explanation to the locals, in parallel with the start of a land demarcation initiative.[49] Sections of the peasant population rejected this initiative, triggering a strong movement to resist the State's plans. Silvino Silvério Marques, then governor of Cape Verde, notes euphemistically how he sent his subordinates to identify the main leaders of the rebellion, who "were removed from the *Rabelados* area and placed in the care of the Administrator of Fogo".[50] Indeed, several peasants were effectively arrested and tortured, and some deported away from their communities, in a process aimed at disbanding the resistance and leaving its leaders in squalor.[51]

In the mid-1960s, the Cape Verdean Júlio Monteiro Júnior was sent by the Ministry of Overseas Territories to study the *Rabelados* on the assumption that greater knowledge about this "religious sect" could help to contain and neutralise the movement. Monteiro Júnior's work was only published in 1974 and gives us an explanatory framework of the phenomenon. According to him, the number of *Rabelados* was estimated at between 1,500 and 2,000 people, although he notes that "there are thousands of individuals with the same 'mentality' on the main Island".[52] This was because the process that gave rise to their community, far from being the result of the determined action of one or other religious leader, was rooted in the socio-economic and cultural specifics of the peasants on the island as a whole. Contrary to some missionaries, who have accused the group "of being communist-inspired" and highlighted its opposition to the church, the government and the "whites", Monteiro emphasised the

138   *The Struggle and Cabral's Afterlives*

socio-religious nature of the movement and understood that what was needed was to encourage measures of a socio-economic nature.[53]

The term *rabelado* seems to have appeared for the first time in writing in the report made by Father Moniz to the Administrator of the municipality of Tarrafal in 1959, and from 1961 on the term became official, with the events that then took place. Over time, the *rabelado* communities came to accept the term and give it a new meaning that referred to the realm of the sacred; they understood the word not as referring to rebellion (*rebelado*), but to revelation (*revelado*).[54] Some of their distinctive customs include the adoption of the Bible and some ancient books (religious or not) as sources of knowledge, holding their own religious ceremonies, the use of a wooden cross, the type of dwelling (called *funku* and made of cane, leaves and sisal), the refusal to give their first name when directly questioned (presenting themselves as the *Rabelado* of Our Lord Jesus Christ), and their estrangement from the State with their rejection of government jobs, formal education and health care.

Luís Gomes de Pina, known as Nhonhô Landim, had been a sacristan for one of the "old priests", Father Joaquim Furtado, and was the first *Rabelado* chief.[55] In 1962, he was one of the leaders deported by the colonial power to the island of Fogo. He was succeeded by Nhô Fernando, and the return of Nhonhô Landim led to the coexistence of the two leaders until the latter gave way to Nhô Fernando.[56] Although contacts between the *Rabelados* and the PAIGC during the liberation struggle are relatively unclear, it is known that they would have existed. According to Pedro Martins, there were close contacts with the *Rabelados* by PAIGC clandestine militants in the archipelago.[57] Jorge Querido, a prominent member of the PAIGC indicates that political work in Santiago from 1963 on, first clandestinely in Portugal and then in Cape Verde, enabled the movement's message to gain acceptance in rural areas.[58]

Euclides Fontes, who returned to Praia in May 1974 after being deported to São Nicolau prison (Angola) for his political activities, recalls his encounter with the *Rabelados* in the months immediately following the 25th of April. Following a rally in Praia attended by some *Rabelados*, Fontes went to the Espinho Branco community to speak with chief Nhô Fernando. In the author's view, the conversation held attested to the millenarianism of the group, for whom Cabral was "the Messiah who would join them, the chosen people, to save Cape Verde after centuries of suffering and oppression of all kinds". Fontes recalls that Nhô Fernando asked him "if he knew where Cabral was, and when I told him that he had been murdered, he laughed and said that he was somewhere, waiting calmly to return at the opportune moment".[59] He also remembers that he gave them a PAIGC flag, which they carried every Sunday when they went to their religious ceremonies and that, when they passed by the party headquarters in Calheta, they took off their hats as a sign of respect and sang a hymn to the party.[60]

The Struggle and Cabral's Afterlives 139

Nevertheless, it is certain that the essential element in their relationship with the struggle did not occur fundamentally through militancy or organisation, but rather through a singular and somehow detached appropriation from the "real PAIGC". In fact, from early on, the figure of Cabral and the symbolism of the PAIGC struggle, embodied in the flag, assumed a place in affirming the identity of the community. When Nhô Fernando died, in August 1979, the newspaper *Voz di Povo* dedicated a news article to the "undisputed leader of the community and the rebellion against the colonial power". It stated that, after 1974, PAIGC militants found in Nhô Fernando "an interpreter of the liberation ideals defended by the Party" and that, in "his mystique", they considered Amílcar Cabral "the black God that they always dreamed of using to oppose the European religion brought by the colonisers", flying "the flag with the coveted Black Star".[61]

Public representation of the *Rabelados* fluctuated between the perception of a community far from civilisation, backward and closed in on itself, and an almost heroic vision associated with anti-colonial resistance and the "sanctification" of Cabral and the PAIGC flag. Over the decades, the *Rabelados* have been perceived as the "alternative inside"[62] the Cape Verdean community, as excluded and discriminated against as much as they have been the target of attempts at integration. It is important to note that, over time, the *Rabelados* have undergone a gradual process of opening up, accentuated in the last two decades by the presence of the artist and sociocultural activist Maria Isabel Alves ('Misá') in the community. Espinho Branco, where the *Rabelarte* association is located, gathering together the work of young *Rabelado* artists, is today regularly visited by Portuguese and foreign citizens. Cultural activity in the community has made connections with activist sectors in Praia, thereby gaining international recognition. At the same time, the process of social advancement, migratory impulses, the erosion of certain forms of sociability and religiosity, access to education and health services, as well as to new communication technologies, have all changed the interaction and self-representation of the community that, with the emergence of younger generations, has progressively opened itself up to the outside world.

The trips we made to Espinho Branco, in February 2017 and May·2019, gave us an insight into this phenomenon. The community is constantly visited by locals and foreigners. A small stone residence was advertised on the Airbnb website, and you could book overnight stays there for about 20 euros a day. The *Rabelarte* project occupies a central position as a workshop and store where it is possible to buy the works of art made in the community. In several of them, the PAIGC flag appears, either representing community activities in which it is involved – such as traditional funerals, where the deceased follows the flag in a sugarcane casket or *djangada* (picture on the left, by Kanhubai) – or adorning a musical

Figure 4.7 The Presence of the PAIGC Flag in Artwork Done by Youth From the Rabelados Community in Espinho Branco, May 2019.

Source: Photographs by Inês N. Rodrigues.

instrument or the drawing of two mermaids (by Josefa) at the entrance to the *Rabelarte* facilities (Figure 4.7).

PAIGC's flag is, for the Espinho Branco *Rabelados* a symbol with a double meaning: a way of paying homage to Amílcar Cabral – a hero and a friend to the community – and an image representing resistance (of the *Rabelados* themselves too).[63] Although he is more commonly seen in painting, Cabral is also a permanent reference point in the community, possessing a symbolic place that blurs the traditional boundary between life and death. Márcia Rego attests to divergences in the *Rabelados* communities as regards Cabral's status, with some considering him a divine entity and others a man endowed with exceptional qualities.[64] The author reports that, while attending a mass, she saw a picture of Cabral and António Mascarenhas Monteiro (the president elected with the support of the MpD), which led her to ask the chief whether Cabral was a saint or not:

> The chief responded that their pictures were there because they were both very good men. He listed all the reasons why Cabral was good, among which was the fact that he believed all men and women were equal, and that people should stop exploiting and mistreating each other. I told him I had heard the *Rabelados* believed Cabral had not really died, and that he had been seen in his community, to which he shrugged, gave a half-smile and uttered a mysterious "who knows" (m'ka sabi, literally meaning "I don't know").[65]

The Struggle and Cabral's Afterlives 141

In an article published in 1995 in the newspaper *A Semana*, a member of the *Rabelados* community explained that "Amílcar Cabral didn't die, we believe he is still alive, we believe in him and the PAIGC because they brought us freedom and justice. Jesus carried out work at the level of faith and Cabral performs practical work".[66] In an interview with the authors, Fico and Josefa, two *Rabelados* born in the post-independence period and belonging to the new generation of artists, note their strong relationship with the figure of Amílcar Cabral. Fico claims that "the Rabelados have always fought alongside Cabral". He adds: "when I was eight or nine years old, I remember people making fun of me, throwing stones, saying that Cabral is dead... And the *Rabelados* said no, Cabral is not dead! His body died, but his spirit did not die".[67] Josefa associates the emergence of Cabral and the *Rabelados* as directly related historical processes. With Cabral the *Rabelados* became "real Rabelados" and that is the reason why they claim that "Cabral did not die [Cabral ka mori]" and that is why they always carry the "Cabral flag" and associate it with the Bible.[68]

One somewhat unusual example of Cabral's presence also emerges in the realm of spiritualism. João Vasconcelos studied Christian rationalism in Cape Verde, a spiritualist current created in Brazil in the early 20th century that gained some prominence in Cape Verde, particularly on the island of São Vicente, where it took hold more than a century ago. In sessions held in Christian Rationalist centres, inferior spirits and superior spirits – or spirits of light – appear, who, as Vasconcelos notes, are often deceased people linked to spiritualism and also doctors, writers, or politicians from the archipelago. Amílcar Cabral is one of these spirits, along with Renato Cardoso (the PAICV minister and leader who was assassinated in the late 1980s under circumstances that were never fully clarified, mentioned in Chapter 2), which adds to the fact that they fall "into another category, which encompasses the spirits of progressive politicians who died violently and sometimes in murky circumstances". This includes, for example, Martin Luther King, John Kennedy and Olof Palme. His appearance in the sessions, notes João Vasconcelos, has less to do with his biographical profile and more to do with "the norms of conduct that human beings must follow in order to avoid the harassment of evil and hasten their spiritual development".[69] One of the branches of Christian rationalism in São Vicente – located on Mindelo's Avenida da Holanda, in one of the oldest houses on the island – features Amílcar Cabral as its "astral president", that is, a kind of spiritual tutor for the centre, who would often appear there to leave messages and communications.[70]

The new heirs: Protest and appropriations

The examples mentioned above remind us that memorialisation processes follow less linear paths than one might suppose from an analysis of their most obvious public expressions. Besides these, a constant and

142   *The Struggle and Cabral's Afterlives*

growing presence of the figure of Amílcar Cabral occurs in the urban culture – in rap, clothing, murals – in Cape Verde and also in Guinea-Bissau.[71] His figure is also mobilised by Afro-descendant sectors linked to rap music and anti-racist activism, as part of their identity and as a source of pride and inspiration.[72]

In Cape Verde, these representations emerge from the sectors of politicised youth and / or related to the diaspora. Rap music, but also public petitions, cyber activism and the reappearance of cultural manifestations of an Afrocentric and / or Pan-Africanist tone, as well as community youth activism, are some of the types of emerging activities that Redy Wilson Lima identifies.[73] This political-cultural scenario finds expression and connection in the *Marxa Kabral*, a demonstration held annually on 20 January – the date of Cabral's assassination – as a protest and political performance in his memory. According to Lima, the first event took place in 2010, organised by the *Djuntarti* association and by the *artivist* Dudu Rodrigues, under the slogan "20 di Janeru: Manifeztasom Kultural", as part of the Creole hip hop movement, with a march, lectures and a musical show.[74]

The *Marxa Kabral* was resumed on a regular basis in 2013, organised by *Korrenti di Ativiztas*[75] and sectors of the youth of Praia. Led then by sociologist UV (João José Monteiro), a component of this activist sector would create the *Pilorinhu* association in 2014. The association occupied an abandoned building in Achada Grande Frente that since then functions as housing and a space to promote education, local knowledge and training (courses in capoeira, theatre, carpentry, circus arts, handicrafts, etc.). Providing scholarly aid to children and social and medical support to the general population of the community are fundamental components of the association's work.[76] *Pilorinhu*, together with other structures such as the Pan-Africanist Movement, has been the driving force behind *Marxa Kabral*.

Each year there is a different theme which is intended to promote discussion, and the march passes through some of the capital's main streets for about two hours. In addition to the considerable presence of children, young people and cultural displays such as *tabanka*, the *Marxa* is attended by a veritable kaleidoscope of Pan-Africanist militants, cabralists, socialists, cultural activists, members of neighbourhood associations, members of the *Rabelados* communities, politically committed citizens, etc. These are groups with different cultural relationships with institutional power, with different histories and from different social and ideological backgrounds. Sometimes, there are also readings and appropriations of varying intensity on the two elements common to all of them: Africanness and Amílcar Cabral.

The event has introduced a sort of counter-memorialisation of Cabral. The historical leader is celebrated in his words, in his image and in his public representation, with the *Marxa* passing by the statue that represents

The Struggle and Cabral's Afterlives 143

him. The same element also appears in the noisy ascent to Plateau, where the statue of Diogo Gomes stands, breaking with the imaginary border that existed, and still exists, between the Creole property-owning elite and a substantial part of the population that felt forbidden to occupy this central space of a "divided city".[77] At the same time, the *Marxa* is also a clear affirmation of Africanness, evident in the choice of clothing, hairstyles and music, in the slogans and the use of capoeira as a globalised symbol of black resistance. The Africanness that has emerged here represents both a "return to the source" and an appropriation through globalised issues. The *Marxa Kabral*, like other protests that have taken place in the city of Praia in recent years, is thus associated with a broader gesture of dispute over the memorial landscapes that constitute – and have constituted – the country, suggesting that it is necessary to return to Amílcar Cabral and the heritage of the struggle in order to articulate the concerns of the present.

A cursory look at the themes of each annual *Marxa* demonstrates just that. In 2019, the focus was on combating xenophobia and valuing the "African brothers" that make up a proportion of the emigration in the country (namely Senegalese and Guineans); in 2020, the 8th *Marxa* took place highlighting the role of women in the liberation struggle "*Mudjer na luta pa libertason*" [Women in the struggle for liberation]; finally, in 2021, the theme chosen – "*Pensa ku bu kabesa*" – echoes a well-known Cabralist assertion, which urges the people to "think through their own minds". As in the previous year, when the role of women was highlighted, in 2021 this will also be in evidence, not directly in the theme chosen, but in the composition of the poster, which features the image of Titina Silá's face. In 2022, the 10th *Marxa Kabral* was held under the aegis of a "homage to all the liberation struggle combatants", albeit not in the format of a march, due to COVID-19 constraints, but with several activities in *Pilorinhu*'s space such as art exhibitions; debates; and capoeira, *batuku* and other sociocultural actions. In recent years, the *Marxa* has adopted as its common motto "*Amílcar Cabral, unifikador di povu*" (Amílcar Cabral, unifier of the people).

The *Marxa* also emerges as a mnemonic performance that is sometimes a parallel, sometimes an alternative, to the political elite's appropriations and institutionalisation of the figure of Amílcar Cabral. This became particularly evident in the 2019 edition, one of the events we had the opportunity to follow. Every year, on the morning of 20 January, there is an institutional and official ceremony to lay flowers and pay tribute to Amílcar Cabral at the memorial dedicated to him, with the presence of the State's leading figures, representatives of foreign nations and organisations, and some former combatants. While previously the ceremonies had never clashed – the *Marxa* route passed only at a distance from the memorial – as part of the 7th *Marxa*, the demonstration made a spontaneous and unplanned detour toward the monument before the official

144 *The Struggle and Cabral's Afterlives*

ceremony had ended (Figure 4.8).[78] The police very quickly created a barrier, preventing the demonstrators from proceeding to the statue, and generated a division of clearly drawn lines between the two public performances (the "ceremony of power" and the "youth demonstration"). The *Marxa*'s inability to get near the figure of the man it honours ended up creating a certain friction with the authorities. Although the leaders of the demonstration had rerouted it to the previously stipulated route approved by the Municipality of Praia, the friction continued for the rest of the way. It was not a conflict desired or expected by most of the organisation, that considers it part of a momentaneous "disorganisation".[79] The truth is that the event revealed more sharply some of the traits of *Marxa* as a counter-memorialisation of Cabral.

By demanding the right to access Cabral while the "politicians" were there, *Marxa* staked a claim to be one of Cabral's legitimate heirs. The police barrier accentuated this clear and impassable line. At the same time, one of the interesting aspects of the march, as mentioned above, is the transgression of the imaginary lines that define the occupiable and forbidden spaces of the capital, not only in their unsuccessful attempt to approach Cabral's statue but also in the climb to Plateau itself. As Capinero (Adérito Gonçalves Tavares), activist and former president of *Pilorinhu* said, it was a particularly "symbolic" moment: "as we went up to Praia, we didn't just take half the road; we took the whole road".[80] In 2020, after the 2019 events and in articulation with the municipal authorities, the *Marxa* made a stop by the memorial (see Figure 4.9). In fact, the figure of Cabral is the metaphor for the connection to Africa, but also the vehicle for criticism of the betrayal by the ruling powers, evident in the constant – and historic – cry of "*Cabral ka mori*" (Cabral did not die). For Capinero, speaking about Amílcar Cabral is "to bring hope to the people and to show that changes are possible".[81] Zanildo Vaz Moreno, *Pilorinhu*'s current president, notes: "we do not consider Amílcar Cabral a God but, as young people, we follow his legacy".[82]

Defining themselves as "young people", those responsible for organising the *Marxa* seek to claim a space of social legitimacy as legatees of a heritage that was passed on to them in an incomplete form.[83] In this sense, the notion of youth here is above all a political tool, strategically evoked to define a movement of political and cultural differentiation vis-à-vis institutional politics. It aims to actualise the idea of Cabral as an articulator of political yearnings as urgent as they are forgotten or betrayed. In fact, in general terms, the relationship between history and youth – or between memory and generations – has had at least two significant lines of theoretical analysis: one which focuses on examining the relationship between State institutions and citizens (in the school setting, for example) in the production, reproduction and recreation of representations of the past; and another, that follows the theories on "post-memory", which analyse the (im)possibility of transmitting, receiving and appropriating narratives about violent pasts.[84]

The Struggle and Cabral's Afterlives 145

Figure 4.8 Marxa Kabral and Official Ceremony of Homage to Cabral, 20 January 2019

Source: Photographs by M. Cardina.

146 *The Struggle and Cabral's Afterlives*

Figure 4.9 8th *Marxa Kabral*, 20 January 2020.
Source: Photograph by Inês N. Rodrigues.

However, the sharing and intergenerational displacement of the memory of the liberation struggle in Cape Verde, namely from *Marxa*, does not fit strictly or exclusively into either of these two lines. As a positive memory, which celebrates the achievement of independence and the utopian vision of its hero-martyr, the past of the struggle is explicitly the target of commemoration by the State at certain times, despite all the significant ambiguities that should be analysed (and of which we have given some examples in the previous chapters). Simultaneously, it is a memory valued and praised by the activist youth associated with the *Marxa Kabral*, who take possession of it by establishing critical and alternative ways of re-signifying the legacy and importance of the anti-colonial leader. While it is true that the perceptions of Cabral socialised there are, to some extent, distinct from the view that the State, parties or combatants publicly hold about him, it is also true that, especially in structures such as the Amílcar Cabral Foundation, where the weight of combatants' memory is critical, there are activities organised in common with some of the *Marxa* activists or with organisations that participate in it. In 2022, FAC and ACOLP both joined the *Marxa* initiatives, which was considered by Zanildo Vaz Moreno as "very relevant".[85]

In this case, the construction of identity through the relationship with the past develops largely through public memories of significant political

The Struggle and Cabral's Afterlives 147

dimension, but is produced and shared in other societal arenas and instances. Can one, in this sense, speak of the existence of a contemporary "public post-memory" of the liberation struggle in Cape Verde?[86] The struggle – and Cabral as its founding spectrum – is, in this context, a significant mnemonic device for activist sectors. Or as an instance of what Hayden White called the "practical past" – that is, the past that groups, individuals or institutions design to produce statements likely to impact the everyday dimension of their lives or the management of disruptive events.[87] As a mnemonic device, Cabral allows us to trigger a nostalgia of hope that, instead of being historical, or merely evocative, is defined from an iconic dimension capable of inspiring interventions in the present.

For one section of Cape Verdean youth, Cabral is a living myth, a figure that still questions a Cape Verdean society marked by persistent fractures and a complex appropriation of the memory of the liberation struggle. By producing a commemorative counter-performance to the ritual of the State, *Marxa* suggests the possibility of reinventing Cabral as a catalyst for a political critique coming from social and generational sectors that did not directly experience the struggle, even though they feel like the "new heirs" to it. To this extent, Cabral has been sketched out not only as the name of a successful anti-colonial struggle, but also as an "operating concept" whose evocation makes it possible to politically articulate present yearnings and future desires.

Notes

1 The movie was directed by a collective of young film-makers – Flora Gomes, Sana Na N'Hada, José Columba and Josefina Crato – sent to Cuba by Cabral in 1967 to study cinema. Amílcar Cabral had not been unaware of the importance of images in the construction of the future nation. It is significant that, only months after his assassination, the unilateral declaration of independence ceremony on 24 September 1973, was preceded the previous day by the screening of the documentary filmed by Flora Gomes during the Second Congress of the PAIGC, which took place between 18 and 22 July 1973, in the liberated regions of eastern Guinea. Part of the material filmed in the 1970s and 1980s was deposited at INCA (National Institute for Cinema and Audiovisual), created in 1978 in Bissau, and has been recovered, through a process of digitisation and treatment carried out in Berlin in recent years at the Arsenal Institute. One of the records of this process can be found at: Filipa César, Tobias Hering and Carolina Rito, org., *Luta ca caba inda: time place matter voice. 1967–2017* (Berlin, Archive Books, 2017). On the place of cinema in the liberation struggle in Guinea and in Guinean nation-building, see for example: Paulo Cunha and Catarina Laranjeiro, "Guiné-Bissau: do cinema de Estado ao cinema fora do Estado", *Rebeca - Revista Brasileira de Estudos de Cinema e Audiovisual* 5, no. 2 (2017): 1–23.

2 César, Hering and Rito, *Luta ca caba inda*, 231.

3 Statements made by Flora Gomes in the documentary made as part of the CROME project *Guiné-Bissau: da memória ao futuro* [Guinea-Bissau: from

148 *The Struggle and Cabral's Afterlives*

memory to the future]. Directed by Diana Andringa (Lisbon and Coimbra: Garden Films / CES, 2019), Youtube, https://www.youtube.com/watch?v= CYSJA6b3YEM, 44:05–45:12 min.

4 Other historical figures associated with the struggle and considered Guinean national heroes are also buried inside Amura Fort (such as Domingos Ramos, Pansau Na Isna, Titina Silá, Osvaldo Vieira, Francisco Mendes and Rui Demba Djassi), as well as former Heads of State. The fort is also home to a new "Museum of the National Liberation Struggle", with a narrative on the evolution of the struggle and an exhibition of weapons and other equipment used in the fight against colonialism, as well as the studio-container used in the broadcasts of *Rádio Libertação* and Cabral's old Volkswagen.

5 As Verdery also states, "by arresting the process of that person's bodily decay, a statue alters the temporality associated with the person, bringing him into the realm of the timeless or the sacred, like an icon". Cf. Katherine Verdery, *The Political Lives of Dead Bodies. Reburial and Postsocialist Change* (New York, Columbia University Press, 1999), 5 and 33.

6 The figure of Amílcar Cabral – in all its different dimensions – has given rise to numerous studies, from different angles of analysis and different disciplines, as attested by the extensive archive of secondary sources compiled and disseminated by António Duarte Silva in the *Malomil* blog (available at: http://malomil.blogspot.com/2013/01/amilcar-cabral-roteiro-de-fontes.html). Besides the works mentioned there, for a more recent up-to-date study of Amílcar Cabral, see Aurora Almada e Santos and Victor Barros, "Introduction. Amílcar Cabral and the Idea of Anticolonial Revolution", *Lusotopie* 19 (2020): 9–35. In a study carried out under the aegis of the Amílcar Cabral Foundation and Rosa Luxemburg Foundation, Ângela Coutinho has identified a list of 445 texts, in different languages, about Cabral and the liberation struggle. Ângela Benoliel Coutinho, "A produção científica internacional sobre a 'Cultura' no pensamento de Cabral", *Novas Letras - Revista de Letras, Arte e Cultura* 5 (2021): 14–17.

7 Robert Young, *Poscolonialism. A very short introduction* (London, Oxford University Press, 2003), 17.

8 There are a number of examples of this. The documentary *Cabralista*, by Valério Lopes, with voices from various parts of the world, is one of them. See the project at: https://cabralista.com. It is also worth noting the large and growing bibliography on the writer and academic projects that take him as their subject, such as *Amílcar Cabral: from Political History to Politics of Memory*, which ran from 2016 to 2019 at the Institute of Contemporary History (IHC) at the NOVA University of Lisbon (Universidade NOVA de Lisboa), funded by the Portuguese Foundation for Science and Technology. More recently, the Amílcar Cabral Prize was instituted in Lisbon by the IHC and the *Padrão dos Descobrimentos / EGEAC* to honour academic works by young historians on anti-colonial resistance.

9 Cf. "Governo manda erigir um memorial em homenagem a Amílcar Cabral", *Voz di Povo*, no. 610, 24 January 1987; "Brasil. Identidade cultural no critério de escolha", *Voz di Povo*, no. 634, 9 May 1987.

10 Small island located a few meters off the coast, in front of Gamboa beach. In 2015, Macao Chinese businessman David Chow signed an agreement with the Cape Verdean government for the concession and construction of the archipelago's largest development there. This is a hotel-casino, currently being finalised, which will connect the tiny island to the mainland via a small bridge, owned by CV Entertainment Co., a subsidiary of Macau Legend. The sale of the *djéu* provoked several protests and a transitional

The Struggle and Cabral's Afterlives 149

takeover of the rock by a group of activists, some of them active in the *Marxa Kabral*, which will be covered in more detail later. Cf. "Ativistas contra casino de David Chow", *Ponto Final*, no. 3289, 5 August de 2015.

11 Statement by Pedro Pires in João Pedro Abreu Martins (with Catherine Borja), "Memorial Amílcar Cabral: O projeto de Óscar Niemeyer", in *Brasil – Cabo Verde: tópicos de relações culturais*, eds. Bruno Miranda Zétola and Mónica Andrade (Praia: Embaixada do Brasil em Cabo Verde, 2018), pp. 249–270.

12 "Em homenagem a Amílcar Cabral, Leão Lopes anuncia criação de um monumento ao herói", *Voz di Povo*, no. 1290, 15 September 1992; "Monumento a Cabral em 1994", *A Semana*, no. 72, 1 September 1992. The following year a committee was appointed to review the construction of the monument. *Boletim Oficial, Iª Série, Despacho Ministério da Cultura e Comunicação*. 26 July 1993, no. 27, p. 346.

13 "Memorial Amílcar Cabral. O reconhecimento dos cabo-verdianos", *Novo Jornal de Cabo Verde*, no. 298, 8 July 1995. That same year, on the occasion of the 20th anniversary of independence, a bust of Cabral was inaugurated in Assomada (Santa Catarina), on Santiago Island, with the support of the Angolan government. Measuring about 1 metre 20 centimetres, the work was created by the Angolan General Rui Matos. He started it in 1986, after spending about a month working in Cape Verde on the project design. He returned to Angola with the work still unfinished, but various problems prevented it from being completed at that time. In 1995, however, he resumed work on the bust and it was completed. "Busto de Cabral já está em Santa Catarina", *A Semana*, no. 214, 10 July 1995. The following year, in September 1996, a statue was also inaugurated at Sal Airport (which also bears his name), designed by the Cape Verdean artist Domingos Luísa.

14 Carla Gonçalves, "Memorial Amílcar Cabral vandalizado e entregue ao lixo", *A Nação*, no. 354, 12 June 2014.

15 Cf. "Memorial Amílcar Cabral divide espaço com mercado alternativo", *A Nação*, no. 386, 22–28 January 2015; "Mercado provisório da Praia: ACOLP continua na luta – IPC baixa guarda", *A Nação*, 4 December 2015.

16 Iva Cabral, interview, Praia, 19 January 2019. Iva Cabral had already publicly expressed this on her Facebook page, which gave rise to some news about this position. For example, "Iva Cabral pede retirada da estátua em memória do pai e combatentes", *A Nação*, 11 June 2015, https://www.anacao.cv/noticia/2015/06/11/iva-cabral-pede-retirada-da-estatua-em-memoria-do-pai-e-combatentes/.

17 Redy Wilson Lima, "E que tal um movimento de cidadania", *Ku Frontalidad*i. June 2018, http://ku-frontalidadi.blogspot.com/2018/06/e-que-tal-um-movimento-de-cidadania.html.

18 For example, Nax Beat, in *Odja Oby Ntedy Dypoz Fala*: "N'ka kre odja statua di Cabral rostu para simiteriu / Di Diogo Gomi rostu para palasiu di governu" (I don't want to see the statue of Cabral with his face towards the cemetery and Diogo Gomes with his face towards parliament). Cited in Miguel de Barros and Redy Wilson Lima, "Rap Kriol(u): o pan-africanismo de Cabral na música de intervenção juvenil na Guiné-Bissau e em Cabo Verde", *Realis – Revista de Estudos Antiutilitaristas e Pós-coloniais* 2, no. 2 (2012): 101.

19 Cf. text of petition available online at https://peticaopublica.com/pview.aspx?pi=PT100526. In August 2021, the instigator of the petition delivered the more than 1,800 signatures collected to the President of the National Assembly.

20 "Diogo Gome mora la di riba / Na ladu di ká' Prizidenti / Mora na mei di 3 Kontinenti / Cabral / Li di baxo ta gritado biba / Diogo di rostu pa

150 *The Struggle and Cabral's Afterlives*

Parlamento / Amilcar di kara pa simitéri / Ma nha genti ma ki mistériu / E sodadi o e skesimentu?" in the original language.

21 "Cf. Ann Rigney, "The Dynamics of Remembrance: Texts between Monumentality and Morphing", in *Cultural Memory Studies: An International and Interdisciplinary Handbook*, ed. Astrid Erll and Ansgar Nünning (Berlin / New York, De Gruyter, 2010), 345–353.

22 Cf. "Cabo Verde tem que conhecer a sua história de uma forma profunda, Abraão Vicente", *Expresso das Ilhas*, June 16, 2020, https://expressodasilhas.cv/cultura/2020/06/16/cabo-verde-tem-que-conhecer-a-sua-historia-de-uma-forma-profunda-abraao-vicente/70013.

23 Abraão Vicente, interview, Praia, 16 January 2020.

24 Maritza Rosabal, then Minister of Education, pointed out the difficulties still existing to produce a historiographical reflection about the past, which, even today, is marked by a "Europe-centric vision". "I said that this cover had to be revised, that it was not admissible. (…) What interests me is how the islands were settled, etc. How does a student from the island of Maio feel if their island is not mentioned anywhere? They have no point of reference. So, it's a very outward-looking view". Maritza Rosabal, interview, Praia, 17 January 2019.

25 See Berber Bevernage and Nico Wouters, eds., *The Palgrave Handbook of State-Sponsored History After 1945* (Londres, Palgrave Macmillan, 2018), 12–18.

26 Abel Djassi Amado, "Os três Cabrais de hoje em Cabo Verde: uma leitura necessária", *Buala*, 23 January 2012, https://www.buala.org/pt/mukanda/os-tres-cabrais-de-hoje-em-cabo-verde-uma-leitura-necessaria.

27 Daniel dos Santos, *Amílcar Cabral: um outro olhar* (Lisboa, Chiado Editora, 2014).

28 "Cabo Verde precisa de libertar-se dos libertadores [entrevista a Daniel dos Santos]", *Expresso das Ilhas*, no. 876, 12 September 2018.

29 "Há uma memória desestruturada dos 15 anos de partido único [interview with Humberto Cardoso]". *Expresso das Ilhas*, no. 739, 27 January 2015.

30 Humberto Cardoso, interview, Praia, 4 July 2019.

31 Cardoso, interview.

32 Cf. "República dividida", *Expresso das Ilhas*, no. 947, 22 January 2020.

33 António Jorge Delgado, "Quem quiser a minha parte do 5 de julho, que tenha bom proveito", *Expresso das Ilhas*, no. 709, 1 July 2015.

34 Delgado, "Quem quiser a minha parte".

35 António Jorge Delgado, interviewed by email, 31 December 2019.

36 Armindo Ferreira, "A Ofensiva dos 'Melhores Filhos' e a Cumplicidade dos 'Filhos Pródigos' e 'Adoptivos'", *Expresso das Ilhas*, no. 898, 13 February 2019.

37 Ferreira, "A Ofensiva".

38 "Emanuel Barbosa: 'não é aceitável que as fotos de Amílcar Cabral estejam afixadas em estabelecimentos do Estado', *Notícias do Norte*, 30 April 2019, https://noticiasdonorte.publ.cv/88699/emanuel-barbosa-nao-e-aceitavel-que-as-fotos-de-amilcar-cabral-estejam-afixadas-em-estabelecimentos-do-estado/.

39 "MpD demarcar-se das declarações de Emanuel Barbosa", *Expresso das Ilhas*, 2 May 2019, https://expressodasilhas.cv/politica/2019/05/02/mpd-demarca-se-das-declaracoes-de-emanuel-barbosa/63623.

40 Marilene Pereira and Coralie Tavares Silva, *A Turma do Cabralinho e o Búzio Mágico* (Praia, Corart & Graphic Design, 2019). Lilica Boal was director of the PAIGC Pilot School in Conakry. Interestingly, the group of adventurers also includes Guinean Titina Silá, a PAIGC fighter

The Struggle and Cabral's Afterlives 151

assassinated on 30 January, 1973 by Portuguese soldiers, a date now celebrated in Guinea as National Guinean Women's Day.

41 Marilene Pereira and Renato Athayde, *Eu, Amílcar* (Praia, Fundação Amílcar Cabral, 2019). The book has a preface written by Iva Cabral.

42 Cláudio Furtado, "Heróis nacionais e a construção do Estado-Nação", *A Semana*, no. 284, 13 January de 1997.

43 Pedro Martins, *Testemunho de um Combatente* (Testimony of a Combatant) (Praia / Mindelo, Instituto Camões / Centro Cultural Português, 1995), 174. In his novel about the Tarrafal concentration camp, Mário Lúcio Sousa uses Pedro Martins as a character to precisely evoke this mythical character of Cabral in the years of the struggle: "Amílcar is a harbinger, he is legend: in the last few years, he has been a kind of vision, disguised as a priest in such and such a valley, dressed as a sister of charity from a faraway place, as a wise old monk in the wilderness, etc. Even today, in the islands, Amílcar stands for everything that is not known for sure. Whenever a mysterious event occurs, a furtive encounter, an unexpected appearance in a valley on one of these islands, people say it was Amílcar, even though he was in Guinea". Mário Lúcio Sousa, *O Diabo foi meu padeiro* [The Devil was my baker] (Lisboa, D. Quixote, 2019), 284.

44 Pedro Pires, interview, Praia, 18 January 2020.

45 Iva Cabral, *A Primeira Elite Colonial Atlântica. Dos "homens honrados brancos" de Santiago à "nobreza da terra". Finais do séc. XV – início do séc. XVII* (Praia, Livraria Pedro Cardoso, 2015), 16–18 and 173–175.

46 António Carreira, *Migrações nas ilhas de Cabo Verde* (Praia, Instituto Cabo-verdiano do Livro, 2nd ed., 1983), 47–48.

47 António Leão Correia e Silva, "Dinâmicas de decomposição e recomposição de espaços e sociedades", in *História Geral de Cabo Verde. Volume III*, ed. Maria Emília Madeira Santos (Lisboa / Praia, Instituto de Investigação Científica Tropical e Direcção-Geral do Património Cultural de Cabo Verde, 2002), 18, 40. See also António Leão Correia e Silva, *Noite Escravocrata. Madrugada Camponesa. Cabo Verde séc. XV–XVIII*. (Praia: Rosa de Porcelana, 2021).

48 As in the revolt of Ribeira do Engenho (1823), of Achada Falcão (1841) or of Ribeirão Manuel (1910).

49 According to Júlio Monteiro, although almost none of the *Rabelados* owned land, the demarcation procedures caused mistrust and were also linked to the numbering of houses for spraying. Júlio Monteiro Júnior, *Os Rebelados da Ilha de Santiago, de Cabo Verde* (Praia, Centro de Estudos de Cabo Verde, 1974), 128.

50 Statements by Silvino Silvério Marques in the film *Rebelados no Fim dos Tempos*. Directed by Jorge Murteira, Lisbon: Quevídeo II Filmes, 2002, Youtube, https://www.youtube.com/watch?v=NWOQdPSvL70.

51 Notwithstanding the time in which it was written and despite not producing concrete data about the repressive violence against the *Rabelados*, Júlio Monteiro also notes that, besides the deportations, several were arrested, interrogated and tortured. Several women were also mistreated by the police, and "some 30 women were arrested, tried and convicted, apparently on charges of disobedience for refusing to provide their identification in the absence of their husband". Júnior, *Os Rebelados*, 137.

52 Júnior, *Os Rebelados*, 54, 151 and 180.

53 As Márcia Rego notes, Monteiro's conclusions are ambivalent: on the one hand, he considered the movement to be "non-political", which would somehow protect it from State persecution, and believed that one of the ways to deal with the community would be to stop understanding it as

152   *The Struggle and Cabral's Afterlives*

"political"; on the other hand, he suggests a series of "socio-economic" measures to provide access to land and improve education, health and working conditions. Besides being the first study on the community, the book actually became a kind of sacred object among the *Rabelados* themselves, as the writer had the opportunity to demonstrate. Márcia Rego, *The Dialogic Nation of Cape Verde. Slavery, Language, and Ideology* (London, Lexington Books, 2015), 138 and 150.

54   Júnior, *Os Rebelados*, 48. As Maria de Lourdes Silva Gonçalves notes, they render their actions sacred through a "contextualised decoding". They are "not the insurgents or rebels they were baptised as, but the 'revealed ones' - Christ's chosen ones whose mission is to preserve and reveal the sacred word". Maria de Lourdes Silva Gonçalves, "Rabelados no Bacio e no Espinho Branco. Pontes e Portas na (re)formulação identitária do grupo", in *Ensaios Etnográficos na Ilha de Santiago Cabo Verde: Processos Identitários na Contemporaneidade*, ed. Maria Elisabeth Lucas and Sérgio Baptista da Silva (Porto Alegre / Praia, Universidade Federal de Rio Grande do Sul and Universidade de Cabo Verde, 2009), 233.

55   According to Júlio Monteiro, when interviewing him in the mid-1960s, he was "86 years old but still lucid and combative", and was considered the "Patriarch of the sect". Júnior, *Os Rebelados*, 60.

56   Françoise Ascher, *Os Rabelados de Cabo Verde. História de uma Revolta* (Paris, L'Harmattan, 2011), 61.

57   Martins, *Testemunho*, 174.

58   Jorge Querido, *Um demorado olhar sobre Cabo Verde – o país, sua génese, seu percurso, suas certezas e ambiguidades* (Praia, Ed. autor. 2.ª ed., 2013), 191–192.

59   Euclides Fontes, *Uma história inacabada* (Praia, Livraria Pedro Cardoso, 2018), 348–349.

60   Fontes, *Uma história*, 373.

61   "Faleceu o chefe espiritual dos Rabelados", *Voz di Povo*, no. 205, 30 de agosto de 1979.

62   João Silvestre T. A. Varela, "Identidade(s) e Nacionalismo(s) em Cabo Verde" (PhD diss. Universidade Federal Fluminense, 2008), 39.

63   Cf. Moisés Lopes Pereira (Tchetcho), interview, Praia, 9 February 2022.

64   Rego, *The Dialogic Nation*, 146.

65   Rego, *The Dialogic Nation*, 151.

66   *A Semana*, February 1995, cited in Celestino Carvalho, "Media e Identidade Cultural de Minorias. Os "Rabelados" da comunidade de Espinho Branco, na Ilha de Santiago – Cabo Verde". (Master diss., Universidade Aberta, 2020), 102.

67   Fico [João Baptista]. Interview, Espinho Branco, 18 May 2019.

68   Josefa, interview, Espinho Branco, 18 May 2019.

69   João Vasconcelos, "Espíritos lusófonos numa ilha crioula: língua, poder e identidade em São Vicente de Cabo Verde", in *A Persistência da História. Passado e contemporaneidade em África*, ed. Clara Carvalho and João de Pina Cabral (Lisboa: Imprensa de Ciências Sociais, 2004), 157.

70   During his stay in Mindelo, Cabral came into direct contact with followers of Christian rationalism. According to Luiz Silva, "expressions such as 'guide and light' or the idea of the creation of a new man are constant in Amílcar Cabral's works, inherited from the rationalist reading done at João Miranda's home, father of the Cape Verdean nationalist, Lineu Miranda". https://caboverdevida.blogspot.com/2011/09/visita-cabo-verde-do-dr-gilberto-silva.html

71   On this subject, see, for example, Miguel Barros and Redy Wilson Lima, "RAP KRIOL(U): the pan-Africanism of Cabral in the music of youth", in

The Struggle and Cabral's Afterlives   153

Claim no easy victories: the legacy of Amilcar Cabral, ed. Firoze Manji and Bill Fletcher Jr (Dakar, CODESRIA / Daraja Press, 2013), 387–404; Ricardo D. Rosa, "Cape Verdean Counter Cultural Hip-Hop(s) & the Mobilization of the Culture of Radical Memory: Public Pedagogy for Liberation or Continued Colonial Enslavement", *Journal of Cape Verdean Studies* 3, no. 1 (2018): 92–113; Redy Wilson Lima, "Di kamaradas a irmons: o rap cabo-verdiano e a (re)construção de uma identidade de resistência", *Tomo* 37 (2020): 47–88.

72 See Barros and Lima, "Rap Kriol(u)", 89–117; Cláudia Vaz and Ricardo Campos, "Rap e graffiti na Kova da Moura como mecanismos de reflexão identitária de jovens afrodescendentes", *Sociedade e Cultura* 16, no. 1 (2013): 129–141.

73 Redy Wilson Lima, "Hip-hop Praia: rap e representação do espaço público", in *Seminário Permanente em Estudos Africanos. Debates #4*, ed. Ana Maria Martinho Gale (Lisboa, CHAM ebooks, 2018), 90–109. On rap in Cape Verde see also Alexsandro Robalo, "Música e Poder em Cabo Verde: das práticas contestatárias dos jovens 'rappers' à potencialidade 'castradora' do Estado", *Desafios* 3 (2016): 103–130; Redy Wilson Lima, "Rap e Pesquisa Etnográfica", *Desafios* 3 (2016): 133–149.

74 According to Lima, the first tribute march to Cabral was promoted by "the *Djuntarti* association, influenced by the *Fidjus di Cabral* association and the community leadership project guided by the *Shokanti* movement" where, through breakdance, graffiti, rap and performing arts, a "space for the youthful demonstration of symbolic insubordination" was created. Redy Wilson Lima, "Jovens, processos identitários e sociedades em movimento: um olhar sócio-antropológico sobre a emergência dos movimentos juvenis identitários na cidade da Praia, Cabo Verde", *African Development Review* 45, no. 3 (2020): 97–120. See also, Redy Wilson Lima, "Marxa Cabral 2022", *Buala*, 19 January 2022, https://www.buala.org/pt/a-ler/marxa-cabral-2022?fbclid=IwAR3NpADAaYSVGyaUn1_BHGZyMnkGxINCbQzPhj1gqmc4AzH7amKpH2gQHMY.

75 *Korrenti di Ativiztas* was set up in 2012 as an offshoot of the Simenti project, aimed at developing the neighbourhood of Achada Grande Frente. With the suspension of funding, some members created *Korrenti di Ativiztas*, with the aim of setting up a network of community leaders. Silvia Stefani, "Resistência Urbana e Ativismo social na Praia: o caso da 'Korrenti di Ativiztas'", *Caderno de Estudos Africanos* 31 (2016): 69–94.

76 Zanildo Vaz Moreno, Amarildo (José Lito Fernandes), Djamine (Éder Jamine Garcia Fortes) and Capinero (Adérito Gonçalves Tavares), interviews, Praia, 9 February 2022.

77 Redy Wilson Lima, "Rap and representation of public space in Praia city", in *'Who we are' – 'Where we are': Identity, urban culture and languages of belongings Lusophone hip-hop*, ed. Rosana Martins and Massimo Canevacci (Oxford, Sean Kingston Publishing, 2018), 216.

78 Previously, in another context, the official ceremony in front of the memorial had been the scene of critical initiatives by political activists, with the "silent protest" by MAC#114 - Movement for Civic Action, on 20 January, 2015, its first public act. Two months later, in March 2015, the movement held a demonstration where around 4,000 to 5,000 protested against the new Statute for Holders of Public Office, which provided salary increases for politicians. There was even talk of the possibility of the movement becoming a political party, given the high profile it enjoyed at the time, but it ended up fracturing and disappeared. Cf. "MAC#114 quer ser a voz dos jovens", *A Nação*, February 15, 2015, https://anacao.cv/2015/02/15/mac114-quer-ser-voz-dos-jovens/.

154 *The Struggle and Cabral's Afterlives*

79 Zanildo Vaz Moreno, interview, Praia, 9 February 2022.
80 Capinero (Adérito Gonçalves Tavares), interview, Praia, 20 May 2019.
81 Capinero (Adérito Gonçalves Tavares), interview, Praia, 9 February 2022.
82 Zanildo Vaz Moreno, interview, Praia, 9 February 2022.
83 In the presentation of the last *Marxa*, the following was written in Cape Verdean Creole (which is, in itself, a political statement, since the norm is to use Portuguese in formal situations and in written texts): the intention was to "keep alive in the memory of Cape Verdean youth the enormous sacrifice made by Amílcar Cabral and his comrades in the fight for the independence of our beloved country, of Guinea-Bissau, and of all Africa". "8ª Marxa Kabral", Facebook, January, 2020. https://www.facebook.com/events/plateau-cabo-verde/8%C2%BA-marxa-kabral/589951608247418/.
84 For a particular critical appropriation of the concept coined by Marianne Hirsch, see, among others: Inês Nascimento Rodrigues, "Heranças de um massacre colonial: cinco notas sobre pós-memória em São Tomé e Príncipe", in *Heranças Pós-Coloniais nas literaturas em língua portuguesa*, ed. Margarida Calafate Ribeiro and Phillip Rothwell (Porto, Afrontamento, 2019), 167–179.
85 Zanildo Vaz Moreno, interview, Praia, 9 February 2022.
86 The possibilities of materialising a "public post-memory" have been enunciated by António Sousa Ribeiro, criticising the idea of the family as a privileged place of memorial transmission. Cf. António Sousa Ribeiro, "Memória", in *Patrimónios de Influência Portuguesa: modos de olhar*, ed. Walter Rossa and Margarida Calafate Ribeiro (Coimbra, Lisboa and Rio de Janeiro, Imprensa da Universidade de Coimbra, Fundação Calouste Gulbenkian and Editora da Universidade Federal Fluminense, 2015), 81–94.
87 Hayden White, "The practical past", *Historein* 10 (2010): 10–19.

Bibliography

Almada e Santos, Aurora and Victor Barros. "Introduction. Amílcar Cabral and the Idea of Anticolonial Revolution". *Lusotopie* 19 (2020): 9–35.

Amado, Abel Djassi. "Os três Cabrais de hoje em Cabo Verde: uma leitura necessária". *Buala*, 23 January 2012. https://www.buala.org/pt/mukanda/os-tres-cabrais-de-hoje-em-cabo-verde-uma-leitura-necessaria.

Ascher, Françoise. *Os Rabelados de Cabo Verde. História de uma Revolta*. Paris: L'Harmattan, 2011.

Bevernage, Berber and Nico Wouters, eds. *The Palgrave Handbook of State-Sponsored History After 1945*. London: Palgrave Macmillan, 2018.

Cabral, Iva. *A Primeira Elite Colonial Atlântica. Dos "homens honrados brancos" de Santiago à "nobreza da terra". Finais do séc. XV – início do séc. XVII*. Praia: Livraria Pedro Cardoso, 2015.

Carreira, António. *Migrações nas ilhas de Cabo Verde*. Praia: Instituto Caboverdiano do Livro, 2nd edition, 1983.

Carvalho, Celestino. "Media e Identidade Cultural de Minorias. Os "Rabelados" da comunidade de Espinho Branco, na Ilha de Santiago – Cabo Verde". Master diss., Universidade Aberta, 2020.

César, Filipa, Tobias Hering and Carolina Rito, org. *Luta ca caba inda: time place matter voice. 1967–2017*. Berlin: Archive Books, 2017.

Cunha, Paulo and Catarina Laranjeiro. "Guiné-Bissau: do cinema de Estado ao cinema fora do Estado". *Rebeca - Revista Brasileira de Estudos de Cinema e Audiovisual* 5, no. 2 (2017): 1–23.

De Barros, Miguel and Redy Wilson Lima. "Rap Kriol(u): o pan-africanismo de Cabral na música de intervenção juvenil na Guiné-Bissau e em Cabo Verde". *Realis – Revista de Estudos Antiutilitaristas e Pós-coloniais* 2, no. 2 (2012): 88–116.

De Barros, Miguel and Redy Wilson Lima. "RAP KRIOL(U): the pan-Africanism of Cabral in the music of youth". In *Claim no easy victories: the legacy of Amilcar Cabral*, edited by Firoze Manji and Bill Fletcher Jr., 387–404. Dakar: CODESRIA and Daraja Press, 2013.

dos Santos, Daniel. *Amílcar Cabral: um outro olhar*. Lisboa: Chiado Editora, 2014.

Fontes, Euclides. *Uma história inacabada*. Praia: Livraria Pedro Cardoso, 2018.

Gonçalves, Maria de Lourdes Silva. "Rabelados no Bacio e no Espinho Branco. Pontes e Portas na (re)formulação identitária do grupo". In *Ensaios Etnográficos na Ilha de Santiago Cabo Verde: Processos Identitários na Contemporaneidade*, edited by Maria Elisabeth Lucas and Sérgio Baptista da Silva, 229–262. Porto Alegre and Praia: Universidade Federal de Rio Grande do Sul and Universidade de Cabo Verde, 2009.

Lima, Redy Wilson. "Di kamaradas a irmons: o rap cabo-verdiano e a (re)construção de uma identidade de resistência". *Tomo* 37 (2020): 47–88.

Lima, Redy Wilson. "Hip-hop Praia: rap e representação do espaço público". In *Seminário Permanente em Estudos Africanos. Debates #4*, edited by Ana Maria Martinho Gale, 90–109. Lisboa: CHAM ebooks, 2018.

Lima, Redy Wilson. "Jovens, processos identitários e sociedades em movimento: um olhar sócio-antropológico sobre a emergência dos movimentos juvenis identitários na cidade da Praia, Cabo Verde". *African Development Review* 45, no. 3 (2020): 97–120.

Lima, Redy Wilson. "Marxa Kabral 2022". *Buala*, 20 January 2022. https://www.buala.org/pt/a-ler/marxa-cabral-2022.

Lima, Redy Wilson. "Rap and representation of public space in Praia city". In *'Who we are' – 'Where we are': Identity, urban culture and languages of belongings Lusophone hip-hop*, edited by Rosana Martins and Massimo Canevacci, 205–221. Oxford: Sean Kingston Publishing, 2018.

Lima, Redy Wilson. "Rap e Pesquisa Etnográfica". *Desafios* 3 (2016): 133–149.

Martins, João Pedro Abreu (with Catherine Borja). "Memorial Amílcar Cabral: O projeto de Óscar Niemeyer". In *Brasil – Cabo Verde: tópicos de relações culturais*, edited by Bruno Miranda Zétola and Mónica Andrade, 249–270. Praia: Embaixada do Brasil em Cabo Verde, 2018.

Martins, Pedro. *Testemunho de um Combatente*. Praia and Mindelo: Instituto Camões and Centro Cultural Português, 1995.

Monteiro Júnior, Júlio. *Os Rebelados da Ilha de Santiago, de Cabo Verde*. Praia: Centro de Estudos de Cabo Verde, 1974.

Pereira, Marilene and Coralie Tavares Silva. *A Turma do Cabralinho e o Búzio Mágico*. Praia: Corart & Graphic Design, 2019.

Pereira, Marilene and Renato Athayde. *Eu, Amílcar*. Praia: Fundação Amílcar Cabral, 2019.

Querido, Jorge. *Um demorado olhar sobre Cabo Verde – o país, sua génese, seu percurso, suas certezas e ambiguidades*. Praia: Self-published, 2013.

Rego, Márcia. *The Dialogic Nation of Cape Verde. Slavery, Language, and Ideology*. London: Lexington Books, 2015.

Ribeiro, António Sousa. "Memória". In *Patrimónios de Influência Portuguesa: modos de olhar*, edited by Walter Rossa and Margarida Calafate Ribeiro, 81–94. Coimbra, Lisboa and Rio de Janeiro: Imprensa da Universidade de

156　*The Struggle and Cabral's Afterlives*

Coimbra, Fundação Calouste Gulbenkian and Editora da Universidade Federal Fluminense, 2015.

Rigney, Ann. "The Dynamics of Remembrance: Texts Between Monumentality and Morphing". In *Cultural Memory Studies: An International and Interdisciplinary Handbook*, edited by Astrid Erll and Ansgar Nünning, 345–353. Berlin /New York: De Gruyter, 2010.

Robalo, Alexsandro. "Música e Poder em Cabo Verde: das práticas contestatárias dos jovens 'rappers' à potencialidade 'castradora' do Estado". *Desafios* 3 (2016): 103–130.

Rodrigues, Inês Nascimento. "Heranças de um massacre colonial: cinco notas sobre pós-memória em São Tomé e Príncipe". In *Heranças Pós-Coloniais nas literaturas em língua portuguesa*, edited by Margarida Calafate Ribeiro and Phillip Rothwell, 167–179. Porto: Afrontamento, 2019.

Rosa, Ricardo D. "Cape Verdean Counter Cultural Hip-Hop(s) & the Mobilization of the Culture of Radical Memory: Public Pedagogy for Liberation or Continued Colonial Enslavement". *Journal of Cape Verdean Studies* 3, no. 1 (2018): 92–113.

Silva, António Correia e. "Dinâmicas de decomposição e recomposição de espaços e sociedades". In *História Geral de Cabo Verde. Volume III*, edited by Maria Emília Madeira Santos, 1–66. Lisboa and Praia: Instituto de Investigação Científica Tropical and Direcção-Geral do Património Cultural de Cabo Verde, 2002.

Sousa, Mário Lúcio. *O Diabo foi meu padeiro*. Lisboa: D. Quixote, 2019.

Stefani, Silvia. "Resistência Urbana e Ativismo social na Praia: o caso da 'Korrenti di Ativiztas'". *Caderno de Estudos Africanos* 31 (2016): 69–94.

Varela, João Silvestre T. A. "Identidade(s) e Nacionalismo(s) em Cabo Verde". PhD diss., Universidade Federal Fluminense, 2008.

Vasconcelos, João. "Espíritos lusófonos numa ilha crioula: língua, poder e identidade em São Vicente de Cabo Verde". In *A Persistência da História. Passado e contemporaneidade em África*, edited by Clara Carvalho and João de Pina Cabral, 149–190. Lisboa: Imprensa de Ciências Sociais, 2004.

Vaz, Cláudia and Ricardo Campos. "Rap e graffiti na Kova da Moura como mecanismos de reflexão identitária de jovens afrodescendentes". *Sociedade e Cultura* 16, no. 1 (2013): 129–141.

Verdery, Katherine. *The Political Lives of Dead Bodies. Reburial and Postsocialist Change*. New York: Columbia University Press, 1999.

White, Hayden. "The practical past". *Historein* 10 (2010): 10–19.

Young, Robert. *Poscolonialism. A Very Short Introduction*. London: Oxford University Press, 2003.

Legislation

Boletim Oficial da República de Cabo Verde, no. 27, 26 July 1993.

Newspapers

Expresso das Ilhas, A Nação, Notícias do Norte, Novo Jornal de Cabo Verde, Ponto Final, A Semana, Voz di Povo.

Interviews

Baptista, João [Fico]. Audio-recorded interview with Miguel Cardina and Inês Nascimento Rodrigues. Espinho Branco, 18 May 2019.

The Struggle and Cabral's Afterlives   157

Cabral, Iva. Audio-recorded interview with Miguel Cardina and Inês Nascimento Rodrigues. Praia, 19 January 2019.

Cardoso, Humberto. Audio-recorded interview with Miguel Cardina and Inês Nascimento Rodrigues. Praia, 4 July 2019.

Delgado, António Jorge. Written interview with Miguel Cardina and Inês Nascimento Rodrigues. Email, 31 December 2019.

Fernandes, José Lito (Amarildo). Video and audio-recorded interview with Miguel Cardina, Inês Nascimento Rodrigues and Diana Andringa. Praia, 9 February 2022.

Fortes, Éder Jamine Garcia (Djamine). Video and audio-recorded interview with Miguel Cardina. Praia, 9 February 2022.

Josefa. Audio-recorded interview with Miguel Cardina and Inês Nascimento Rodrigues. Espinho Branco, 18 May 2019.

Moreno, Zanildo Vaz. Video and audio-recorded interview with Miguel Cardina, Inês Nascimento Rodrigues and Diana Andringa. Praia, 9 February 2022.

Pereira, Moisés Lopes (Tchetcho). Video and áudio-recorded interview with Miguel Cardina, Inês Nascimento Rodrigues and Diana Andringa. Praia, 9 February 2022.

Pires, Pedro. Audio-recorded interview with Miguel Cardina, Inês Nascimento Rodrigues and Bruno Sena Martins. Praia, 18 January 2020.

Tavares, Adérito Gonçalves Tavares (Capinero). Audio-recorded interview with Miguel Cardina. Praia, 20 May 2019.

Tavares, Adérito Gonçalves Tavares (Capinero). Video and audio-recorded interview with Miguel Cardina, Inês Nascimento Rodrigues and Diana Andringa. Praia, 9 February 2022.

Vicente, Abraão. Audio-recorded interview with Miguel Cardina, Inês Nascimento Rodrigues and Bruno Sena Martins. Praia, 16 January 2020.

Film / Video

Andringa, Diana, dir. *Guiné-Bissau: da memória ao futuro*. Lisbon and Coimbra, PT: Garden Films and CES, 2019.

Gomes, Flora and José Bolama, Josefina Crato and Sana na N'Hada, dir. *O Regresso de Amílcar Cabral*. Bissau, GB: Instituto Nacional de Cinema e Audiovisual, 1976.

Lopes, Valério, dir. *Cabralista*. Cape Verde and Luxemburg: Medeo, 2011.

Murteira, Jorge, dir. *Rebelados no Fim dos Tempos*. Lisbon, PT: Quevídeo II Filmes, 2002.

EPILOGUE

The liberation struggle has become a central mnemonic device in the post-colonial life of Cape Verde. In pursuing this line of thought, this book has sought to construct a history of the memory of the liberation struggle, focusing on the ways in which it has been remembered and activated as part of the socio-political disputes that have marked the archipelago since 1975. Taking the *struggle* as an interpretative code, it is possible to glimpse a kind of alternative history of the archipelago, which in turn allows us to problematise, albeit in general terms, the political role of memory in the formation of contemporary states and nations. We therefore set out to scrutinise nearly half a century of political memories and memory policies in Cape Verde, examining the different occasions, actors, stages and contexts that formed the basis for producing and negotiating distinct evocative repertoires about the struggle and the country. We took a particularly close look at the discourses and actions of the State, its rulers and political decision-makers, in conjunction with former combatants, with civil society and with the various forms of expressing the anticolonial imaginary within the country.

"Birth certificate" of Cape Verde as an independent nation, the evocation of the liberation struggle played, immediately after 1975, a decisive role in legitimising the new political actors but also in the political, cultural, social and economic redefinition of the archipelago. It provided a framework for governing and building the post-independence State, in which the presence of the imaginary of the *struggle* was part of the effort to make the new country viable. The political transition in the early 1990s brought with it a questioning of the place of the liberation struggle, its protagonists and the dominant vision it had sought to express about the country. In an adverse international context, anti-colonialism was giving way to attempts at recovering pre-independence figures and moments, in a repositioning of the nation's memorial landscape that included dynamics of "de-Africanisation" and "de-Cabralisation". Later on, more or less over the last decade, the struggle regained its status as a particularly active signifier in the archipelago and its "public postmemory", being enacted by movements and performances such as *Marxa Kabral*. This

Epilogue 159

allows politicised sectors of the new generations to relate to the memories inherited from the past, re-conducting and transforming them as dialogically in the present.

The importance of the liberation struggle lies not only in the value it has been given historically. In fact, as this book seeks to demonstrate, it has become a decisive catalyst for political, social, historical and cultural narratives, (re)positions, agendas and options. It was in this sense that the liberation struggle has been defined here as a mnemonic device: it is both a historical event that is enshrined in the origins of independent Cape Verde and a memorial event that expresses itself as a stage for ideological disputes. The *struggle* as a mnemonic device is a disseminator of strategic multi-directionalities, the object of political uses and a generator of multifaceted senses of the future.

ACKNOWLEDGEMENTS

We would like to thank the following people:

All the interviewees, duly listed in the bibliography, for sharing their memories and knowledge.

The staff of the National Archive, the National Library, the Institute of Cultural Heritage (IPC) and the Archives of the National Assembly and the Presidency of the Republic, who kindly opened their doors to us in the city of Praia, Cape Verde. Very special thanks also go to the Association of Liberation Struggle Combatants (ACOLP), the Amilcar Cabral Foundation (FAC) and the Pedro Pires Institute (IPP) for the generosity and trust with which they received us, for their willingness to answer our questions and requests and for the experience in co-organising events over these last few years. We are also grateful to the Amilcar Cabral Chair and the University of Cape Verde (Uni-CV) for the timely and meaningful joint initiatives.

We would like to make a special mention of the friends that Cape Verde has given us along this (and other) path(s), for their support and friendship: Ângela Coutinho, Catarina "Pinina" Ressureição, Celeste Fortes, César Schofield Cardoso, Crisanto Barros, Eurídice Monteiro, Indira Pires, Irene Cruz, José Neves, Luhena Correia de Sá, Odair Barros-Varela, Olívio "Baka" Pires, Patrícia (Patti) Anahory, Redy Wilson Lima and Tatiana Neves. A special mention to Pedro Pires and Carlos Reis, who kindly hosted us over the years and shared their memories. It has been a privilege. A word of appreciation and recognition to Adérito Gonçalves Tavares (Capinero), Éder Jamine Garcia Fortes (Djamine), José Lito Fernandes (Amarildo), Zanildo Vaz Moreno and all the members of Associação Pilorinhu for receiving us and letting us know about the inspiring work they have been doing.

To Adelaide Monteiro, Amélia Santos, Ana Cristina Duarte Ferreira, Ângelo Lopes, Antonieta Lopes, Astrigilda Silveira, Carlos Santos, Clara Marques, Djalita Fialho, Edson Brito, Edson Moniz Moreno, Irlando Ferreira, Iva Cabral, João Lopes Filho, João Pedro Campos, João Pedro Martins, Jorge Querido, José Martins, José Vicente Lopes, Júlio Martins,

Acknowledgements 161

Lívio César Duarte Spencer, Lourenço Gomes, Luís Miguel Lima, Maria do Carmo Piçarra, Marilene Pereira, Martinho Robalo de Brito, Matilde Santos, Nélida Brito, Nuno Martins, Pedro Martins, Risa Fortes, Rita Raínho, Teresinha Araújo, Tia Loló (Glória Martins) and members of *Rabelados* community from Espinho Branco: we express our gratitude for the readiness with which they made themselves present and available. Our thanks and indebtedness to Diltino Ferreira, our Cape Verdean language teacher for the exciting lessons and for the help in translating the two excerpts of *Os Tubarões* lyrics and the poem "Batuku". And a word of appreciation to Richard Sidaway, who translated a first draft version of this book to English. Many thanks also to the Centro de Intervenção para o Desenvolvimento Amílcar Cabral (CIDAC); Camões, I. P.; the Portuguese Embassy in Cape Verde; the National Center of Arts and Crafts and Design (CNAD), in S. Vicente; and the newspaper *A Nação*.

Thanks to Bruno Sena Martins, companion on trips and in long conversations, for his support and continual suggestions, especially in the initial phase of writing this book. To the whole CROME project team, André Caiado, Diana Andringa, Natália Bueno, Sílvia Roque, Teresa Almeida Cravo, Vasco Martins and Verónica Ferreira, as well as various other colleagues for discussing ideas and concepts with us. To André Queda, who is responsible for the Cape Verde's map artwork displayed in the introduction of this book. To the Centre for Social Studies, the home that encourages us to think. And, of course, special thanks also to our editor Neil Jordan and all the team at Routledge, Memory Studies: Global Constellations series, who made this book possible. We also owe a debt of gratitude for suggestions and encouragement from the anonymous reviewer. The photographs reproduced in chapter one are courtesy of Bruna Polimeni and Fundação Mário Soares e Maria Barroso, as the credits and captions duly indicate. Our gratitude to them, to Fondazione Lelio e Lisli Basso and to Paula Gonçalves, from Fundação Mário Soares e Maria Barroso.

Research for *Remembering the Liberation Struggles. A Mnemohistory of Cape Verde* was conducted within the scope of CROME – *Crossed Memories, Politics of Silence. The Colonial-Liberation War in Postcolonial Times*, a project funded by the European Research Council (ERC), under the European Union's Horizon 2020 Framework Programme for Research and Innovation (StG-ERC-715593) based at the Centre for Social Studies of the University of Coimbra. Chapter Two is partially based on preliminary ideas presented by Miguel Cardina and Inês Nascimento Rodrigues in an article originally published as "The mnemonic transition: The rise of an anti-anticolonial memoryscape in Cape Verde", *Memory Studies* 14, no 2 (2021): 380–394. SAGE Publishing. DOI: 10.1177/1750698020927735.

INDEX

Note: *Italicized* page numbers refer to figures. Page numbers followed by "n" refer to notes.

Abel Djassi Pioneers Organization 25, 32, 33
Accra 29
Achada Grande Frente 129, 130, *130*, 142
ACOLP (Association of Liberation Struggle Combatants) 93, 95, 96, 99, *99*, 102–105, 125, 134
Adi, Hakim 123
Afonso, Diogo 64, 67, *67*
Africa 1, 5, 9, 60; colonial presence in 3
African Commandos 36
Africanness 40, 69, 74, 77
Agamben, Giorgio 6
Agrarian Reform (1981) 37, 62, 70
Algeria 5, 123
Algiers Agreement 18
Almada, David Hopffer 33, 117n62
Almada, Janira Hopffer 117n62
Almeida, Germano: *Morte do Meu Poeta, A* [My Poet's Death] 70; *O Dia das Calças Roladas* [The Day of the Rolled-Up Trousers] 70; *O Meu Poeta* [My Poet] 70
Alves, Maria Isabel ('Misá') 139
Amado, Abel Djassi 131
Amado, Leopoldo 35
Amílcar Cabral Foundation *see* FAC (Amílcar Cabral Foundation)
Amílcar Cabral Memorial, Praia 9, *125*
Amílcar Cabral: um Outro Olhar [Amílcar Cabral: a Different View] (Daniel dos Santos) 131–132
Amura Fort 121, 148n4
Andrade, Mário Pinto de 4, 101
Andrade, Mayra 68

Angola 3, 5, 30-31
Anjos, José Carlos Gomes dos 41, 78
anti-colonialism 8, 79, 158
anti-colonial struggle 3, 5, 15, 19, 20, 31, 35, 59, 60, 66, 101, 111, 121, 129, 147
Antilles 2, 39
anti-totalitarianism 59
Araújo, Amélia 100
Araújo, Ana Lúcia 12n14
armed struggle 3–6, 9, 18, 20, 23, 24, 26, 31, 35, 42, 47n43, 60, 64, 71, 72, 74, 78, 91, 93, 94, 96–98, 100, 101, 105, 106, 108, 122
Arrighi, Giovanni 59
Arsenal Institute 147n1
assimilation 39, 40
Assistência Disaster 30–31
Assmann, Jan 7
Athayde, Renato 135
Aventura e Rotina [Adventure and Routine] (Gilberto Freyre) 39
Azevedo, Osvaldo 84n58
Azores 74

Badiu/Badio 29, 40, 124, 136
Bairro Craveiro Lopes (Bairro Kwame Nkrumah) 69
Baltasar Lopes da Silva Foundation 66
Bank of Cape Verde 22
Bankslave 130
Barbosa, Emanuel 134
Barbosa, Jorge 84n58
Barbosa, Kaká 68
Barlavento 1
Barros, Crisanto 24, 51n111

Barros, Victor 21–22, 45n28
batuku 30, 31, 33, 34, 41, 49n69, 68, 143
Batuku (Kaoberdiano Dambará) 30, 31, 161
BBC World Histories Magazine 123
Belgium 48n61
Bella, Ahmed Ben 101
Bevernage, Berber 7
Bissau 35, 36, 50n97, 11n6, 121, 147n1
Boal, Lilica 134–135
Boa Vista 1
Branco, João 34
Brazil 2, 129
Brito, Alcides 49n71
Brito, Wladimir 73
Bulimundo 34

Cabo Verde. Os Bastidores da Independência [Cape Verde. Independence Behind the Scenes] (José Vicente Lopes) 105
Cabo Verde. Subsídios para a História da nossa Luta de Libertação [Cape Verde. Subsidies for the History of our Liberation Struggle] (Jorge Querido) 97
Cabo Verde. Um corpo que se recusa a morrer. 70 anos contra fome, 1949–2019 (Cape Verde. A body that refuses to die. 70 years against hunger. 1949–2019) (José Vicente Lopes) 22
Cabral, Iva 125, 126, 149n16
Cabral, Lopes Amílcar 3, 8, 9, 11n6, 15, *16*, 18–21, 25, 28–29, 34, 35, 40, 41, 43, 47n43, 101, 105, 112, 140; afterlives 121–147; alternative representations 135–141; anti-democratic stance 36; assassination of 4, 31, 107; birth of 4; early life 4; memory 123–131; portrait *26, 27*; questioning 131–135
Cabral, Luís 11n6, 35, 36
Cabral ca mori/Cabral ka mori 32, 141, 144
Cabralist 112, 142, 143
Cabralista (Valério Lopes) 148n8
Camões, Luís Vaz de 66, 67, *68*; *Os Lusíadas* 64
"Campo de Trabalho de Chão Bom" *see* Tarrafal Penal Colony
Canaries 74

Cântico da Liberdade [Hymn of Freedom] (Amílcar Spencer Lopes) 76
Cape Verde: archipelago 1; armed struggle 3–6, 9, 18, 20, 23, 24, 26, 31, 35, 42, 47n43, 60, 64, 71, 72, 74, 78, 91, 93, 94, 96–98, 100, 101, 105, 106, 108, 122; cultural heritage 34; ecological vulnerability 19; end of union with Guinea-Bissau 35–37, 42, 74; flags *73*; GDP 79n4; and Guinea-Bissau, bi-national unity between 28, 36, 43n10; independence 3, 15, 18, 29, 33, 72, 158; liberation struggle 1–10, 31; Ministry of Education and Culture 31; mnemonic transition 59–78; mobilisation and clandestine struggle 5; political transition 8, 60–64, 81n26, 107, 158; population 1, 31; State 95
Cape Verdean Armed Forces 5
Cape Verdean Association of Ex-Political Prisoners 102
Cape Verdean Book Institute 41
Cape Verdean Women's Organisation 32
Capinero (Adérito Gonçalves Tavares) 144
capital: cultural 24, 62; economic 62; foreign 61; symbolic 24, 25, 71, 122
Cardoso, Humberto 70, 132; *O Partido Único em Cabo Verde: um assalto à esperança* [The Single-Party in Cape Verde: an assault on hope] 132
Cardoso, Renato 31–32, 62, 141
Carnation Revolution 3, 5, 31
Carreira, António 84n58
Castelhano, Mário 98
Castro, Fidel 71
Catholic Church 24–25, 62, 137
Celestino, Celso 94–95
Centeio, Sérgio 101
Chabal, Patrick 45n28
China 9, 124
Chissano, Joaquim 71
Christian rationalism 141
Chow, David 148n10
CIDAC (Amílcar Cabral Information and Documentation Centre) 35, 50n97
Cidade Velha 136
Cidra, Rui 48n63, 50n84

164   Index

CILSS (Inter-State Committee for
Drought Control in the Sahel) 79n4
civil society 61, 63, 94, 158
Claridade 38–41, 65, 66, 106, 128
Claridosos 72, 81n28
CNCV (National Commission
of Cape Verde) 24, 37
Coat of Arms *73*
Codé di Dona 106
Coelho, João Paulo Borges 5–6
Coimbra 97, 148n3
coladeira 41
Cold War 22, 59
colonialism 5, 8, 15, 18, 20, 21, 28, 69,
94, 129, 148n4; Portuguese 1, 9, 25,
31, 60, 84n58, 93, 108, 111
combatants *see* LSC (Liberation
Struggle Combatants)
Conchiglia, Augusta 101
CONCP (Conference of Nationalist
Organizations of the Portuguese
Colonies) 4
Conference of Nationalist
Organizations of Guinea and the
Cape Verde Islands 20
Congregation of the Holy Spirit 137
constitutional transition 81n26
Correia e Silva, António 2, 38, 51n112,
61–62
Correia e Silva, Ulisses 115n36
Council of the Revolution 35, 36
Coutinho, Ângela 18, 26, 148n6
Crato, Josefina 147n1
Craveiro Lopes District (Kwame
Nkrumah District) 68, 69
Creole 29, 34, 110, 143; identity 40,
69, 130
Cuba 5, 49n69
cultural nationalism 31
currency (the *escudo*) 77, *77*, 106

Dakar 17, 20, 29, 43n10
Dambará, Kaoberdiano (Felisberto
Vieira Lopes) 31, 34; *Batuku* 30, 31,
161; *Noti* 29
Dantas, Agnelo 36
Davidson, Basil 101
de-Africanisation 9, 77, 124, 158
de-Cabralisation 70, 77, 124, 158
Delgado, António Jorge 132
democratic legitimacy 64, 69
"Dimokransa" (Káká Barbosa) 68
Diouf, Abdou 71
Directorate General of Culture 32

Djarama 33
Djassi, Abel 33
Djassi, Rui Demba 148n4
Djuntarti 142, 153n74
domination 5, 109, 135, 136; colonial
15, 18, 27–29
dos Santos, Daniel: *Amílcar Cabral:
um Outro Olhar* [Amílcar Cabral:
a Different View] 131–132
Duarte, Abílio 15, 24, 41

Eastern Europe / Eastern Bloc 59,
121–122
Economic Community of West
African States 129
economic liberalisation 60
EMPA (*Empresa de Abastecimento
Público*, Public Supply Company) 22
Entre Duas Bandeiras [Between
Two Flags] (Teixeira de Sousa) 64
Erll, Astrid 79n4
Espinho Branco 139, 140
Estado Novo regime 3, 97, 98
EU (European Union) 73, 82n45, 129
Eu, Amílcar (Marilene Pereira) 135
Europe 5, 60
Évora, Cesária 106, 134
exploitation 5, 104, 135, 136, 140

FAC (Amílcar Cabral Foundation) 99,
102, 134, 146, 148n6
FAIMO (*Frentes de Alta Intensidade
de Mão-de-Obra*, Labour-Intensive
Work Fronts) 22, 62
famines 16, 19–22, 31, 36, 38, 39, 45n28,
48n61, 51n112, 91 (*see also* hunger)
Fanon, Franz 123
FARP (People's Revolutionary
Armed Forces) 15, 33, 36, 71
Faustino, Manuel 48n63, 97, 101,
113n10; *Jorge Querido: subsídios sob
suspeita* [Jorge Querido: subsidies
under suspicion] 97
Feindt, Gregor 7
Fernandes, Gabriel 52n124
Fernandes, José Lito (Amarildo)
153n76
Fernando, Nhô (Rabelados) 138, 139
Ferreira, Armindo 82n45, 133
Fico (João Baptista) 129, *130*, 141
Fidalgo de Barros, António 62
Fidjus di Cabral 153n74
fighters 24, 26, 29, 31, 44n16, 69, 75,
84n58, 101, 108, 110, 130, 134

Index 165

Figueiredo, João de 66
finason 30, 32, 68
First Republic 42, 60, 62, 63, 65, 70–72, 74, 78, 91, 92, 109
FITEI (*Festival Internacional de Teatro de Expressão Ibérica*, International Festival of Iberian Expression Theatre) 34
FNLG (National Front for the Liberation of Guinea) 43n10
Fogo 1, 2, 10n2, 64, 66, 81n28, 137, 138
Fonseca, Aguinaldo 40
Fonseca, Jorge Carlos 81n26, 101, 105–108, 110, 113n10
Fonseca, Luís 92, 102–103
Fontes, Euclides 138
forced labour 19, 20
forced migrations 19, 106
foreign capital 61
Fortes, Celeste 100
Fortes, Éder Jamine Garcia (Djamine) 153n76
Fortes, Paula 100
Forti, Dina 101
Foucault, Michel 6
FRAIN (African Revolutionary Front for National Independence) 4
France 5
Freedom and Democracy Day 107
FRELIMO 5
Freyre, Gilberto 39
funaná 33, 34, 41, 50n84, 106
Fundação Mário Soares e Maria Barroso *16*, *26*, *27*
Furtado, Cláudio 25, 75, 97
Furtado, Joaquim 138

Gil Eanes High School, Mindelo 25, 51n116
Global South 59, 69
Gomes, Diogo 64, 66–68, *67*, 126–127, 143
Gomes, Flora 121, 147n1
Gonçalves, António Aurélio 84n58
Gonçalves, Bento 98
Gonçalves, Maria de Lourdes Silva 152n54
Gonçalves, Vasco 15
Górna, Ada 68
Górny, Krzysztof 68
Graça, Aires Leitão da 17
Graça, José Leitão da 17, 105

Graça, Maria Leitão da 17
GRIS (Revolutionary Group of Socialist Intervention) 46n34
Guinea-Bissau 3, 5, 8, 9, 17, 26, 33, 73, 75, 95, 142; armed struggle 72; and Cape Verde, bi-national unity between 27, 28, 36, 42, 74; end of union with Cape Verde 35–37, 121; independence 44n13
Guinea Conakry 4, 5, 92, 95
Guinean Armed Forces 121
Gulf of Guinea 2, 19
Gusmão, Xanana 71
Guterres, António 71

Hirsch, Marianne 154n84
historical justice 65, 79n3
Hobsbawm, Eric 59
Holland 5, 129; Cape-Verdean migrants 63
House of the Students of the Empire/*Casa de Estudantes do Império* 4, 40
Human Development Index 79n4
hunger 8, 19, 20, 22, 106, 109

IAC (Amílcar Cabral Institute) 25, 47n46
Ignatiev, Oleg 101
Ilhéu de Contenda [Teixeira de Sousa / Leão Lopes] 81n28
INCA (National Institute for Cinema and Audiovisual) 147n1
Independence Day 132–133
Inocêncio, Manuel 84n67
International Monetary Fund 59–60, 129

JAAC (Amílcar Cabral African Youth) 25, 32
Já está em USA 149n13
John Paul II, Pope 62, 80n21
Jorge Querido: subsídios sob suspeita [Jorge Querido: subsidies under suspicion] (Manuel Faustino) 97
Josefa (Rabelado) 140, *140*, 141
Júnior, Júlio Monteiro 137–138

Kanhubai 139
Kany, Inocêncio 4
Kaoguiamo 31
Kennedy, John 141
King, Martin Luther 141
Kondé, Kwame (Francisco Gomes Fragoso) 34

166 *Index*

Korda Kaoberdi [Wake Up Cape Verde] 34
Korda Skrabu! Unidade Guiné-Cabo Verde [Awaken, Slave! Guinea-Cape Verde Union] 31
Korrenti di Ativiztas 142, 153n75
Koudawo, Fafali 61, 62, 81n26

Labanta Braço 32
Landim, Nhonhô (Luís Gomes de Pina) 138
legitimacy: democratic 64, 69; of independence 64; political 5, 70; symbolic 5
Leite, Luís Sousa Nobre 113n10
liberal capitalism 59
Liberation Script 6
liberation struggle 158; centrality of 17–28; as cradle of the independent nation 15–43; memorial flows 26–17; as mnemonic device 1–10, 16, 21, 147, 159; in mnemonic transition 8–9, 59–86; recalibrating memory 37–42; "return to Africa" through music 28–34; between two ruptures 42–43
Liceu Domingos Ramos see Liceu Nacional da Praia
Liceu Gil Eanes 47n43
Liceu Nacional da Praia 47n43
Liceu Nacional de Cabo Verde see Liceu Gil Eanes
Lima, Redy Wilson 126, 142, 153n74
Lisbon 4, 24, 32, 35, 48n63, 97, 148n8
Lisbon Agreement 18
LOPE (Law on the Political Organization of the State) 17, 43n6
Lopes, Amílcar Spencer: *Cântico da Liberdade* [Hymn of Freedom] 76; "Peace and Labour" 76
Lopes, Francisco Craveiro 68, 69
Lopes, Gilson Varela 126, 127
Lopes, João 39
Lopes, José Vicente 20, 40, 65; *Cabo Verde. Os Bastidores da Independência* [Cape Verde. Independence Behind the Scenes] 105; *Cabo Verde. Um corpo que se recusa a morrer. 70 anos contra fome, 1949–2019* 22
Lopes, Leão 81n28, 124
Lopes, Manuel 84n58
Lopes, Pedro Gregório 73–74, 84n66
Lopes, Valério: *Cabralista* 148n8

Lopes da Silva, Baltasar (Baltasar Lopes) 38–39, 41-42, 51n116, 66-67, 77
Lopes da Silva, Osvaldo 24
LSC (Liberation Struggle Combatants) 9, 15, 18, 35, 43, 44n16, 50n84, 71, 72, 78, 83n56, 90–112, *104*; composite memorial framework 111–112; construction of 91–99; diversification of the image 105–111; political disputes 99–105; public recognition 99–105; struggle and image of 90–112
Luísa, Domingos 149n13
Luso-tropicalism 39, 40, 52n118
Luz, Silvino da 24

MAC (Anti-Colonial Movement) 4, 11n6
MAC#114 153n78
Macaronesia 74
Madeira 74
Maharaja Ranjit Singh 123
Maio 1, 62, 150n24
Manalvo, Nuno 69
Mariano, Gabriel 84n58
Marques, Silvino Silvério 137
Martins, Carlos Alberto (Catchás) 34
Martins, Ovídio 31, 34
Martins, Pedro 84n58, 97, 135, 151n3
Martins, Vasco 85n76
Marxa Kabral/Marxa 142–147, *145, 146*, 149n10, 158
Matos, Rui 149n13
Mausoleum of Amílcar Cabral *122*
memorialising State 7
memoryscape/memorial landscape 6–9, 60, 61, 64, 69, 77, 78, 80n11, 127, 143, 158, 161
Memory Studies 60
Mendes, Francisco 148n4
Meyns, Peter 97
MFA (Armed Forces Movement) 3
Mindelo 1, 18, 34, 47n43, 64, 65, 67
miscegenation 17, 39, 40
MLG (Guinean Liberation Movement) 11n6
MLICV (Movement for the Liberation of Cape Verde Islands) 43–44n10
mnemography 7
mnemohistory 7, 12n17
mnemonic device, liberation struggle as 1–12, 16, 21, 147, 159
mnemonic hegemony 8, 95
mnemonic signifier 7

Index 167

mnemonic transition 8–9, 59–78;
change in national symbols 72–77,
73, 77; political transition 61–63;
reasons and circumstances 77–78;
remembrance, new paradigm of
69–72; removed images, return of
64–69
mobilisation 7, 16, 32, 94, 123;
political 5, 21, 31
modernisation of popular music 33
Moita, Luís 50n97
Molden, Berthold 8
Moniz, Father 138
Monteiro, António Mascarenhas 63,
66, 71, 72, 84n58, 95, 140
Monteiro, Eurico 96, 113n10, 114n19
Monteiro, João José (UV) 142
Monteiro, Júlio 151n49
Monteiro, Leão do Sacramento 66
morabeza 31, 110, 129
morna 41, 106, 134
Morte do Meu Poeta, A [My Poet's
Death] (Germano Almeida) 70
Mozambique 3, 5; liberation
struggle 31
MpD (Movement for Democracy)
63, 66, 69, 71, 72, 74–78, 82n42,
95, 96, 100, 104–106, 113n10,
114n19, 115n36, 134, 140; Political
Committee 70
MPLA (People's Movement for the
Liberation of Angola) 101
multidirectional memory 21
multi-party systems 8, 59, 94, 111, 115n36
Murteira, Jorge 151n50
Museum of the National Liberation
Struggle 148n4
Música cabo-verdiana. Protesto e Luta
[Cape Verdean Music. Protest and
Struggle] 31

Na Isna, Pansau 148n4
Na N'Hada, Sana 121, 147n1
National Assembly 17
National Heroes' Day 26, 107, 125
national symbols, change in 72–77,
73, 77
nation state, building 17–28
neoliberalism 59, 61, 78n3
Neto, António Agostinho 4, 101
Neves, José Maria 106, 115n36
Nha Nácia Gomi (or Inásia Gómi,
born Maria Inácia Gomes
Correia) 68

Niemeyer, Óscar 9, 123, 124
Non-Aligned Movement 22
Noti (Kaoberdiano Dambará) 29

OAU (Organization of African Unity)
18, 44n13
O Dia das Calças Roladas [The Day of
the Rolled-Up Trousers] (Germano
Almeida) 70
O Meu Poeta [My Poet] (Germano
Almeida) 70
Oporto 46n34
*O Partido único em Cabo Verde: um
assalto à esperança* [The Single-
Party in Cape Verde: an assault on
hope] (Humberto Cardoso) 70, 132
oppression 20, 31, 59, 70, 111, 138
Oramas, Óscar 101
Order of Amílcar Cabral (Medal of
the) 71, 83n56, 100, 101, 107
O Regresso de Cabral [The Return of
Cabral] 121
Os Lusíadas (Camões) 64
Os Tubarões 32

PAI (African Party for Independence)
4, 11n6
PAICV (African Party for the
Independence of Cape Verde) 8, 25,
37, 41, 42, 83n48, 132; LSCs 94, 95,
99, 103, 105–107, 115n36, 117n62;
mnemonic transition and 63, 69,
70, 72, 74, 75, 77, 78, 80n21, 80n23;
National Council 61; political
transition 61
PAIGC (African Party for the
Independence of Guinea and
Cape Verde) 3, 9, 11n6, 15, 18, 20,
22, 24, 25, 27, 31, 35–37, 44n13,
48n61, 51n116, 102, 105, 123, 132,
138–141; armed struggle 4, 47n43;
combat zones in Guinea 91; cultural
services 29; flag 140, *140*; hegemony
5; liberation struggle 132; LSCs
90–96, 101, 103, 105, 113n10, 115n36;
mnemonic transition and 69, 70,
71, 73, 77, 78, 83n55; mobilisation
50n93; Pilot School 100; Second
Congress 37–38, 147n1; Superior
Council of Struggle 47n46; Third
Congress 33
Palme, Olof 141
PALOPs (Portuguese-speaking
African Countries) 79n4

168   *Index*

Pan-Africanism 73
Pan-Africanist Movement 142
PCD (Democratic Convergence
  Party) 113n10, 114n19
"Peace and Labour" (Amílcar
  Spencer Lopes) 76
People's National Assembly 93
Pépé Lopi 32
Pereira, Aristides 11n6, 18–19, 22, 36,
  41, 42, 44n13, 62, 63, 80n21, 93, 105,
  106, 112n6, 134
Pereira, Marilene: *Eu, Amílcar* 135;
  *Turma do Cabralinho e o Búzio
  Mágico, A* [Cabralinho's Gang and
  the Magic Whelk] 134
Pereira, Moisés Lopes
  (Tchetcho) 152n63
PIDE and PIDE/DGS 93, 97
Pilorinhu 129, 142, 143, 144
Pinto, Serpa (Alexandre) 64, 66, *68*,
  81n29
Pires, Pedro 17, 20–21, 24, 32, 36,
  37, 45n30, 69, *99*, 99–101, 108–109,
  115n36, 134, 136
Pires, Olívio 24, 50n84
pluralism 94
Poesia cabo-verdiana. Protesto e Luta
  [Cape Verdean Poetry. Protest and
  Struggle] 31
Polimeni, Bruna *26*, 101
political appropriation 1, 7
political autonomy 28, 31, 41
political disputes 99–105
political liberalisation 60
political mobilisation 5, 21, 31
political transition 8, 60–64, 81n26,
  107, 158
Portugal 2, 5, 129; colonialism 1, 9,
  25, 31, 60, 84n58, 93, 108, 111;
  liberation struggle 3; Luso-
  tropicalism 39; mobilisation and
  clandestine struggle 5; National
  Assembly 65
Portuguese Colonial Empire,
  legitimacy of 39
Portuguese Communist Party 98
Praça Nova (Praça Amílcar
  Cabral) 67
Praia 1, 9, 15, 31, 139; Amílcar
  Cabral Memorial 9, *125*;
  Information and Propaganda
  Sub-Commission 33; Municipality
  144; Praia-80 Festival 33

privatisation 59
protest 141–147
public recognition 99–105

Querido, Jorge 84n58, 97, 98, 138; *Cabo
  Verde. Subsídios para a História
  da nossa Luta de Libertação* [Cape
  Verde. Subsidies for the History of
  our Liberation Struggle] 97
Querido, Jorge (Ioti Kunta) 29
Quina, Carolina 50n97

Rabelados community, culture
  and art 129, *130*, 136-142, 151n49,
  151n51, 151n53
race/racism 5, 77, 129; ostracism 66
Rádio Barlavento 18, 39
Rádio Libertação 29, 100, 148n4
Rádio São Vicente 18
Rádio Voz do Povo 18
Rai di Tabanka [King of Tabanka] 34
Raínho, Rita 100
Ramos, Domingos 148n4
rap 126, 142, 153n74
Readjustment Movement 35
re-Africanization 8, 28
recalibrating memory 37–42
Rego, Márcia 9, 77, 140, 151–152n53
Reis, Carlos 96, 103, 104
remembrance, new paradigm
  of 69–72
removed images, return of 64–69
Rendall, Daniel 49n72
Republic Week 106-107, 132
"return to Africa" through music 28–34
revolutionary national
  democracy 22
Rhode Island 17
Ribeira Brava 1
Ribeiro, António Sousa 154n86
Rigney, Ann 127
Rodrigues, Dudu 142
Rodrigues, Sarmento 39
Rosabal, Maritza 150n24
Rosa Luxemburg Foundation 148n6
Rosário, Gualberto do 72, 82n45, 90
Rothberg, Michael 21
Rotterdam 48n61
Rudebeck, Lars 101

Sá da Bandeira, Marquês de 65, 67
Sabino (Simões) 129, *130*
Sal 1, 105

Index   169

Sampaio, Jorge 71
Santa Catarina 149n13
Santa Luzia 1
Santa Maria 123
Santiago 1, 2, 10, 10n2, 31, 33, 64, 74,
   136; cultural traditions 34
Santo, Alda Espírito 101
Santo Antão 1, 109
Santos, António Almeida 101
Santos, Jacinto 72
Santos, Marcelino dos 4, 101
São Filipe 66
São Nicolau 1, 97
São Tomé and Príncipe 3, 19, 30, 101;
   labour crisis 44n19
São Vicente 1, 10, 17, 18, 34, 67, 69,
   74, 109, 141
Sarney, José 123
Seminario-Liceu de São Nicolau
   47n43, 137
Senegal 4, 5, 17, 43n10
Senghor, Léopold 4, 11n6
Silá, Titina 130, 135, 143, 148n4, 150n40
Silva, Adriano Duarte 65, 148n6
Silva, Coralie Tavares 134
Silva, João Pereira (Djunga de
   Biluca) 31
Silva, João Pereira 83n48
Silva, Luiz 152n70
Silveira, Onésimo 31, 40, 67, 70, 105
slavery 3, 5, 12n14, 15, 20, 21, 52n124,
   106, 127, 129; abolition of 44n19, 65
Soares, Mário 66, 71
social memory 60
Sousa, Julião Soares 11n6, 45n28
Sousa, Mário Lúcio 127, 151n43
Spain 2
Statute of the Liberation Struggle
   Combatant 71, 90–94, 96, 101–103,
   113n10
Strella anti-aircraft missiles 4
Super Mama Djombo 33
Sweden 5
symbolic capital 24, 25, 71, 122

tabanka 33, 34, 43n2, 142
Tamm, Marek 7
Tarrafal Penal Colony 18, 97, 98, *98*,
   102, 114n34, 135, 151n43
Tavares, Álvaro 95
Tavares, Eugénio 77
Tavares, Lucílio Braga 84n58
Tavares da Silva, Adalberto Higino 76

Teixeira de Sousa, Henrique 81n28,
   81n30; *Entre Duas Bandeiras*
   [Between Two Flags] 64; *Xaguate* 64
Testemunho de um Combatente
   [A Combatant's Testimony]
   (Pedro Martins) 97
Tomás, António 11n6
*tortura em nome do partido único.
   O PAICV e a sua polícia política,
   A* [Torture in the name of the single-
   party. The PAICV and its political
   police] (Onésimo Silveira) 70
Touré, Sékou 4
Traverso, Enzo 79n3
Turma da Mônica, A [Monica's
   Gang] 134
*Turma do Cabralinho e o Búzio Mágico,
   A* [Cabralinho's Gang and the Magic
   Whelk] (Marilene Pereira) 134

UCID (Independent and Democratic
   Cape Verdean Union) 37, 63, 94, 104
UDC (Cape Verdean Democratic
   Union) 17, 18, 43n10, 81n28
Um Brasileiro em Terras Portuguesas
   [A Brazilian in Portuguese Lands]
   (Gilberto Freyre) 39
UN (United Nations) 18
UNESCO: Memory of the World
   Register 134
Unity Council 50n91
Universal Declaration of Human
   Rights of 1948 109
UPG (Union of the Peoples of
   Guinea) 43n10
UPICV (Union of the People of the
   Cape Verde Islands) 17, 18, 44n10,
   63, 92, 101, 105
UPLG (Popular union for the
   Liberation of Guinea) 43n10
USA 129; Cape-Verdean migrants 63;
   diaspora community 74; Embassy
   125
USSR 59

Vasconcelos, João 28, 141
Vaz Moreno, Zanildo 144, 146
Veiga, Carlos 63, 69, 71, 107
Veiga, Manuel 106
Verdery, Katherine 121–122
Veríssimo, Érico 101
Vhils 130, *130*
Vicente, Abraão 127

170 Index

Vieira, Nino (João Bernardo) 35, 36, 121
Vieira, Osvaldo 148n4
violence 5, 8, 16, 20, 31, 35, 36, 39, 50n93, 59, 70, 79n3, 98, 151n51

White, Hayden 146
World Bank 59

World War II 3, 22
Wouters, Nico 7

Xaguate (Teixeira de Sousa) 64
Xalabas di Kumunidadi 129

Young, Robert 123

Printed in the United States
by Baker & Taylor Publisher Services